The Complete Bearded Dragon Care Book

2022 Edition

Jacquelyn Elnor Johnson
Author of I Want A Bearded Dragon

Cataloguing in Publication Data

Jacquelyn Elnor Johnson

The Complete Bearded Dragon Care Book

Description: Crimson Hill Books trade paperback edition | Nova Scotia, Canada

ISBN: 978-1-990291-43-2 (Paperback - Amazon)

BISAC: JNF003190 Juvenile Nonfiction: Animals - Reptiles & Amphibians |
JNF003170 Juvenile Nonfiction: Animals – Pets |
JNF051150 Juvenile Nonfiction: Science & Nature – Zoology

THEMA: YNNM - Children's / Teenage general interest: Reptiles & amphibians |
YNNH - Children's / Teenage general interest: Pets & pet care |

Record available at https://www.bac-lac.gc.ca/eng/Pages/home.aspx

Cover Image: Raphael Kaiser (Snap_it), pixabay.com

Interior Art: Kaitlin Bauer, KaitlinBauer.com

Book design and formatting: Jesse Johnson

Crimson Hill Books
(a division of)
Crimson Hill Products Inc.
Wolfville, Nova Scotia
Canada

Crimson Hill
Books

CONTENTS

INTRODUCTION

Looking for a pet that's always eager to see you and enjoys hanging out together?

Easy to care for, this pet you're longing to get wouldn't take up much space. They also wouldn't mind being left on their own during the day, but would be even happier once you're home [illegible]

This pet we're talking about would never get fleas. They'd never need to be brushed. Or taken to obedience classes. Or for walks.

They'd never rip up the cushions or scratch the furniture.

They wouldn't ever bark or yowl. In fact, they'd hardly make any sound at all!

This pet would live indoors, but also enjoy some outdoor play in warm weather. They'd even love car-rides!

This fantastic pet would be friendly, smart, curious and just interesting to get to know.

If you're saying a big YES to most or even all these great pet qualities, it could be that the best pet for you, the one that ticks every one of these boxes, is – a lizard!

And not just any lizard, but the sweetest, most playful and friendliest of all lizard pets, the bearded dragon.

Hundreds of thousands of people, just about world-wide, have discovered how much pleasure there can be in having a pet bearded dragon.

Also, for all these reasons, there's been an explosion in the popularity of this pet in this century. With just a bit of knowledge and good care habits, you, too, can discover what's turned them from wannabe pet owners to raving bearded dragon fans!

If you want to learn what you need to know about how to care for your bearded dragon, what odd and amusing things they do and why you'll lose your heart to your dragon, here's the book you need!

Turn the page to find out what bearded dragons eat, how to set up their vivarium, which dragon you might choose, how to give them the good care that will keep them healthy and everything else beginning or intermediate-level dragon lovers need to enjoy many happy years with their best lizard friend!

DO BEARDIES LIKE TO BE PETTED?

Strangely enough, for a lizard, the answer is yes, most beardies like to be gently stroked on their back or head while you're holding them.

If your pet doesn't like this, it could be they just don't know you well enough yet. Be patient. Most bearded dragons take time to get to know and trust a new owner and new home.

ONE
Welcome, Beardie Lovers!

If you were to name the one coolest pet of this year, this decade, or even this century, what would it be?

Since you're reading this, I think you've already cast your vote for the bearded dragon. This gentle, mild-mannered, easy-going and friendly lizard makes a great pet choice for lots of people. In this century, beardies have become particularly popular with young adults and teens.

Bearded dragons are more exotic than such 'traditional' pets as dogs or cats, yet far easier to care for than other non-traditional pets, such as snakes and other types of pet reptiles. But beardies aren't just a lizard starter-pet, though many people who are into reptiles, and lizards in particular, begin their pet adventure with a beardie.

What beardies are is an all-around great pet choice. With good care routines, you and your beardie could have a sweet friendship for years to come.

Thank you for choosing this book – there are others on the shelves and at bookstores you might have chosen instead. So what's different here?

This book is the most complete how-to for new beardie owners, or people who've had their beardies for a while and want to be sure they're doing everything right.

It isn't just a book of colour pictures to flip through. In fact, there are no photos at all in this book. That's on purpose. There are LOTS of places online to find pictures of pets, including bearded dragons.

THIS book is about getting you ALL the most up-to-date information. It's designed to be an easy read.

Although bearded dragons have been pets for decades, there's still more that's not known or entirely understood about them. They remain something of a mystery in the way they see and think about their world. That just makes them all the more interesting to get to know!

In adopting a bearded dragon, you're not just getting a pet. And you're not just getting a cool pet. You're joining a world-wide community of pet owners who are fascinated by what beardies can do. This tribe of global beardie-lovers actively share what they're learning.

THE PROMISE OF THIS BOOK

This is a real-world, practical guide of immediately useful information about getting your bearded dragon and enjoying him or her. It's designed to give you what you need to know to transform you into a confident bearded dragon owner with a healthy, happy pet.

This book is organized to make it easy to dip into for fast need-to-know information. Or take a more leisurely stroll through the whole book. It includes the most reliable information available today from herpetologists and other experts including experienced beardie breeders and owners.

It's designed to be fast to read. This book is all about the hobby of keeping pet bearded dragons for beginner and intermediate bearded dragon owners.

WHAT ARE BEARDIES?

Bearded dragons are a group of lizards that live in the wild only in Australia and a few nearby islands.

They aren't dragons, so they can't breathe fire, fly or do any of the other heroic feats that dragons do in folklore, fantasy fiction and movies.

And, in another naming fib, they aren't exactly bearded, either. They don't have flowing face hair. What they do have is scales all over their bodies, including a wide band of spiky scales from ear to ear below their chin. When angry, or excited, or ready to attack an enemy, these scales darken and enlarge, looking curiously like Santa's beard, only spiky and black.

All of the beardies available as pets are captive-bred. This means they were bred from wild dragons in the last century. The dragon you own, or you will get soon, has wild animal ancestors, but is now several generations away from its wild heritage. He or she couldn't live in the wild. They wouldn't survive. They only know how to be a pet.

WHAT IS HERPETOLOGY?

The study of reptiles, and their very distant cousins the amphibians, is called "*herpetology*." People who study these animals are called "*herpetologists*." And if you go to a reptile show, it's likely to be called a "*herps*" show.

The word comes from "*herpeton*," which is a Greek word that means "*creeping animal*." Today we know that reptiles don't creep. Instead, they walk, run, jump, fly or slither. We still use that old Greek name for reptile topics, whether you're a scientist who studies them or being fascinated by them is your hobby.

WHAT MAKES BEARDIES ATTRACTIVE PETS?

In addition to all the nice-to-know features you've just read about, beardies are fun to have because:

Bearded Dragons are smart.

Adults know their own names and can learn a few other words.

They're curious.

They love exploring.

They like people.

Bearded dragons bond with their owners, but they aren't needy or clingy. They do quirky, funny things like waving their arms and asking for treats.

They have distinctive personalities.

Like dogs or cats, beardies are individuals. They will be as outgoing as you want them to be.

They don't have dander, so it's impossible to be allergic to a bearded dragon.

They don't smell when you give them and their feeder insects proper care.

They don't make any noise, or any sound at all.

They sleep at night, so they're awake when you are.

They can bite or nip, but hardly ever bite people.

They won't bite you unless they are seriously annoyed with you.

They are fairly low-maintenance when you have a good care routine.

They're a medium-small sized pet that lives in a relatively small space.

Beardies are used to living alone. You don't need to have two so they can keep each other company.

They are beautiful. Fancy breeds, called morphs, come in many patterns and colours.

They're alert, active and a lot of fun.

BUT A BEARDIE MAY NOT BE RIGHT FOR YOU

Beardies have plenty of advantages as your first or next pet. But they may not be meant for you. Here's why:

By law, you cannot have a bearded dragon as a pet in some places.

The reason is the fear that careless owners will release pet beardies into the wild, or let them escape. In places with a similar climate to what bearded dragons require, this could present challenges for the native creatures.

One place with this law, for this reason, is Hawaii.

You might live in a part of the world where having bearded dragons as pets is allowed, but only with a permit. This is because they are classified as exotic pets.

Check if you'll need a pet permit before you get your pet.

A bearded dragon, like every pet, should never be an impulse purchase.

Think carefully about any pet before you adopt.

- Are you ready to commit to caring for and loving this pet? You'll be providing everything they require for a comfortable, safe and happy life, 24/7 for many years to come. Do you have the time to do this?

ARE BEARDED DRAGONS SMART?

All species evolve to be as smart as they need to be to find water, food, shelter and healthy mates and defend themselves from enemies.

Some learn to do much more, such as craft tools (crows), navigate during long journeys (elephants and birds that migrate) or race or do tricks (dogs and horses).

Pet bearded dragons can't do any of these things, but they can bond with their owners and learn some words, including their own names.

- Can you afford to keep them? Bearded dragons are NOT an inexpensive pet to get or to keep.
- Do you have space for their vivarium, in your family room or bedroom?
- Are your answers to the questions above likely to stay the same for the next 10 years or more?

Bearded dragons are not an inexpensive pet to get or to keep.

The initial cost of getting your pet could be as inexpensive as $60 or so, up to several thousands of dollars for a rare hybrid (morph) bearded dragon. (All of these costs are in U.S. dollars).

You can expect to spend another $800 or more to get your pet properly set up at home. If you want a fancy set-up, the cost could be much more.

A vet visit will cost $100 to $150.

Their food will vary in cost, but expect to spend $50 to $80 per month.

Power (electricity) for their lights is another cost. Other costs are replacing the heat and UV lamps from time to time and pet licensing, if that's required where you live.

There are ways to save money, but in general it's best to assume that it will cost $1,000 or so to get your pet and everything they need and then expect to spend, on average, $100 per month, all in.

They have exacting climate needs. You have to get their vivarium conditions including heat, UV (ultra-violet light) and humidity exactly right and be able to keep them there. Dragons have a narrow range for these in their environment in order to survive.

Their climate range is even narrower than the fairly limited conditions that are the range for human survival. This means the home you live in comfortably isn't quite the same as the comfort level your dragon must have. If you can't create the mini-world they need to be healthy within your home, they aren't the right pet for you.

You will need to find a qualified reptile veterinarian before you get your pet.

General small animal vets tend to deal mostly with dogs and cats and have little or no experience with lizards. You will need to find a vet that specializes in reptile pets and they are fairly rare.

If you live in a small town or rural area, there may not be a vet who knows about beardie illnesses to turn to when you need help for a pet in distress.

It's a sad fact that more than half of lizard pets die within a few years of their owners getting them. One reason for this is owners not having the help of a veterinarian. Another is not recognizing when their pets are in trouble. There's more about beardie health in Chapter 8.

How do you feel about insects?

Bearded dragons LOVE insects.

As babies or juveniles, they eat mostly live insects, with some vegetables.

As adults, they eat mostly veggies, with some live insects. So if you have a beardie, you also have insects. You need to care for these insects until they get eaten.

If just the thought of handling insects sounds disgusting, and you really don't want to try getting used to handling them, maybe getting a beardie isn't the best idea for you.

Bearded dragons are not a good choice in some homes. If there are babies, children younger than five years old, women who are pregnant or people who have a compromised immune system or a chronic illness, a lizard pet could be a 'wait till later' choice.

This is because young children may not be able to be gentle with a small pet, though most children over age five can learn to sit still with a beardie and hold him or her correctly. Older kids can help with the vivarium set-up, changing their water and feeding. Beardies that are gently handled as a pet from the time they are juveniles are just as affectionate to children as they are to teens or adults.

Though you can't be allergic to a beardie, some people are allergic to the bugs their pets eat. There is also a slight, but real risk of catching salmonella from reptile pets. (More about this in Chapter 8).

Like all reptiles, bearded dragons are cold-blooded.

This means they don't have the ability (as mammals do) to control their own body temperatures. They must seek heat to warm up. When they get too hot, they need to move to shady places to cool down.

WHAT DO BEARDIES SEE?

Bearded dragons have eyesight that is better than human eyesight in some ways. They have better night vision than we do and can see in the ultraviolet light spectrum as many animals (including dogs and cats) can, but humans can't.

Beardies see in colour but have poor depth perception. Their 'third eye,' on the top of their heads, is a shadow- and motion- sensor.

A spot in the sun or in the shade is easy enough for wild bearded dragons to find in their native land. It takes more effort to create both warmer and cooler spots in a pet vivarium (that's their tank).

Beardies poop often, on everything in their vivarium.

You'll be poop-scooping once a day for adults, or twice a day if you get a baby or juvenile beardie. It only takes a few minutes for daily cleaning, but still. Think about if you can commit to doing your beardie's housekeeping every day for years to come.

Beardies don't smell if their enclosure is kept clean. Some types of feeder insects do stink if you don't keep up with their cleaning and care. Feeders can also be noisy.

Are you AND your roommates, or your family, going to be able to handle this?

If you love your beardie, you can learn to get used to handling live insects. With proper care, they can be clean and non-smelly. Do you have the time to do this, as well as wanting to make insect care a regular routine in your life?

Beardies take time.

This isn't a pet you can mostly ignore. Are you ready to spend 10 minutes or so every day cleaning the vivarium, plus an hour every weekend caring for your pet and your feeders?

Though they're content in their vivarium most of the time, a beardie that doesn't get a break out of their tank and with you for an hour or more every day is not going to be happy. And when they aren't happy, just like any other pet (and like people, too) they tend to get sick.

They don't live for a long time.

The average pet bearded dragon lives for between 4 and 8 years, though some can live as long as 12 years.

Considering all this, is a bearded dragon really right for you? Are you ready to commit to all the care and love a little dragon deserves? Remember, they are depending on you to be their sun, their shade, their dinner and snacks – their morning and their evening, their fun and their world. Their everything.

No one is born already knowing how to be a good pet parent. The good news is that it's a skill almost anyone can learn.

Are you up to the challenge and excited about this opportunity to bond with a creature so different than you?

If your answer is, "YES," let's move on to Beardie Basics!

TWO
Beardie Basics

Maybe you know someone who has a bearded dragon and as soon as you met their pet, you knew you had to have a beardie of your own.

Or perhaps, for you, it was love at first sight at a herp show.

Or you've just seen pictures of beardies on Insta or watched YouTubes about them and thought about how cool it would be to have one.

Possibly, you've already got your beardie, but realize there's more you need to know about them. That's one of the cool things about having a pet – there's always more to discover about them!

WHAT ARE POGONAS?

There are eight types of lizards in the Pogona group, all of which are commonly called bearded dragons. Almost all pet beardies are just one of these eight types. They all evolved to live on the dry and rocky scrublands and nearby woodlands that form a broad band across Australia. This band stretches from the south coast to the southeastern region of the North, totaling nearly a third of Australia.

This part of the continent isn't desert. But it is hot and dry by day and cool at night. Here, many types of agamid lizards, all known as "dragons," evolved over sixty million years.

Until very recently, not much was known about Australia's unique reptiles. Instead, both scientists and the world were captivated by the unusual and downright weird mammals of this island continent. Like the lizards, they too developed to suit their environments.

They remained far from the threat of invading predators until the arrival of settlers from Europe. Those settlers brought animals such as cows, sheep, cats and dogs with them. All these were and are a threat to the native animals.

The native people, who got to Australia around 50,000 years ago are today known as Aboriginals. These native people had long known about the dragons. They depicted them in rock paintings and included them in their legends. Aboriginal knowledge about bearded dragons and other reptiles of Australia and Tasmania was largely dismissed as ridiculous and too fantastic to be believed by the Europeans.

The new settlers, struck by the oddness of kangaroos, koala bears, and that strangest of all animals, the platypus, pretty much ignored the lizards. Often spotted sunning themselves on rocks or low branches of the type of eucalyptus or gum trees known locally as mallee, Pogona lizards soon became as common a sight to the newcomers as robins back home.

Yet it wouldn't be until the 1960s that Australian naturalist, herpetologist and writer Eric Worrell published the first book based on careful research about Australia's fascinating reptiles.

BEARDIES BY THE NUMBERS

8 to 10	Number of years well-cared for pet beardies live, on average
3 to 4	Length of newborns, in inches (or almost 8 to 10 cm)
18 to 24	Length adults can grow to, in inches (or 45 to 60 cm). Usually, males are larger than females.
1/2	Amount of their length that is their tail.
10 to 20	Weight of a healthy adult, in ounces (350 to 600 grams)

WHAT ARE BEARDED DRAGONS?

Let's start with what is easy to see about them. Like almost all reptiles, bearded dragons have wide, triangular heads. Their legs join to the sides of their bodies and are covered in scales. They are short, can move surprisingly quickly and are cold-blooded. This means they can't regulate their own body temperatures, as mammals can by or sweating to cool down.

HOW DO SCIENTISTS CLASSIFY PET BEARDED DRAGONS?

Domain:	Eukaryota
Kingdom:	Animalia
Phylum:	Chordata
Subphylum:	Vertebrata
Class:	Reptilia
Order:	Squamata
Suborder:	Iguania
Family:	Agamidae
Subfamily:	Amphibolurinae
Genus:	Pogona
Species:	Pogona vitticeps (the Central Bearded Dragon)

Though they are good climbers, they prefer to live mostly on or near the ground. And though they have a mild venom and do bite their enemies, they rarely bite humans. Their venom is too weak to harm people, but it does stun the small animals that wild beardies eat, such as mice, hatchling birds and baby lizards.

They are curious and can be social, yet they prefer to live alone.

Dragons are indifferent parents. The father's job is done after breeding. The mother buries her eggs in a sand nest and leaves the hatchlings to fend for themselves. She might check back once or twice, then wander off and forget about them.

Bearded dragons are most active during the day and generally sleep at night. In the summer heat, they're most active in the early morning or late afternoon.

They eat a variety of foods. Wild beardies eat fruits, leaves, ants and beetles, and small animals, including other lizards. Their natural enemies are birds, goannas (monitor lizards), snakes, dingoes (wild dogs), wild cats and foxes.

Like their distant relative, the chameleons, they have the ability to change colour.

Wild bearded dragons range in colour from brown to grayish-brown, but they are able to change colour to blend in with their surroundings. Central Bearded Dragons can become almost as red as the sands of Central Australia. Dragons in Southern Australia turn yellow to match the sands there.

These animals can change their skin colour faster than humans can change their clothes.

For the past few decades, scientists have wondered how bearded dragons do this trick so quickly and so accurately. Is it possibly caused by their hormones? Can only Central dragons turn red and only Southern ones turn yellow? And how do they even know what colour they are?

It seems they are able to turn the colour of what they see around them. But how?

Is it evolution, colour-consciousness, or maybe a blend of both?

"It's very handy for bearded dragons that they can change their skin colour. They can become flashy orange with jet-black beards to warn rivals off their territory, become camouflaged to hide from predators and darken themselves to absorb more heat from the sun," says Devi Stuart-Fox, an associate professor at University of Melbourne's School of BioSciences. She is one of a team of biologists studying how, when and why bearded dragons change colour. The teams' findings were published in *Journal of Experimental Biology* in 2017 (*phys.org/news/2017-03-lizards-local-colour.html*)

"They are able to assess their surroundings and then trigger a response in their skin." Not only can they change colour, some lizards can change the crystal formations inside their skin cells, which changes the way light reflects off their skin.

The University of Melbourne research team captured adult bearded dragons in Central and in Southern Australia. They chose only males, because males are easier to spot as they patrol their territories. The scientists put all the 22 bearded dragons they caught to a colour test. What they wanted to know was what would happen when each dragon was placed on a red sand, yellow sand or black sand background.

Each was left, on each colour, for 45 minutes while time-lapse cameras recorded their colour changes.

The results are astonishing. All the lizards could change, somewhat, to all three background colours. However, the Southern lizards were better at matching the yellow sands of the South; the Central lizards were better at turning as red as the sands of Alice Springs. While black sand was something neither type had ever seen, the Southern lizards were better at matching it, perhaps because there are more trees and vegetation in the South.

LIFECYCLE OF A BEARDED DRAGON

Baby beardies are born from eggs 55 to 75 days after their mother lays the eggs. Hatchlings are a bit more than 3 inches (7.6 cm) long at birth and are nervous and jumpy.

They are Juveniles when they grow to 5 to 15 inches (13 to 33 cm) long. Juveniles have huge appetites, grow rapidly and will attack other Juveniles.

When they are 12 to 14 months old they become Adults. Active and usually easy-going Adults are able to reproduce from the time they are between 12 and 18 months old until they become Seniors.

Senior dragons are more than 6 years old. Females slow down and stop breeding at age 7 or 8.

All bearded dragons can become darker when they want to blend into the background, when stressed or confronted by an enemy, or when they are outside (or under a UV light) and need to absorb more sunlight to warm up.

Also when threatened, they can darken and enlarge the band of spiky scales that cover their chins from ear to ear to create the beard that gives them their name. The beard scales aren't sharp enough to be a weapon. It seems that deploying your beard, especially if you're a male confronting another male dragon, is a show of strength, power and superiority.

> **WHERE TO SEE WILD DRAGONS**
>
> If you travel to Australia, you can see protected bearded dragons in their natural habitats at these Bush Heritage reserves:
>
> In Western Australia at Charles Darwin, Cherininup, Eurardy, Kojonup and Monjebup Reserves.
>
> In Queensland at Carnarvon, Cravens Peak, Ethabuka and Yourka Reserves.
>
> In New South Wales at Scottsdale Reserve.
>
> In Victoria at Nardoo Reserve
>
> In South Australia at Bon Bon and Boolcoomatta Reserves.
>
> You can find out more about visiting these reserves at **bushheritage.org.au**

When a younger male encounters a larger, older or healthier male bearded dragon with beard unfurled, the younger one may wave his hand to show, in body language, that he's no threat. Female beardies also may wave a hand, for the same reason.

In all the types of beardies, the colour and patterns change as they grow from baby to juvenile to adult. Males are usually more brightly coloured than females.

Baby beardies are almost identical, from the same clutch of eggs. Until they are older juveniles or adults, it's difficult to tell the difference between males and females.

After many generations of the original wild ancestors (they were stolen by tourists in the last century) being selectively bred, you now see their much more colourful descendants. These pet dragons are called morphs. Morphs are in a much broader range of brighter colours and patterns than their ancestors, from white to yellow, orange and red-orange. There is now an almost-pure black beardie and some breeders are trying for a blue beardie.

One of the strange things about some morphs is that their beards don't turn black when they're angry and ready to attack. Instead, they turn a darker shade of the morph's colour! So you can have a tangerine beardie that gets a deep orange beard. Or a deep gold beard, on a citrus yellow beardie. Will blue beardies have navy blue beards, if such an animal is ever created? It *might* happen!

Breeders have also created animals with smoother scales, called leatherbacks. Or with [illegible] to create more interesting and exotic pets. Their striking appearance and rarity means if you want a morph, expect to pay much more than you would for the standard beardie you might see at a pet store.

HOW DID BEARDIES BECOME PETS?

Sometime in the 1970s, or perhaps the early 1980s, someone, likely a tourist, captured a few wild bearded dragons and took them back to Europe to breed as pets. They soon became popular pets in Europe, particularly in Germany, and then Britain. However, they didn't become popular as pets in United States until the 1990s.

It wasn't until the 1960s that Australian authorities passed laws protecting their reptile wildlife from poachers. This also limited the number of animals available for scientists to study and slowed down the effort to gain more knowledge about them.

There is still a lot we don't know about bearded dragons, as they behave in their natural world.

Though humans and lizards have lived close to each other for many thousands of years, in many ways they still remain mysterious. One of the pleasures of being a beardie owner or breeder is continuing to learn about them and add to our knowledge of how these animals think and experience their world.

DO BEARDED DRAGONS LIKE MUSIC?

Beardies have good hearing but are sensitive to sudden or loud sounds. Most seem to enjoy music that is soft, calming and what you might call easy listening. However, some seem to enjoy pop, blues or country music.

How to tell what your pet's musical preferences are? If they turn towards the music, lie down and close their eyes, they're digging it!

Capturing wild animals to 'turn into' pets remains a problem, in Australia as elsewhere. Authorities still stop people at Australia's airports as they attempt to board with snakes or lizards captured for pets or breeding. These captures must be traumatic for the animals, as well as (deservedly) for the thieves.

It isn't only exotic animal poachers who are a threat to wild dragons.

Though beardies aren't considered to be endangered, they have suffered from loss of their natural habitat to land clearing and cattle grazing.

The greatest threat to bearded dragons, and all of Australia's creatures (and many of the human population) is caused by climate change. Australia is getting hotter, and drier, with catastrophic weather events such as the flooding of 2021. Annual fires have become more widespread and devastating.

In 2020, bush fires claimed the lives of millions and possibly billions of Australian creatures. This includes an unknown number of wild bearded dragons.

MEET All THE POGONAS!

The eight – or some experts say there are nine – Pogona dragons (experts can't agree on this; some even say there are just seven) used to be collectively known as the genus *Amphibolurus*. You'll see them described that way in books published before 2012. They also have gained a lot of names, just to make things more confusing. Here are the eight pogonas, plus one, as they're known today:

P. vitticeps, commonly called the **Inland Dragon**, or **Central Dragon**, or **Yellow-headed Dragon**. Almost all pet bearded dragons are this species.

P. barbata, the **Common Bearded Dragon** or **Eastern Dragon**, is rare as a pet, but [illegible] vitticeps.

P. henrylawsoni is the **Rankin's Dragon**, or **Lawson's Dragon**, or **Black-soil Bearded Dragon**. That's not the end of the list of names for this animal because, perhaps unfairly, it's also known as the **Dumpy Dragon**. It's only half the size of P. vitticeps. Also rare as a pet and difficult to breed.

P. minima, the **Western Bearded Dragon**, is not the smallest, despite their name.

P. minor, the **Dwarf Dragon**, is sometimes also called the **Western Bearded Dragon**, just to confuse things.

P. mitchelli, the **Northwest Bearded Dragon** or **Mitchell's Dragon**.

P. nullarbor, the **Nullarbor Bearded Dragon**.

P. microlepitoda, the **Kimberly Bearded Dragon**, or **Drysdale River Bearded Dragon**.

P. vittikens is Number 9, not usually classed as a species because it's a hybrid of P. vitticeps and P. minor. Unlike most cross-breeds, it is able to reproduce.

THREE
Get Set To Get Your Pet!

The box your new pet will live in is called a vivarium. This is a Latin word that means "place of life." It's a good name, since your bearded dragon will spend most of his or her life in the vivarium you create and manage for their comfort and safety.

For an adult beardie, this box, or vivarium, needs to be no smaller than 6 feet long by 2 feet wide (or 1.8 metres by .6 metre). That's about three times as long as the average adult dragon. It's also close to the length, but half as wide, as a double bed. It really isn't much space, but to your pet, it's their entire world except for times when they get to come out and play in the 'outside' world with you.

In the wild, bearded dragons have lots more room to enjoy. This includes places to climb and bask, undisturbed, in the warmth of the sun. When they get too hot, they can find their favourite cool shady places in small burrows or rock crevices. If they're hungry, they go scouting for insects. Thirsty? Time to lick water droplets from leaves or munch on some juicy plants.

Wild bearded dragons not only choose to roam around their territory, they have to. They must control their body temperatures as well as find water and food. They constantly seek out places that are warmer, or cooler, because they have no other way to control their body temperatures. Without warmth, they cannot survive.

Humans tend to take body temperature for granted. If you're feeing a little chilly, you can shiver to warm up. Or start a fire. Turn up the heat. Move around. Put on more clothing.

If you're too hot, you sweat to cool off. Or have a refreshing dip in the lake or a shower.

Or you could just stop moving around. Wear lighter clothing. Turn on a fan or the AC.

As a human, we have bodies that help moderate our body temperatures. We also have lots of options for getting more comfortable.

For many creatures, that's not true. Bearded dragons, like all reptiles except birds, are cold-blooded. This means they have only one option to warm up, which is go sit in the sun. To cool off, they must find a sheltered, shady spot.

Needing to do this to survive may seem like a serious disadvantage, but actually, it helps them. Creatures that don't need to spend energy warming or cooling themselves can get by on less food. They need to eat less often.

They don't use precious food energy in trying to warm up or cool down. They simply move out in the sun, or back into the shade.

That is, if they're wild. Reptiles that live in zoos or are pets need everything they'd naturally find in their wild homes, but in the very much smaller but more controlled space of a vivarium.

This isn't merely a matter of comfort. A beardie that doesn't get enough warmth and ultra-violet light will stop eating, because, without both, they aren't able to digest their food and convert it to energy. They will become weakened and die.

Their species has evolved, over millions of years, to thrive in very specific conditions. As a pet owner, it is up to you to provide these exact conditions. Not doing so is not only unfair, it is cruel. It will mean they live shorter, less healthy lives.

WHAT COMES FIRST – YOUR VIVARIUM OR YOUR BEARDIE?

It's much better to get your vivarium first. Set it up and get it running correctly before you get your pet. Critically, for a reptile pet, you need to get the heating and ultraviolet (UV) lights right. Humidity and the daylight/nighttime light cycle also matters to a beardie's good health.

Once you've got your setup working as it should, you can enjoy getting to know your new friend and relax, knowing you're giving them their happy, healthy place. As their owner, as well as best friend, you owe them this.

NEW OWNER SHOPPING LIST

This isn't everything you'll need, just the essentials for your pet's new home.

1. Tank or vivarium that is the right size for their age.
2. Hood top or screen top for the tank or vivarium that closes securely.
3. [illegible]
4. UV tube and fixture, set up on separate dimmer switch.
5. Basking platform – rocks for a baby, a branch for juvenile or adult.
6. A cool hide that is larger than they are.
7. Digital thermometer with probe or heat gun-style thermometer.
8. UV light meter.
9. Humidity meter.
10. Plant misting bottle.
11. Newspaper or paper towel for substrate.
12. Cleaning supplies – bleach, rubber gloves, cleaning rags.

You'll also need appropriately-sized insects, greens, calcium supplement and reptile multi-vitamin (See Chapter 6).

What do pet bearded dragons need to be healthy and happy?

The short answer is they need what all living creatures need. This is: fresh air, clean water, healthy food they like, warmth, places to cool off and sleep and protection from their enemies. In your home, enemies might include other beardies, your other pets and small children.

> **START SMART!**
>
> A home that's ready to welcome your new pet will mean fewer worries for you as a caring and kind pet owner.
>
> There will be less visits to the vet, and you will have a pet that lives a good and long life.

Given the opportunity to breed, female dragons also need a safe place to lay their eggs.

It would make life easier if I could give you an exact perfect bearded dragon set-up. This advice would include precisely what you must do to be ready to put your new pet in their new home. This isn't possible, and here's why: your set-up and routine will be determined by the age of your dragon and also by the climate you live in and the season. This includes not only the region of the country, but also how warm you keep your home in winter (or the cool season) or how cooled your home is in summer as well as at night. Humidity also plays a role.

The good news is it IS possible to give you a list of what you'll need and why to create a healthy mini-biosphere in your vivarium that is ideal for a bearded dragon. It isn't a long list, and it needn't be expensive, but you do need the right gear, connected and used in the right way, to have a healthy pet.

Dragons on the dessert? That's a myth!

It's a mistake to think that bearded dragons are a desert creature, so all they need is some sand, rocks and then all you do is crank up the heat.

They have actually evolved to live in places that are semi-arid, or on the edges of semi-arid places. Semi-arid is the scrubby land that humans might call good for grazing cattle or sheep, but not good for growing food. The ground tends to be dry. It is warmer during the day and cooler at night. There are places to climb, such as rocks and fence posts.

Like humans, bearded dragons need the changes of the seasons. They also need a daylight/darkness cycle. Like us, they are active during the day and sleep at night. The range of temperatures and humidity most humans generally find comfortable isn't that far off from what bearded dragons require, but it also isn't exactly the same.

Since you are sharing your home with a bearded dragon, you'll need to create the ideal dragon-friendly conditions in your tank or vivarium. Fortunately, the technology and tools to do this have never been better. These tools are more widely available and also more affordable than ever before. In this you – and your pet – are truly lucky!

Our knowledge of these animals has grown, especially in this century. The technology to care for them has improved vastly in the four decades or so since they first became [illegible] pet owners.

But all this good health and happiness doesn't happen by accident.

It would be convenient if you could simply buy a pet kit that would be Everything, Everywhere. It would work for every bearded dragon and suit, exactly, you as a pet owner, where you live, the age and size of your pet, the climate of your home, in every season. Unfortunately, this simply doesn't exist. Despite this, pet stores (especially in U.S. and Canada) and general online stores continue to offer such 'everything, everywhere, for every dragon' kits.

Almost always, if you are buying an 'everything' beardie starter kit or tank equipment from anywhere except the major pet product manufacturers that specialize in reptile pets or a dedicated reptile pet store, the kits or set-ups will waste your money and could endanger your pet. They most often contain products designed for turtles, snakes or other pets, but not suitable for bearded dragons.

So, what to do?

It's so tempting to go get your pet first, then do your set-up, but this is going to cause a lot of stress for you and for them. There are many beginning pet owners who, sadly, still rely on the trial-and-error method, resulting in their own frustration and, worse, pets that suffer. Or you can get the right information and get your set-up working correctly before you bring a pet into your life and your home.

The smart solution to this challenge is to:

1. buy the necessary basics,
2. set them up properly,
3. take the right measurements to be sure they are working exactly as they should, and
4. make adjustments to your setup as required.

No one gets this exactly right on the first try, so you need to make informed choices and then test, test, test. And adjust, as required.

Keeping good records will help you establish and maintain the optimum vivarium conditions. Once you've got daytime heat, night heat (if you need it), UV light and humidity under control, you'll be ready to meet your new pet! The testing will become a part of your regular pet care routine.

Buy the best quality. This is particularly important for lights. Know that you will probably need to upgrade your lights and maybe your vivarium over time.

The basics you must have are:

1. A **Vivarium**, or tank. This is the box that is the walls and floor of your pet's new home. The size you need depends on the age and size of your pet. Generally, a vivarium needs to be three times as long as the length of your pet, tail included. For safety, only one pet per vivarium.
2. A **Tank Hood** or **Screen Tank Top**. This is the vivarium's ceiling. It protects your pet from danger. If you choose to have a tank hood, it also holds the lights.
3. **Lights**. There are two types. One supplies heat. The other is for ultraviolet (UVA and UVB) light. Beardies can't digest their food without heat. They will weaken and die without UV light because it gives them the ability to absorb and use Vitamin D. Without enough of this vitamin, bearded dragons can't absorb calcium, leading to them becoming paralyzed.
4. **UV meter, Thermometer and Hygrometer**. These tools measure the UV output of your light and the levels of heat and humidity in the tank.
5. **Basking branch** or rock pile so they can get close but not too close to their lights. Adults need a branch. A rock pile works for the younger ones.
6. A **Cool Hide**. This is down at the cooler end of your vivarium. It's where they go to chill, sleep, or get some privacy.
7. **Substrate**. This is what's on the floor of the vivarium or tank.
8. **Tank Décor**. Everything else you might choose to put in their vivarium for your adult pet's comfort and pleasure, or just to make it more interesting to look at. Younger dragons are disturbed by tank décor, while the adults seem to enjoy it.

These are the critical basics and all you need to start with. It's more than you need for either a baby or a juvenile bearded dragon, since very young beardies can be overwhelmed and even frightened in a tank that is too large or has too much stuff in it.

WHAT DO BABY DRAGONS NEED?

Minimalist is the way to go for babies. They need just a smaller tank, a basking rock under their UV and heat lights and a cool hide. As they get a bit older, they'll need more space. By the time they are well into adulthood (at about two years old) you can introduce more stuff into your larger vivarium, perhaps creating the tankscape of your dreams.

Adult dragons want their tank to change a bit from time to time. You can do this each time you do a total clean of their vivarium.

THE TANK, OR VIVARIUM

Size matters when it comes to our homes and that's also true for lizards. For a baby, a medium fish tank will do, but this is just a temporary home. By the time they're a juvenile, they'll need an upgrade. At this point, you could buy the adult size (6 feet or 1.8 m long) vivarium and block off a third of it until they're older and need all the space.

Babies can get along in a plastic box as long as the lights are placed so they can get to the ideal position under their lights to bask. Make sure the lights aren't so close that the box starts to melt.

The disadvantage is you can't see into a plastic box, you can only see your pet from the top.

Some owners use a fish tank for their juvies or adults, but that isn't recommended because fish tanks tend to be deep, but not very wide.

Deep, not wide is ideal for fish. Lizards need the opposite, that is, a home with more floor space, but not so much height. A narrow but tall tank will give them a lot of space they can't use. It will also be more challenging to position your lights correctly and more difficult to control the humidity in the tank.

Too much humidity just sounds like a muggy summer day to humans. For pet lizards, it can lead to bacteria and mould growing in their home. Both of these are dangerous to their health.

Juveniles and adults need a vivarium that has at least one side that is glass, because you want to be able to see them. And they want to see you. The [illegible] expensive) open at the front as well as the top, which makes feeding, giving them water and cleaning much faster and easier.

The vivarium needs to be deep enough to allow space for your pet to climb their basking rocks or branch and bask in the ideal position while not getting too close to the lights. You don't need to worry about them escaping. They can't climb glass or wood sides. (If you have a pet that is trying to do this, it's a sign of trouble. See the section on glass surfing in Chapter 5).

WHAT NOT TO PUT IN YOUR BEARDIE'S VIVARIUM:

- Anything with sharp or jagged edges
- Anything made of cardboard (they will quickly destroy it)
- Anything made with evergreen wood
- Anything made with toxic plastic
- Another beardie (unless briefly, for mating)
- Any other type of pet (such as an anole or a snake). This would cause stress for both animals.
- Soft toys

And never leave live (uneaten) insects in the vivarium after they've eaten all they want. The insects can and will attack a sleeping dragon!

SAFE PLANTS FOR YOUR VIVARIUM

Lots of owners prefer a natural-looking vivarium, with a branch or rock pile (or both), and possibly pebbles, natural-looking hides and possibly some plants.

What type of plants?

Plastic plants only look natural from far away. To your dragon, they will smell odd, taste bad and could be poisonous. Silk plants aren't any better as a terrarium choice. They are also made with unhealthful chemicals that make them smell and taste bad, could be harmful and silk plants shred.

So that just leaves live plants. If this is your choice, be aware that you will have to check that they've not been sprayed with pesticides. If you're not sure, wait three months before giving the plant to your pet. Before you do, remove all the soil the plant comes with and repot it. You're doing this because nurseries put plenty of fertilizer into plant pots but this fertilizer could be (likely is) a danger to your pet. So you need to repot with organic, clean, non-fertilized soil (not soil from your garden. It will be full of bacteria and possibly mites and other dangers).

Choose from the short list of safe plants for beardies. Wash the leaves with warmish water and a sponge. Know that you'll be washing and replacing your terrarium plants frequently, since beardies climb over and poop on everything in their home.

Safe plants are **Clover**, **Fennel**, **Ivy**, **Herbs** (such as mint, oregano, thyme, sage or basil), **Succulents** (such as miniature snake plants (sansevieria)), **Miniature Pansies, Nasturtium** or **Geraniums**. All these are safe for beardies to eat.

The only usual tank escapees are grasshoppers or crickets if you use them as feeders and let your pet hunt for them, rather than using tongs to offer them to your beardie. Both these feeders are well-known for getting out of the vivarium and into your floors or walls, or anywhere there is a dark place to hide.

Be aware that all babies and most juveniles are very twitchy and jumpy and may try to leap up when you open their tank or vivarium. For them, a tank that only opens at the top is the best choice.

WHAT GOES ON TOP OF THE TANK?

Your tank needs a top that attaches securely. Some owners chose to have a simple screen

This works, and it is cheaper than a tank hood, but choosing a screen top also has problems. Putting a screen between your lights and your pet means the lights will be less efficient.

You'll be wasting light that isn't getting to your dragon. Many owners also find lights that clamp onto the upper sides of their vivarium, or hang from above, are less attractive than the next option. If you decide you want a screen top, choose a more open (larger size) mesh, because it allows more light to get into the vivarium.

Tank hoods have become less expensive in the past few years and so have the lights that fit in them, making them the more popular choice among beardie owners. They work more efficiently and they are also the sleeker, better-looking option. They fit more tightly than screens and hold the lights in the optimal position, rather than having to hang from above or perch to the side.

Tank hoods are hinged, making cleaning easier than needing to re-position your lights every time you clean the tank, which can happen with hanging or clamp light fixtures.

THE BENEFITS OF WOOD VIVARIUMS

Wood vivariums have a lot of advantages, in addition to being attractive. They are the best and easiest for controlling heat and humidity. They have glass on only one side (the front), which reduces the chance your pet could become stressed by seeing their own reflection.

You might think this is funny, but seeing their own reflection is actually a danger to your pet. They think they're seeing an approaching enemy animal. They want to escape, but in a vivarium there isn't anywhere to go. A beardie that is always afraid (or suffering from stress) is going to be much more likely to get seriously sick.

Wood vivariums with lights in the hood are stackable, if you want to have more than one beardie. It is never good to have more than one pet per vivarium or tank except during the brief periods when two animals share a space for mating. The reason is the stronger, larger or older one will attack their tank-mate. The smaller or younger animal will be constantly stressed.

Another advantage is that in a wood vivarium, you will achieve the heat you need with a lower wattage bulb, therefore saving on your power bill.

You could build your own vivarium, or you might choose to buy one. Prices recently online are in the $300 and up (or £200-plus) range. This is for the box only, and doesn't

TWEAK YOUR TANK!

Check your daytime temperatures at least one hour after your pet wakes up in the morning or no less than one hour before bedtime.

Test again after lights out when your dragon is sleeping.

You will probably have to make adjustments in the lights, heat, humidity and everything else in your pet's vivarium, but that's normal. No one gets their tank set up 'perfectly' on the first try!

include shipping or taxes.

Inside the vivarium, you need controlled temperatures, with a warmer end and a cooler end. The middle area is for the food and water dishes and possibly, for adults, a nesting or digging box. Or another hide.

TANK PLACEMENT

Put your pet's tank in a place where you can enjoy seeing each other all the time. Dragons want to be part of the family.

Your vivarium shouldn't be where there's a draft, right next to a room heater or air conditioner or in direct sunlight. It also shouldn't be in a dark corner, a spare room, or an unheated or damp room, such as a garage or basement.

Tanks that are entirely glass (such as fish tanks) can be dangerous if placed next to a window. Glass enclosures tend to collect heat, something like being locked in a car with all the windows closed on a hot summer day.

The tank also needs to be in a place that is dark and quiet at night and bright during the day. It usually isn't a problem to have the vivarium in a room where the TV is on in the evening, unless you like to have your TV really loud. When they get tired, most beardies will put themselves to bed in their cool hide, even if the family is still up.

Like cats or dogs, beardies soon adjust to family sounds, routines and odours. Also like other pets, they are comforted by a predictable routine.

TANK LIGHTS

Tank lights do two critical jobs for your pet. One type provides Ultraviolet light (UVA and UVB) and the other gives them heat.

YOU'LL NEED A LIGHTING SCHEDULE.

It is easiest (for you) and feels most natural for your pet if you set it up like this on timers:

	UV and Basking Lights ON:	Lights OFF:
Spring and Fall	7 am	7 pm
Summer	7 am	9 pm
Winter	7 am	5 pm
During Brumation (See Chapter 5)	All lights turned off	

Bearded dragons, like people, are diurnal. This means they naturally wake up not long after sunrise and go to sleep just after sunset. For this reason, you will need to remember to turn on their UV and heat lights each morning, just after dawn and turn them off each evening, just after sunset.

The easier option is to plug all your lights into timers and program your timers to change with the seasons.

Remember that beardies can't digest their food until they warm their bodies, so they can't eat until two hours <u>after</u> lights go on in the morning and must stop eating at least two hours <u>before</u> lights off in the evening.

You could also choose to plug your lights into a surge control/dimmer. This makes it easier to increase or decrease the heat/UV as needed and also protects from power differences, but not power outages.

Some owners like to have red lights turned on at night, or blue lights that "look cool," or "moonlight lights" or even black lights above the tank for a kind of lizard monster-scape.

This might sound like fun for you, but not for your pet. To them, it is unnatural, therefore weird as well as scary. Fight or flight is their natural response to being afraid. When they can't do either, in the small space of a vivarium, they are stressed.

Beardies can see in colour, though probably not in exactly the same way, or the same colours humans see. Their vivarium needs to be away from TV, computer or other electronics screens and anything else that you could call a night-light.

THE HEAT LAMP

Beardies must have heat from a heat lamp positioned

needs to warm the tank to about 100 degrees F. (38 degrees C) on the warm side of their tank and allow the vivarium to be about 75 to 80 degrees F. (24 to 27 degrees C) at the cooler end of the tank. This is the right range of temperatures for an adult. Babies need it to be a bit warmer than this – say around 110 F. or 43 C. No dragon can thrive when the temperature dips below 65 degrees F. or 18 degrees C.

PET HEATING MISTAKES

It might be tempting to use hot rocks or under-tank heating pads to keep your pet warm

Neither is a good idea. Beardies have tender bellies, easily burnt by the rock heaters some pet suppliers (notably pet stores) still recommend.

Under-tank heaters can also overheat the vivarium, including the cool end. Beardies need heat from above, not from below their feet.

For your daytime heat, you could use a 30 watt or 60 watt floodlight bulb or a curio cabinet bulb or spot floodlight bulb. These bulbs screw into a light fixture, such as a ceramic or reflector or angle light or clamp light, or directly into the tank hood.

Both your UV light and heat light are turned off at night. If you like your home cooled below 65 F (18 C) at night, as some people do for comfortable sleeping, your dragon will be too cold. Give him or her a CHE heat lamp (it creates no light) for night-time heating. For convenience, you can also put this light on a timer and adjust seasonally.

If you use a mercury vapour-type light for UVB, you probably won't also need a heat light during the day, as the mercury vapours are a large round bulb (they look like a floodlight) and they emit both UV and heat.

To get the right amount of heat, you may need to experiment with different bulbs. You could also find that you need to vary the size and wattage of bulb you use, depending on the season. You will also have to measure the heat output at your pet's basking spot. Do this daily while you are getting your vivarium set up and, once it is working properly, measure UV output and heat at least twice a week.

THE UV LIGHT

Your tank must have an Ultraviolet (or UV) lamp at the top of the tank. Wild beardies get all the UV rays they need naturally, from the sun.

That's why they bask. Basking is sitting on a branch or a rock and snoozing while their bodies collect warmth and healthy UV rays. The UV rays give them natural vitamin D, which helps their bodies absorb and use calcium, critical for bone health.

Today, most lights are combination UVA/UVB lights, though you will still find lights that are only, or mostly, UVB.

The bulbs are either fluorescent, or mercury vapour. The mercury lights are designed for mounting three to four inches (8 to 10 cm) above a screen lid or outside and above the tank. The fluorescents mount directly in a screen hood, so are inside the vivarium.

Properly deployed, either type works fine. Your pet can be healthy and happy either way,

MAKE YOUR UV LIGHTS LAST LONGER!

Here's a tip for making your UV tube-style lights last longer. Flip them, end to end, once every three months. When your UV tube falls below 70 percent output, it's time to replace it.

so it's your choice.

A third light design, coil-style lights, have a very high output. This too-strong light can damage your pet's eyesight. Another reason to avoid them is they can overheat and explode.

Properly installed (follow the instructions that come with your lights exactly) and used,

Your UV light coverage needs to be about two-thirds to three-quarters (or 66 percent to 75 percent) of the length of their vivarium, leaving the cooler end of their home beyond the lights.

In their vivarium (or tank), the maximum distance between your pet and their UV light is 10 inches (25 cm). The ideal distance, beardie to UV light, is six or seven inches (15 cm to almost 18 cm). Letting them get less than 6 inches from their lights is dangerous because they could get burnt.

You need to measure the UV output of your lights, because they start strong and over time give out less UV, even though they still appear to be working. The usual life of a UV light is six to 12 months, though some last only half that amount of time. Then they must be replaced. Most experienced owners put a date on their bulbs, keep records and also have spare bulbs on hand.

The UV light needs to produce UVA and UVB output ideal for bearded dragons at their basking spot. To test for this, and be sure your lights are working, you'll need a UV light meter. The major light suppliers (such as Zoo Med) sell these, available on their websites or at reptile pet supply stores.

All lights made by the quality brands come with warranties and detailed instructions for mounting them correctly.

Here are some trusted brands of UV lights for reptile pets, including lights specifically for bearded dragons, for either hanging above or placing in the tank hood, as chosen by experienced dragon owners. These are in no particular order. They're all good choices:

- **High Intensity Self-Ballasted Light for Bearded Dragons by Tekizoo**. Combo UVA/UVB with a compact size. Compatible with most sizes and types of vivariums. Requires very specific positioning.
- **ReptiSun 10.0 UVB Reptile Lamp by Zoo Med**. Output is 10% UVB and 30% UVA, considered by many pet owners to be ideal. Compact, reliable and durable. It comes in a choice of sizes to suit the size of your vivarium.
- **Compact 70 Watt Mercury Vapor Bulb by Mega-Ray**. Efficient, effective, very compact and long-lasting UVA/UVB bulb, all of which makes it a high quality choice.
- **Bearded Dragon UVB Fluorescent Bulb 18 Inch by Zilla**. Powerful and consistent full-range lighting, which many owners claim makes for a more active and happier dragon. Emits all the UVA and UVB you need for an average of 3,500 hours of bulb life. One of the longest-lasting choices. This one is a long bulb, so it's not compact. It's meant to be used in fluorescent fixtures for larger tanks.
- **100 Watt UVA/UVB Mercury Vapor Bulb for Reptiles by Evergreen Pet Supplies**. Dual light that is known for reliability. Compatible with different sizes of tanks and set-ups. This one isn't compact, so not for the smaller tanks of babies.

Don't be too concerned about the bulb wattage. What matters more is getting the bulb that is:

1. the right size for your vivarium, and

2. it delivers the right amount of UVA and UVB light for the season when your pet is active and eating.

Remember that your UV and recommended daytime heat lights are turned off during brumation. That's the beardie form of hibernation during the coldest months of the year, when beardies mostly doze and stop eating. They don't need heat or UV light when they aren't eating.

Pet lighting is one of those things that sounds more complicated than it actually turns out to be.

What matters is that your pet gets warmth and UVB during the day, and light-free warmth (if needed) at night.

Here's what's critical to know about your lights:

1. Choose a quality brand
2. Get the light that is suited to your set up (tank screen or tank hood) and the length of your tank (so, for example, choose the UVB light that provides 48 inches of coverage for a 72 inch long vivarium), and
3. Follow the directions that come with the bulbs <u>exactly</u>.

If you have an active pet that is basking for at least four hours a day, eating well and pooping normally, you've got your lights, heat and humidity right.

If you've got a pet who isn't basking, eating and pooping, the most likely reason and very first thing to check is your lights.

If they are right, check the heat. Then the humidity. Beardie problems are usually one of

MERCURY VAPOURS MAY NOT BE YOUR BEST CHOICE!

Mercury vapour lights have plenty of fans. But they also have plenty of foes. Why?

On the plus side, they can last a long time. They provide both heat and UVB light, which is a lot to get in one bulb.

The downside is they can be expensive, costing as much as two to three times what you'll pay for the other styles of UV lights, and this isn't the only reason to choose a different option.

It can be difficult to position combo-lights correctly for both the right amount of heat and UV coverage.

They gradually reduce and then stop putting out UVB, usually long before they stop putting out either light or heat. Unless you test and keep track of your lights including replacement dates, you could easily forget to replace the bulb, meaning your pet doesn't get the UVB they need.

If you're the organized sort of pet owner who tests light levels and temperatures regularly and keeps on top of your light replacements, and you don't mind the price, mercury vapours could work for you.

these three (usually, the first one).

Over time, with experience and as your pet ages, you might change your lighting set up. Most pet owners do. Don't be too concerned about this. Get it right to start, and go from there.

A LITTLE NIGHT HEAT

Most humans sleep more comfortably in rooms that are cooler than daytime temperatures. Most pets are also used to warmer days and cooler nights, and this includes bearded dragons. The problem is the human idea about comfortably cool to be able to sleep soundly isn't the same as

nighttime comfort.

SOME LIKE IT HOT – BUT NOT TOO HOT!

Keep your beardie in their comfort zone:

<u>Cool Side of the Vivarium</u>

For babies: 80 degrees F. to 85 degrees F. (27 to 29 degrees C.)

For adults: 70 degrees F. to 80 degrees F. (26 to 32 degrees C.)

<u>Warm Side</u>

95 degrees F. to 104 degrees F. (26 to 32 degrees C.)

<u>Basking Spot</u>

105 degrees F. to 110 degrees F. (40 to 43 degrees C.)

If you like it cooler than 65 F. (or 18 C.), that's fine, but your beardie is going to need a little night heat. This comes from a bulb that does not emit any light, just some warmth.

This is called a ceramic heat emitter, or CHE. You can put your CHE on a timer to come on an hour or so after bedtime and lights-out, and put it on a dimmer to control the heat. You need the CHE to give your dragon nights of no more than 70 F. (or 21 C.)

TAKING YOUR TEMPS

Checking temperatures in the three zones of your vivarium (warm, cool, in-between) will be a part of your daily routine.

Don't rely on the strip thermometers, the kind that you stick on the glass. They are rarely accurate. All they measure is the glass and the area very close to where they are placed. Much better to buy a digital probe thermometer. Or invest in an infra-red thermometer. They will give very accurate readings.

WHAT ABOUT HUMIDITY?

Just like us, beardies don't like muggy weather. But too dry also doesn't suit them. For babies, about 65 percent humidity is right. Closer to 40 percent is what adults need. Either too much (more than 70 percent) or too little (less than 20 percent) humidity can lead to respiratory (breathing) problems.

You'll need to check the humidity daily. The tool you need to do this is a hygrometer. Buy one and follow the instructions that come with it.

To add to the humidity in your vivarium, you could do any of these:

- Give them a shallow water dish, such as a jar lid with water changed twice a day.
- Mist them during the day. Never mist if it is less than 90 minutes before lights out.
- Give them a bath, during the day and well before bedtime.
- Use a humidifier in the room where their vivarium is.
- Buy a reptile humidifier. This goes in the tank. They come with complete instructions for use.

IDEAL HUMIDITY FOR DRAGONS

Babies and younger juveniles are most comfortable in 35 to 55 percent humidity.

Adults prefer it to be a bit drier, at around 30 percent humidity.

To decrease the amount of humidity for your beardie, do any of these:

- Remove the water dish from the tank.
- Remove live plants from the tank.
- Use a dehumidifier in their room.

BASKING BRANCHES

Bearded dragons climb to get close to their sunshine or UV light.

Give your beardie some smooth, rounded rocks or a big climbing branch, a bit wider than their body, or both. One should be directly under their heat and UV lights.

If you choose a climbing branch, make sure it did not come from an evergreen tree.

Cedar is poisonous to bearded dragons. Other evergreen wood, such as pine, hemlock or yew will make them sick. That's also true of driftwood.

Be sure your basking branch has no peeling bark or anything sharp like thorns or smaller branches.

The safest basking branches have been disinfected before they're sold specifically as basking branches for reptiles.

Good choices for your pet's climbing branch would come from any of these types of trees:

- Oak
- Maple
- Aspen
- Dogwood
- Apple, cherry or any other fruit tree.

HOW TO DISINFECT A CLIMBING BRANCH

Suppose you can't find a climbing branch you like at your local reptile pet supplies store, or online. However, you've got some driftwood, or a branch from a backyard tree, or just a piece of climbing branch another pet owner gave you. Should you use it? Is it safe?

The answer is maybe, if…

You can't use it if it is ocean driftwood, but fresh water driftwood might be OK if you disinfect it.

Don't use it if it's one of the woods that are poisonous to dragons. Fruitwood, particularly cherry or apple, is a much better choice.

It will already be disinfected if you've just bought it from a reputable reptile pet store or online supplier (not a neighbourhood pet shop). It's safe to use.

Here's how to disinfect a climbing branch:

1. Wash thoroughly with warm water and dish detergent.
2. Scrub clean with a brush. A toothbrush or vegetable-cleaning brush works.
3. Rinse.
4. Allow to dry.
5. Wrap in tinfoil (aluminium wrap) and put in a warm oven (about 250 degrees F). Bake for one hour.
6. Discard the tinfoil. Allow the branch to cool for 24 hours before it goes into your vivarium.

Rocks that have been cleaned and disinfected, with no sharp edges, are safe.

If you put anything made out of plastic in the tank, make sure it's made out of non-toxic plastic.

ALL ABOUT BEARDED DRAGON HIDES

It isn't possible to give your dragon more hides than he or she is wishing for. The average vivarium simply doesn't have the space for multiple hides, but it does need to have at least one, which is the cool hide. Better is to have two, one cool and the other not directly under your UV or heat lamps. Hides need to be a place where your dragon can get completely out of sight and relax or sleep in comfort and peace.

This is relatively easy to provide for a tiny baby or small juvenile. Once your pet reaches adult size and length, it becomes more of a challenge. This is another reason why a tank that is less than six feet long (or 183 cm) is simply too cramped for an adult beardie.

Your cool hide is the most important. Beardies need to cool down to relax and sleep. It is also their nature to prefer to run from danger and hide, rather than stand and fight. Not having a comfortable place to cool off and relax is stressful for dragons.

You can find cool hides made of ceramic or plastic at pet supply stores. If you buy plastic, be sure it is the newer, safer, non-BPA plastic. Generally, these are fine for the youngsters. For adults, you may need to improvise, perhaps with a partly broken flower pot set on its side. Or some sort of box.

Do not place a hide directly under the basking light, especially if the hide is a bowl or flowerpot or anything ceramic. These can easily overheat and burn your pet.

Remember that they climb over and poop on every single thing in their vivarium. Your hide-building materials will need to be sturdy as well as dragon-proofed with smooth edges, made of safe materials and washable.

WHAT ABOUT SUBSTRATE?

Substrate is the ground beneath their feet. This is another beardie care topic where there has been controversy in recent years.

DANGEROUS SUBSTRATE!

Any of these, used as substrate, are dangerous for your pet:

- Corn husks
- Walnut cobs
- Alfalfa pellets
- Kitty litter
- Wood shavings, bark or mulch. Cedar is particularly toxic to beardies.
- Potting soil or garden soil

Bearded dragons in their natural habitat (that is, Australia) live in places that are somewhat dry or semi-dry, but they are not a desert animal. In the wild, they might encounter some sand, but it is more likely what they are used to is harder-packed ground. When you think about farmland for grazing animals such as cows or sheep or scrubby woodland on the edges of farmland, this is closer to the natural habitat for most of Australia's wild dragons.

Could you recreate this, or something like it, in your tank? Yes you could. But it's far easier, and also looks pleasing to pet owners, to just use sand. That's what a lot of beardie owners did until it became clear that impaction is a common problem with bearded dragons. There's more about this danger in Chapter 8. Basically, impaction is pets accidentally eating sand along with their food. This causes them to become bloated with sand. They can't get rid of it. Impaction kills them.

Babies and juveniles are more likely to eat sand than adult dragons.

Seeing that these pets were prone to eat their sand, some pet food producers started selling sand for tanks with added calcium or other supplements. You can still see these products for sale and even recommended as "safe" substrate, which isn't true. There are far better and healthier choices.

In this century, more study of dragon behaviour and health has revealed that impaction is not caused by simply having edible – or any kind – of sand as your substrate. But that doesn't mean it's safe!

The danger is that sand creates sand dust as your pet moves around and digs in their vivarium. The dust gets in their eyes, so it can create eye problems. When they breath this dust in, they can get respiratory infections. For this reason, if you have sand in the tank, it should be just a very small area. For pets that like to dig (as many dragons do), there are safe choices for their digging box or area.

Other substrate options are:

1. **Shredded paper** such as newsprint, recycled paper, butcher paper, baking parchment paper, or paper towel. All of these are odour-free and absorbent. Be careful about using shredded paper, because feeders can easily hide (crickets, particularly, always scurry off to the darkest place they can find). These are the only substrate choices that are safe for a baby or young juvenile. Of these, newsprint is the best and cheapest. For babies, you will need to replace it daily. It doesn't look natural and isn't very attractive, but it works.

2. **Small river stones** that have been cleaned and disinfected or aquarium rock. Unlike gravel, the rounded edges won't hurt your pet's feet and most dragons like an area of very small stones to walk on. The disadvantages are stone substrate will add weight to your tank and is harder to keep clean. If you are using a fish tank as their home, it won't be strong enough, structurally, to support stone substrate. Feeder insects may be able to hide in the stones. Your pet will dump water on them. It is easier for bacteria and other nasties to grow in stone substrate, causing illness.

3. **Reptile carpet** or cage mat is very similar to outdoor carpet. It looks somewhat natural, but you will probably have to take it out and wash it frequently, perhaps daily. When it starts to fray, replace it. Pets can and will eat any frayed bits or loose threads.
4. **Ceramic tile** can be a good choice for adult pets, but must be fitted so there are no cracks where insects, water or waste could gather. Beardies don't enjoy walking on a smooth surface, particularly, but it is safe for them.
5. **Bare tank floor** is the safest and easiest to clean.

There is no one, ideal, reptile substrate. Each presents challenges for pet owners. You will probably test-drive a few before finding the one that is safe and both you and your pet like.

Remember that beardies can, and will, swallow anything small in their tank.

This includes sand, small stones, pieces of paper, carpet threads or anything else that's there. A healthy pet should be able to handle very small amounts of any non-food they swallow by accident. A highly-stressed pet will be less able to (this is the real cause of impaction). A pet that is getting enough water to drink is much less likely to become impacted.

To be sure he or she is getting that water, you'll be misting your pet, meaning the substrate will get wet. Some of the substrate options can remain damp, allowing moulds to grow.

Combine that with a pet that eats a lot and poops a lot, and you will be spot cleaning daily and disinfecting the entire tank once a week or so. Whatever you put in the tank, you'll be cleaning it fairly often.

So, what do breeders use for substrate? After all, they have multiple pets, making multiple tanks to clean daily. Here's what breeders say they use, after having tried all the options:

For Babies and Young Juveniles:

Paper towels, with edges taped down so feeders can't hide under it. Replace daily.

For New Adults:

Shelf paper, because it is easy to clean and also not expensive to replace often.

For Adults, particularly Gravid (pregnant) Females:

Give them plastic containers of washed, sifted play sand (you can buy it at home improvement stores). This gives them somewhere to dig, which most adult dragons love to do and pregnant females must do to create a nest for their eggs.

OTHER TANK DÉCOR

Part of the enjoyment of having a beardie, for a lot of owners, is vivarium décor. It's something like having a really cool room, rather than just a plain box to live in.

Your adult beardie wants variety in his or her tank, but it should be naturalistic. That is, what they'd find in their natural world, not odd plastic castles or other strange (to a lizard) objects.

You might choose real plants or (non-toxic) plastic ones. Safe varieties are fine, though your pet will climb over them and they'll need to be cleaned almost every day. Silk plants are harder for a pet to destroy, but dangerous, because of the chemicals they are made with and also because the material frays and can get caught in their claws. Bearded dragons will also try to eat their tank plants, so choose safe varieties.

SHOULD I GET TOYS FOR MY PET?

Beardies aren't very interested in toys. Their idea of a rockin' good time is to chase a dubia roach or grasshopper (locust) around for a while and then eat it.

Another thing some adult beardies just love, but others don't really care about, is digging.

If you've got a digger, give them an area or nesting box filled with safe material to really get stuck into. Safe materials are vermiculite (buy it at the garden centre) or shredded paper.

When out of their vivarium with you, a toy some beardies have a happy time with is a ping pong ball. Get your pet one, wash and disinfect it and see if he or she enjoys pushing it around.

Stuffed toys aren't a good idea. A toy will need daily washing. Your pet will shred it and the fibres and little pieces could harm them.

BEARDED LADIES

Both male and female bearded dragons are able to darken and inflate their beards when they're angry, sense danger or encounter a rival. Males are more frequent at bearding because they also deploy their beards during courtship.

Bearding is fairly common among wild bearded dragons, but it's rare for a pet dragon to beard.

FOUR

Bringing Your Beardie Back Home!

Once you have your tank set up and you know it's working the way it should, you're one huge step closer to being ready to bring your new pet home!

But first, you must find a vet and think carefully about what sort of bearded dragon you want.

FIND A REPTILE VET

A vet (or veterinarian) is a doctor and surgeon for animals. Since no vet could possibly be expert in every animal, like doctors for humans, vets specialize.

Generally, vets specialize in small animals (primarily dogs and cats) or large animals (primarily horses, cows and other farm animals). There are also vets who specialize in large exotics (such as lions, tigers and elephants) or sea mammals (such as seals and whales).

It's just good sense to know who you're going to turn to, in an emergency, before that crisis happens. It's also sensible to get an annual health check-up with your vet. This gives you an opportunity to bring up any concerns and ask questions.

The challenge is finding a vet who specializes in treating reptiles. They're fairly rare.

If you adopt from a reputable breeder or a rescue shelter, your pet will have been checked out by their vet and have a health record. Experienced, reputable breeders (like most advanced reptile pet owners) are usually very knowledgeable about reptile health.

HOW TO GET A HEALTHY PET PART 1

Don't buy your pet because you feel sorry for how sad, thin and sick they are. This is almost guaranteed to lead to heartbreak.

If you're buying a baby, buy the biggest, most active one. They're the alpha lizard that has gotten most of the best food and is probably the healthiest.

Choose the beardie that has:

- Bright, clear eyes. Their eyes aren't watering or swollen or red.
- A good appetite.
- Healthy poop, once a day or every other day. Feel their belly. If it feels hard, they could be impacted and need the vet.
- A rounded body with a plump belly and wide tail.
- Their backbone (spine) doesn't stick out.
- Their skin looks healthy. Don't buy a pet with crusty skin. This is yellow fungus, caused by living in a dirty tank. It's very contagious. Pets usually don't survive yellow fungus. Also make sure there are no black spots on their skin. Black spot is a skin infection.
- There are no cuts, scrapes or sores on their body.
- Fingers, toes and tail tip aren't damaged.
- They don't have swollen elbows (this could be a sign that they have bone disease).

HOW TO GET A HEALTHY PET PART 2

- They're active.
- They hold their head up.
- They're curious and alert. They want to meet you.

Beyond determining that your future pet is healthy, here are some important questions to ask. Is the dragon you want to buy:

1. Eating normally?
2. Basking?
3. Pooping?
4. Happy to be held? Are they calm, not nervous?

Even with a clear health record from either a rescue centre vet or reputable breeder, it's good to take your new pet to a reptile vet about two weeks after you adopt them. This gives your beardie time to settle into their new home. By then, you'll be able to answer the three basic health questions the vet will ask. These are:

- Are they eating the right amount of the right foods for their age?
- Are they basking at least six hours a day?
- Are they pooping normally?

Bearded dragons are hardy animals. As pets, they live in a controlled environment where you protect them from being attacked by a rival or burnt by a hot rock or other disasters they might suffer in the wild.

HOW MUCH WILL THIS PET COST?

<u>For your bearded dragon</u>:

Cost depends on:

1. **Age**. Babies are cheaper than juveniles or adults because babies are harder to keep alive.
2. **Where** you get your beardie. Cost is higher in England or Japan, for example, than in US.
3. The **type of dragon**. Standard beardies are the cheapest; the rarest morphs are the most expensive.

<u>For their terrarium set-up</u>:

Good used equipment is hard to find, but it will cost about half as much, or less, than you'll pay for a new tank, lights, meters and everything else you'll need. For your set-up, expect to spend about US $500 to $1,300, or slightly more in pounds or euro.

<u>For their food:</u>

Budget about US $30 per month for insects and US $20 for supplements. They'll also eat small amounts of the same fresh fruits, vegetables and greens that you eat (or should eat).

<u>Plus, you'll pay for</u>:

Vet visits. About US $100 to $150 for a qualified reptile vet, or about the same in pounds or euro.

HOW MUCH WILL THIS PET COST?

Your **power bills** will go up for their heat and UV lights. By how much? About US $200 per year is average.

Tank upgrades. Varies, depending on what you choose to do. You'll have to replace UV bulbs and possibly heat bulbs, at a cost of $60 to $100 per year.

Estimates vary, but if you want to know **how much it costs to keep a bearded dragon per year** (after you have your pet and your vivarium set up), that would be in the neighbourhood of US $1,000.

While your beardie will avoid these dangers, there are other possible dangers caused by being your pet.

Even the most cautious and conscientious beardie owner can run into problems with what reptile pets are susceptible to, including mould, parasites and infections (See Chapter 8).

To go to the vet, put your beardie in a cardboard or plastic box with air circulation holes or in a pet carrier, the type used for cats. No, they won't like it, but it is much safer for them to travel this way than allowing them to ride unrestrained in the car. Check local laws. In many places, pets in cars are required to be in a harness (dogs, mainly) or in a pet carrier.

Remember to take a sample of their most recent poop so the vet can do a fecal exam. You do this by scooping a small amount into a very clean plastic container with a tight lid.

As with any animal, a fecal exam (this means their poop) can reveal a lot about their health.

WHICH BEARDIE DO I BUY?

In Europe and Britain, the usual way to get a beardie is adopting from either a pet rescue shelter or directly from a breeder. However, if you live in United States or Canada, in addition to these two sources, you could also buy your pet from a pet store.

A fourth place to get your pet is from someone else who can no longer care for them, or who has lost interest in having a pet.

There are advantages and disadvantages to each of these sources. Which is right for you?

Consider that you aren't just buying consumer goods, like a phone or pair of gym shoes that you will use for a while and then recycle or discard.

You're buying the companionship of a living creature.

A pet is a major purchase of heart as well as head. Like any major purchase or decision, it requires research, thoughtfulness and commitment.

You are about to add a new member to your family.

There is the time you devote to pet research. Their set-up requires attention to every detail of their environment to give them exactly the home they need. Beyond this, you must be willing to have your heart stolen by one small creature who moves into your life and changes it forever.They will come to own a part of you, just as you own them.

So, where will you find your new four-pawed soul mate?

FIND YOUR PET AT A HERP SHOW

A Herp Show is a trade show for people who appreciate reptile pets. There you can usually see snakes, chameleons, iguanas, anoles and bearded dragons. There may be some very rare animals on display that aren't for sale, but are interesting to meet. It is more likely that most of the animals at the show are for sale.

Generally, these shows are offered once a year, usually in or near a city. Visitors to the show get the opportunity to talk to breeders about the animals they sell. As beardie lovers, they are usually happy to answer questions.

It's also a good place to see creative vivarium set-ups, learn about the latest lighting and other tech innovations and order or buy custom-made vivariums and leading-edge products (often not yet offered in pet supply stores).

You'll also see adult bearded dragons, relaxing amidst the merchandise, content to watch the crowd. Some breeders will be walking around, visiting competitors, with one of their beardies clinging to their shoulder or chest.

A Herp Show makes a fun family day out, even for people who aren't quite smitten (yet) with having a beardie for a family member. You can find out when and where the next Herp Show near you will be with an online search.

PET STORE PETS

In the U.S. and Canada, it's common to see tropical fish, birds, small mammals such as hamsters and guinea pigs and also reptiles sold at pet stores. These pet stores may be small family businesses, or one of the pet supply chain outlets.

Some of these stores do a good job of ethically sourcing their animals, properly housing

DON'T BUY THE ANIMAL THAT:

- Seems to be sleepy or hardly moves.
- Keeps their eyes closed (a sign of stress).
- Is afraid of people.
- Is too thin, with a narrow tail and visible hip bones.
- Has a dirty bum (a sign of parasites).
- Has a dirty tank (a sign of neglect).
- Shares a tank with other animals.
- Has brown streaks on their belly (these are stress marks).
- Always has their mouth open or is gasping (a sign of respiratory illness).
- Is trembling (a sign of bone disease).
- Has a hunchback.
- Don't buy a pet you've never seen, unless you are buying from a reputable breeder.

It's too easy to buy an animal because you feel sorry for it. Sometimes, that works out OK and both you and your new pet are a happy match. More often, sadly, despite your best efforts and possibly some big vet bills, that pet can't be saved.

them and keeping them healthy. Sadly, stores that do a competent job of housing and presenting reptile pets are rare. Far more commonly, pet stores sell animals bred under questionable conditions.

It is common for pet shop staff to have little or no knowledge of bearded dragon care.

They may display several baby dragons in a small fish tank. This is dangerous because babies or juveniles will attack each other. There may be no heat or UV lamp. Interior store lights may be left on 24/7. They may have received no calcium or vitamin supplements. The list of common abuse towards animals for sale in too many general pet stores goes on.

This can be deliberate carelessness or simply happen because pet staff don't know how to house bearded dragons. Not surprisingly, these poor little dragons often die, or are so stressed and sick that they are not likely to survive when unknowing new owners take them home.

Typically, in these pet stores, you will find a baby beardie for $30 to $60. I've heard many stories of new owners who did buy a baby at a pet shop and were advised to buy a "starter kit" not meant for beardies plus a shopping cart overflowing with supplies for their new pet. In other words, the little animal is the bait, tricking shoppers into spending hundreds of dollars on pet gear.

Then these hapless new owners discover that at least half of what they've been sold isn't appropriate for bearded dragons. It also might not be returnable.

Just about every experienced reptile pet owner tells this story. If it didn't happen to them, then they know at least one pet owner who fell victim to this scam. The advice they offer is do your research before you pick your pet.

Shop with a list. Know what you're buying, and why.

Pet supplies stores that specialize in reptiles are generally a giant step up from most general pet stores. There you will find staff who are knowledgeable about the animals they offer for sale. You are more likely to find healthy juveniles or adults. You will pay more for their pets, typically $100 to $150, but you will have these valuable advantages:

- Assurance that you're buying a healthy pet.

- A return guarantee, if anything goes wrong.
- Reliable advice.
- They will also sell healthy live feeder insects (though they will charge more than prices you will see online, if you live in a place where receiving live insects shipped by online suppliers is legal).

RESCUE PETS

Most large pet rescue organizations or charities specialize in dogs and cats, simply because these two are the most popular pets in the world. Some also offer other types of pets, including reptiles. There are also a few smaller local or regional rescues that specialize in reptiles. You can find these by asking friends who own reptile pets or by doing an online search.

Typically, they won't offer babies or younger dragons or the fancier dragons called morphs. Instead, they'll have standards. These are adult animals given up by careless or irresponsible owners who choose not to or can't spend the time or money to get it right.

If you buy your pet from an online marketplace, such as Kijiji, you can expect to get a neglected pet. Usually, sellers there include a setup that doesn't work and needs to be replaced. If you find your new pet is ill (as they likely are) this could get expensive.

Here's a way to make rescue or rehoming less risky. Take the time to find and talk to a reptile vet, reptile specialist or rescue group about dragons they have or know about that need a new home. If the pet you want to adopt has a health condition, get the details about what kind of on-going health care they'll need.

For example, a beardie that has lacked calcium and/or UV light could be partially paralyzed. They'll be a special-needs pet, but could, with care, live for several more years.

BUYING FROM A BREEDER

Ask around, do an online search or go to a Herp Show to find an experienced, ethical breeder. Check out their reviews. Ask beardie owners. Well-respected breeders know their animals and want the best for them as well as for owners.

Breeders will be able to tell you how old the animal you want to adopt is. You can learn about the parents. What food he or she is currently eating. Good breeders will answer all your questions, before and after you buy. One way to identify a good breeder is their genuine passion and enthusiasm for the animals they keep and offer for sale and for people who share their interest in bearded dragons.

Unfortunately, there are also some bad breeders out there. These are people who are breeding animals strictly as a business and money-spinner.

BEARDIE BREEDERS

Here are just a few of the many reputable breeders of morphs, the more exotic (and expensive) bearded dragons. Note that breeders are only able to ship animals within their own countries.

In United States:

- [illegible] website of breeder Joe Cattey in Texas. He also creates beautiful vivariums.
- www.fireandicedragons.com in Pennsylvania.
- www.atomiclizardranch.net in Arizona.
- www.dachiubeardeddragons.com in Pennsylvania.

In Canada:

- www.redhotchilidragons.com in Ontario. Visit this site to see photos of some spectacular reds!

To find more breeders, including ones that may be closer to where you live, do an online search.

They may knowingly sell animals that aren't healthy or haven't been well cared for. Usually, if you've done your pet research, talked to friends with bearded dragons and met some healthy animals already, you'll be able to spot the signs of poor care and poor health.

Then, there's a danger you can't spot, and it's common among unethical breeders. This is inbreeding, to get a specific body colour or pattern. In the quest to produce an ultra-exotic or even one-of-a-kind animal that will command a high price, there are breeders who will do almost anything.

The problem is that inbreeding produces serious health flaws. We see it in purebred dogs today, as a result of careless inbreeding that has resulted in serious hereditary flaws. Just some of these are Dalmatians, prone to deafness; Boxers, who suffer high rates of heart disease and cancer; German Shepherds, known as are many larger breeds for hip dysplasia and Irish Setters, where the result is far too many develop epilepsy.

All of this would have been avoided with responsible breeding. Could the same happen with other pets? Absolutely. It appears that it is happening now in reptile pets, including bearded dragons.

Since early in this century there has been a sharp rise in cancer in captive bearded dragons, particularly in the United States. Many experts are pointing to inbreeding as the most likely cause. However, with relatively little study of these animals, and no controls on breeders except their own ethics, there is no proof.

Check to make sure the breeder you choose to get your dragon from has a long and honourable history of breeding reptiles and is passionate about them. These are the breeders who keep careful records of how they have diversified the bloodlines to create healthy dragons.

The breeder who seems to be creating animals merely as a business where the animals are simply a commodity is the one to avoid. If enough pet owners can do this, more of the irresponsible breeders will be driven out of business.

WHAT IS A MORPH?

The baby beardies you most often see for sale at pet stores (in Canada or U.S.) are standards. They are brown with patterns in dark brown, grayish-brown or tan. Their appearance is fairly close to their wild Australian ancestors.

While their colour and patterns will change as they grow to adulthood, just as is true of all bearded dragons, these standard babies will still be brown/tan on their backs and creamy/tan on their bellies as adults.

Morphs are hybrids specifically created by breeders for specific desirable colours or patterns. The rarer and more exotic their colouring or markings, the more in-demand and expensive these animals are. This is similar to the demand for very rare breeds of dogs or cats.

You can see photos of morphs online and may even see a few at a Herp Show or private zoo. However, most morphs belong to either breeders or wealthy pet owners.

So, what's so special about morph beardies?

They eat, bask, breed and generally act just like any other pet beardie. The only difference is their skin colour or pattern.

COLOUR MORPHS

Breeders love to invent fanciful names for the animals they create.

There are creamy-white or almost-pure-white animals, called Snowies, among other names. They aren't albinos, so they don't have pink eyes. They are truly and entirely almost-white.

There is an almost pure black beardie, with black eyes.

And there are various shades of orange, reddish-orange and yellow.

Generally, the most expensive morphs are very pure white, orange or red. Pure blue and pure purple morphs do exist, but for reasons breeders haven't worked out yet, these two colour morphs tend to have very short lives.

Hypo morphs are hypo-melanistic. This means a pure and lighter colour that can be pastel. They usually have bands on their tails, but no other markings. They might be light yellow, pale green (bred in England) and yellow, or light reddish yellow. They have clear nails and their beard is usually just a darker shade of their skin colour. Otherwise they look just like a standard beardie.

A **Witblits** dragon has no pattern and can be any colour.

Dunners are dragons that look rough and like they're up for a fight. Not true; it's just that this animal looks rugged and primitive, like some ancient dragon ancestor. This is because the scales on their backs are cone-shaped, making them look tougher than every other type of dragon with their teardrop-shaped scales.

There are some other oddities about dunners. When they have belly stress marks, these marks will be in circles. They have big feet and extra-long toes. They also have unique tail patterns that can look like dots, dashes or long stripes, rather than the pattern of bands that standard dragons have.

Het is another term breeders and experienced pet owners use. Het is short for Heterozygous. It just means that a particular baby carries the gene from one parent for a particular trait. That trait may prove to be dominant, meaning you see it in the baby. Or it is recessive, meaning the baby carries that genetic signal forward to its babies eventually (if it ever breeds as an adult), but that trait is invisible in this bearded dragon, as it will be for all their life.

Leatherback is, despite what the name suggests, a beardie morph with somewhat smooth skin and very bright colours. They have no spikes on their backs, but do have them on their heads and along their sides. Leatherbacks are rarer than hypo morphs.

Translucent morphs are usually hypo, so lighter in colour. Their scales are almost see-through. The babies have almost clear belly skin. Adults have dark eyes and sometimes blue eyelids.

Silkback is the morph with the smoothest, softest skin. They have no spikes or scales. They are more delicate than other beardies and require more care, so are only a good choice for experienced bearded dragon owners.

German Giant was one of the first morphs developed in the last century, in Germany as the name suggests. They were very large, but otherwise typical of standard pet beardies.

As a designed animal, they turned out to be a fad in Europe but unpopular elsewhere and are now rare. Today, there are a few American breeders who create very large versions of red or yellow morphs and call them German Giants.

Zero Morphs are the rarest of the rare dragons. They have no colour or patterns at all, so they are white.

Wero is the hybrid baby of a Witblits and a Zero parent. As an adult, a wero looks like a zero, but it has darker colour blotches near its tail.

Paradox is the strangest-looking morph dragon of all. It looks like a wero or a zero, except that it has bigger, irregular blotches of a pure colour, such as yellow or orange, all over its head and back.

BOY OR GIRL?

Knowing the gender of a baby dragon is guesswork until they become juveniles. This happens at about four months old, or when they're eight inches long. Even as juveniles it's easy to get it wrong as some males are late to reach sexual maturity.

The difference to look for is this. On their tails, just beyond the vent, females have a triangle-shaped bump that points towards the tips of their tails, like this: Δ

Males have two long thin oval bumps with a space between them that hold their hemipenes, from just beyond their vents along their tails, like this: 0 0

Bearded dragons don't like being turned over for you to get a closer look. They also don't like having their tails held up as you try to find out what gender they are, as this can easily hurt them. If you do check for gender, with your pet sitting on a hard surface, gently lift their tail with one hand while holding them (to prevent escape) with the other.

SHOULD I GET A MALE OR A FEMALE?

As adults, males are usually larger, but not always. They usually have brighter colours.

Females, many owners say, are generally more docile, though all beardies are known for their usually easy-going, sunny nature.

Neither gender tends to be healthier than the other.

If you really want to know what gender your beardie is but it's hard to tell, ask your reptile vet next time you and your pet go for a check-up. Or a friend who's an experienced beardie owner can probably help you out.

COMING HOME

Moving to a new home is stressful for anyone, whether they're animal or human. It's especially stressful when you just don't know what's going on and no one can tell you.

To come home, put your new pet in a box with holes big enough for lots of air circulation. Place some shredded newspaper in the bottom. If it is winter, warm up your car first. In summer, you might need some air conditioning.

Once you're home, put the opened box on its side inside the tank. Let your new pet come out of the box when they're ready.

Give them fresh water and some insects to eat and then leave them alone. Don't feed them again until the next day. Don't handle your new beardie for a week or so. They need time to get used to their home and all its strange sounds and smells.

Be patient about taming your bearded dragon. Like any newbie, they need some time to get used to being a member of your family.

It's common for a pet beardie to be stressed, as they adjust to this new vivarium they now find themselves in. They might get stress marks on their belly. They might not want to eat. They might spend a lot of time in their cool hide.

Doing this for a couple of days is normal. However, a baby beardie that doesn't eat for more than two days is a major problem. Babies need to eat a lot, and often. They can quickly go downhill when they don't eat or drink.

Tempt your new pet with right-sized pieces of fruit. Just about every dragon loves cut-up grapes or cranberries. They also like mini-sized insects (for babies) or right-sized (for juveniles and adults), especially crickets or dubias.

Their appetites are usually stimulated when they can chase a live insect. But if they're just ignoring their food, as newbies sometimes do, try offering it with tongs.

If they still won't eat, check that your tank is warm enough, but not too warm. Also check noise levels in the room and the humidity level in the vivarium.

If your vivarium has a glass side or sides, cover the glass with paper for the first several days. This makes a vivarium feel more homey to a new pet.

It will be very tempting to get your new pet out and play with him or her. It is far kinder to leave them alone for the first week or so, letting them get used to their new home at their own pace.

Another temptation is to give your new pet a vivarium that is filled with accessories – rocks, plants, hides, dishes, toys, background wallpaper and more. This is simply too much of too much for your pet. Babies, especially, need a stripped down, very basic home of just their basking spot, cool hide, a lid as a food dish, paper substrate and nothing else.

WILL MY PETS GET ALONG WITH EACH OTHER?

Baby beardies have the instinct to be afraid of cats. This is for a good reason. Feral (wild) cats and foxes in Australia are very fond of eating baby lizards.

Beardies usually get along just fine with dogs.

Always introduce pets to each other gradually. Don't show favoritism. Dogs, especially, are very sensitive to this and can become jealous of a 'new' pet in their home.

Adults can tolerate more, in their larger tank, but do better if they don't have too much to cope with for the first few weeks.

MAKING FRIENDS

Give your juvenile or adult beardie a week or so to get used to their new home. Don't handle them until they know your voice and that delicious insects come from you.

Always, before and after you handle them, wash your hands with soap and warm water. This protects both of you from illnesses.

A beardie that trusts you and wants to come out and play will climb onto your palm. To pick them up, support their belly with that hand, and cradle your other hand over them. You do this because most bearded dragons (and all babies or juveniles) will try to jump away at some point. They might try this several times. The danger is they will fall and could be badly injured.

The correct way to hold them is gently but firmly.

Once they know, like and trust you, they may want to ride around on your chest or shoulder for hours. They might be happy watching TV or playing computer games together. Many owners have noticed that most beardies would rather hang out with their people than with other dragons.

SIGNS OF RELOCATION STRESS

1. **Not eating**. Feed them once when you get home. On Day 2 and for the next few days, tempt them with treats. Don't try to hand-feed an upset beardie because they might bite. Use tongs.
2. **Stress marks**. These are brown lines or ovals on their bellies and chins. This is normal and should go away in a few days.
3. **They hardly move around at all**. A lazy dragon that just lies around, hardly moving, could be stressed. They should be back to their normal, active selves in a few days. If they aren't, check that the heating, UV light
4. **They're a darker colour**. Darkening their skin and sometimes also their beard is a sign of stress. It can also be a sign that they aren't warm enough or they're about to shed.
5. **They hang out all the time in their cool hide**. If they aren't basking, they're stressed. This could also be a sign they're going into brumation, if they're an adult and it's the cool season. Otherwise, if your baby does this for more than two days, or your juvenile for more than a few days, or your adult for more than five days, the first thing to do is check your heat, light and humidity levels.

Be sure there are no stressors, like noise, strong odours, or other pets. This includes being able to see other dragons in nearby glass-sided vivariums, or their own reflection in the glass of their vivarium. That's scary if you're a beardie who suddenly finds himself or herself in a foreign territory with a shadowy rival.

DRAGON-PROOF YOUR HOUSE

Some beardie owners let their pets freely roam around the house. Not letting animals that still have their ancestors' instincts to explore their territory free from their vivariums, at least for a few hours each day, is just cruel, these owners say.

Others disagree. There are just too many dangers for a free-roaming beardie, they say. It's surprising how quickly a bearded dragon can run. They find small spaces to hide and might remain lost for too many hours away from the warmth and safety of their vivariums. There are also other dangers, such as electricity outlets and wires to consider.

So who's right?

Could it be that both these Beardie Freedom strategies are partly right, but partly wrong?

It's true that dragons need some privacy time, in their familiar homes. But they also need stimulation, with attention from you and, if they are a juvenile or adult, time to stretch their legs in a larger space.

Your dragon would like to be out, with you, for an hour a day or more (note: this is not true for babies, who should have very little or no handling).

Before you let your dragon out in the human world, you need to dragon-proof the room (or rooms) they're allowed to be in. Dragon-proofing is a lot like human baby-proofing. You need to make sure there is nothing that could harm them and no small spaces they could get into.

Put covers on electricity outlets (power points). Wrap, cover or get rid of cords. Make sure there are no spots where they could hide, like behind or under large pieces of furniture.

Remove any houseplants from the room.

Close off other pets, such as a dog or cat, in another part of your home.

Most importantly, always stay with your beardie when they're out of their vivarium.

Think about what kind of behaviour could possibly harm them.

Then, prevent it from happening so you and your pet can enjoy some quality time together without worries.

IS YOUR DRAGON STRESSED?

Stress is a life-changer for pets just as much as it is for people.

Here's how to tell if your dragon is suffering stress:

- They're not eating.
- They're lethargic.
- They spend a lot of time in their cool hide.

(Note that the points above are all completely normal when your pet is brumating).

More signs of stress:

- Their behaviour has changed. They seem more nervous or timid.
- They have smelly or runny poop.
- Glass surfing.
- They hiss at you or try to bite.
- Bearding.
- Running away when you approach their vivarium.
- Stress marks on their belly or chin. These are darker or brownish and look like irregular stripes. They fade away naturally when your pet is feeling more secure and content.

FIVE

Acting Up! Bearded Dragon Behaviour

Except for hissing, which they hardly ever do, bearded dragons are a quiet pet. Unlike people and also other pets, they don't use sound to communicate. Also like some other pets, they can't smile or use other facial actions to show their emotions and what they're thinking. Instead, they use body language.

You probably won't be able to translate every body gesture your pet makes. You'd need to be another bearded dragon to be totally fluent in Dragon. But you will begin to understand who they are, what they want and what they're trying to tell you, just as you can with a more conventional pet such as a dog or cat.

Bearded dragons don't simply copy, or mirror, what another dragon is doing. They react to their environment and what they care about. Their actions show this clearly to other dragons, but sometimes less clearly to us.

Many of these signals beardies send each other and understand evolved over many thousands of years to help them live their wild lives. Tame pet beardies may have little need to express the same things their wild ancestors did. Even so, the behaviour remains a part of their repertoire.

These ancestors needed to do what any animal has to accomplish. They needed to find water, food, shelter and, occasionally, an attractive partner to mate with so their species would survive.

A pampered pet, who has all the water and food she or he needs and a comfortable shelter and who is never threatened by an enemy or a rival will live a longer, healthier and calmer life than any wild animal. He or she won't need this bearded dragon language, so might seldom use it with large aliens (that's us, the humans).

Yet you still might see it. So in this chapter, we take a look at translating all the beardie behaviours known to experts, breeders and pet bearded dragon owners. Next time you're wondering *Why is my beardie doing that weird thing?* or *Just what is she trying to say?* remember, your pet still has strong instincts to be a wild animal, but they're now trying to be a tame animal and interact with a human (you), something their ancestors would have found unthinkable!

IS MY BEARDIE SMILING AT ME?

It's amusing to think that generally happy, easy-going bearded dragons are smiling all the time. After all, they look like they're smiling. It's just part of our human brain wiring, to like and trust people who smile.

But no, beardies aren't always smiling. That's just the way their face is shaped.

Beardies show affection for their human friends by running over, when you put you hand down flat in their vivarium, to climb into your palm because they want to come out to play and hang out with you.

Rushing away means they'd just rather have some time to themselves.

WHY DO THEY BLACKEN THEIR BEARDS?

A beardie that has a dark, enlarged beard and a gaping mouth could be upset, or they don't like changes in their territory or they're feeling sick. If there's also hissing, he (or rarely, she) is about to attack a rival dragon. It's usually just a bluff. Beardies try to look scary, but they'd almost always rather run than fight.

Males will sometimes also blacken their beards to flirt with females, maybe in the belief that it makes them appear more handsome and manly. When they do, the object of their desire usually bobs her head up and down or waves a front foot to say something like, "Yeah, you're pretty cute. Maybe we could get together."

Very occasionally, dragons give their beards a stretch, just because they can.

Here's how the bearding works. Beardies have bones running along both sides of their heads. These bones push the skin out as it turns darker, creating the bigger-and-badder beard effect that gives them their name.

WHY IS MY BEARDIE YAWNING?

They do this when they're waking up or maybe when their vivarium lights turn on in the morning. They'll puff their beards slightly and open and close their mouths.

They also open their mouths when bearding, part of the effort to make themselves look larger and fiercer.

Another reason for opening their mouth is to regulate their temperature, since they aren't able to sweat to cool off.

A beardie that keeps his or her mouth open a LOT is something to be concerned about, as this can be a sign of respiratory illness. If your beardie seems to have his or her mouth open all the time, you both need to see the vet.

DO BEARDIES EVER ATTACK PEOPLE?

Very rarely. You'd have to seriously annoy your beardie to ever see them blacken their beard at you.

They do, very occasionally, bite their owners. You should know that male beardies, being generally larger, have a stronger bite. If this happens, wash the wound, apply antiseptic and a band-aid (plaster).

Biting could be their way of trying to protect themselves when you and your pet are just getting to know each other. They don't trust you yet. Rather than just leave them alone, you should put on gardening gloves and handle them gently. This will give them a chance to find out that you aren't going to hurt them.

Hand-feeding also helps build trust with your pet.

WHY IS THAT BEARDIE WAVING AT ME?

Waving one or both front paws in a little circle (it looks surprisingly like the Queen's Wave) can mean a couple of things.

To understand, you need to know that bearded dragons, like many animals in the wild, exist in a hierarchy when they're together. There is a leader, or Alpha animal, and then everyone else has a ranking, from high to low. Every animal knows exactly where they fit in such a society. Subordinate animals defer to their superiors.

Humans use this same group organization, with remarkably similar rules, in politics, the military or para-military organizations such as the police and in their jobs. You take orders from those above you. You give orders to those of a lower rank than your own. The way you talk to and act with superiors is different than what you might say or do with those who report to you.

In their hierarchy, the healthiest, strongest and biggest male is at the top. Females, seniors and all juveniles are, socially speaking, beneath them.

Imagine that two male bearded dragons happen to meet. The older and stronger animal is outraged that a young male has entered his territory. He darkens his beard and does everything he can to make himself look bigger and more threatening, the king of his domain.

The brash youngster who has made this blunder will wave a front paw slowly to say, "I'm so sorry, I didn't mean to offend you. Don't attack me. I'm just a little bearded dragon who is no threat to you."

Then the smaller, younger, less dominant male scurries away. The winner does a victory wave.

In breeding season, females will slow-wave to males, accepting them as mates.

Arm waving isn't only a sign of submission. Fast arm waving plus head bobbing can be a young male trying to proclaim his dominance.

Bearded dragons rarely do the wave for people. If your beardie waves as you approach his vivarium, they don't trust you yet.

IS MY DRAGON NODDING AT ME?

If you have a male, you may see what looks like a dragon nodding his head up and down, as if he is enthusiastically agreeing with you. But that's not likely, as head bobbing is another male-dominance behaviour, as in *I am a mighty dragon, hear me roar!*

You might think this is funny, or kind of pathetic, but in the dragon world, it's a clear message that means, "Scram, buddy. This is MY territory and any females around here are my girls!"

Males will also head-bob at females to show them who's The Dude before mating. The females will accept with slow head bobbing, arm waving and possibly slow push-ups.

WHEEZING, GURGLING, CROAKING OR GASPING

This is a serious sign for concern. It could mean a problem with the temperatures in their vivarium. If that's not the case, they likely have a respiratory infection. See the vet immediately.

IS HE TWITCHING HIS TAIL BECAUSE HE'S HAPPY?

Maybe. More likely, he's just noticed something interesting. Or he's stalking prey, like a cricket. One of the fun things about having a juvenile beardie is seeing how excited they get when they're offered a tasty-looking insect. That's when you're most likely to see some serious tail twitching!

Times when beardies twitch their tails are when they're stalking prey, feel stressed, want to be left alone or during breeding.

STRANGE SLEEPERS

Did your beardie fall asleep standing up, maybe in a corner of their home? This is normal. They sleep at night, like we do, but don't seem to need to lie down to do it.

IS HE TASTING THE AIR?

Yes. Many animals and all reptiles do this. In addition to aromas, how air tastes helps them navigate their territory and avoid danger.

WHY IS SHE LICKING?

For a beardie, licking isn't just about tasting their food. It also helps them figure out where they are and gives them other information about their environment. It could be that, like snakes, they taste the air to find their way around and back to their favourite basking spots or hides.

FOOT STOMPING

This is usually male behaviour when they want to mate or challenge another male.

They bob their heads so energetically that both arms can seem to hop up and down,

WHAT IS BASKING?

Basking is just like you laying out at the beach to catch some rays. While you might do this to get a golden glow, beardies bask to warm up. Unlike humans, reptiles have to bask under the sun, or a UV lamp (it mimics the benefits of sunshine) to be able to warm up because they are cold-blooded.

Sun (or UV) exposure also provides Vitamin D. Without enough of this vitamin, beardies can't metabolize (use in their body) the calcium they eat or digest their food.

WHY ARE THEY HIDING?

Some shedding dragons just want to be left alone. This is also true of animals that are brumating. Being extremely antisocial when they aren't shedding, brumating or laying their eggs is a sign of illness, especially when they aren't eating or basking.

WHY ARE THEY DIGGING IN THEIR VIVARIUM?

Adult females dig to create a cooler, protected nest to lay their eggs. A female doesn't need to mate to have eggs, but if she doesn't mate, her eggs will not be fertile. If your female beardie lays eggs but she hasn't been with a male, you will need to take the eggs away and destroy them. Otherwise, they'd rot.

Both genders may dig to find a cooler place, if their cool hide is too warm. They also might dig before taking a nap or before they go into brumation. Another reason for digging is to escape, or get away from something inside their vivarium.

WHY ARE THEY CLIMBING ON TOP OF EACH OTHER?

If you have two dragons in the same vivarium, you will see one climbing on the other's back. Are they just trying to be friendly? It might look that way to humans, but in the beardie world, the guy on top is trying to get closer to the sun (or UV lamp). He (or she) is asserting dominance over the one on the bottom of the heap.

Though bearded dragons are social, they spend most of their lives alone. They can't live close to each other, with too little territory to be able to spend time apart. That's exactly what happens when you have two beardies in the same vivarium. They are forced to be far too close for comfort, all the time.

One will assert dominance. Usually this is the larger animal over the smaller one, males over females or healthy animals over weaker ones. The alpha beardie gets all the best of what there is to get in their small world. They will eat most of the insects offered. Claim the best hides. Take the prime basking spot. Bite the other dragon, possibly damaging toes and tail tip.

Generally, the stronger animal will terrorize the weaker, smaller or younger one.

The poor creature on the bottom of this pecking order will suffer from stress which will weaken him or her and make them susceptible to injury and disease. For this reason, you should never have more than one beardie per vivarium.

WHY IS MY BEARDIE GLASS SURFING?

Glass surfing is when a beardie presses their entire belly up against the smoother sides of their tank or vivarium. They wave their arms as they push their bodies across the glass. It looks like they're doing everything they possibly can to escape.

And that's exactly what they're doing. They are stressed and desperate, because they are bored or their home is too hot or too cold or there is another dragon in their home constantly threatening them. Or it could be that something else is very wrong in their [illegible]

Glass surfing is a cry for help.

WHAT ELSE CAUSES STRESS FOR DRAGONS?

Like any pet, beardies get used to normal family life noises. They can learn to recognize the sounds of you walking over to their vivarium to say hello and may come rushing out of their hide to greet you!

Too much noise, though, is stressful for humans and also to just about any animal with the ability to hear, including bearded dragons. Beardies have quite good hearing.

If you play video games with the sound turned up, or loud music, or the TV is always turned on or there's a lot of shouting in your house, you're going to have a stressed dragon.

That's also true if they don't get enough fresh water, enough of the right foods or enough variety in their meals.

A tank or vivarium that is too small for an adult, or too large for a baby, is stressful. You should also be aware that, like us all, beardies like their home comforts. A new environment takes some time to get used to.

During that time, they may not want to eat and prefer to just be left alone. Generally, if your vivarium is set up properly for them, they will be happier and more like themselves in a couple of weeks or so.

Beardies like being with people, but not being handled all the time. They also become stressed when they are completely ignored.

Baby beardies are VERY stressed by cats, because feral cats hunt and eat baby beardies in the wild. If you also have a cat, it's best to keep your pets apart until your beardie becomes an adult. Since cats don't bother attacking adult lizards, they usually get along just fine if you wait to introduce your pets until they're both adults.

Signs of stress in beardies are weight loss, not eating, pacing and glass surfing.

Stress is bad. It makes a bearded dragon more prone to having parasites as well as causing other health problems. Just as in other kinds of pets and in humans, high stress causes suffering and it can, eventually, lead to an early death.

WHY ARE THEY BULGING THEIR EYES?

Eye bulging seems to be a normal part of shedding. That's when reptiles shed their old skin, allowing them to grow larger.

Shedding usually starts with the eye bulging to loosen the old skin around their eyes.

Babies and juveniles are growing much faster than adult beardies, so they shed more often. All bearded dragons shed, throughout their lives.

You'll see your beardie rubbing up against their hide or basking branch when they're shedding, probably because the old skin is itchy and they want to be rid of it.

WHY ARE THEY FLATTENING THEIR BODY?

Males do this to make themselves look bigger and more threatening to rivals. They may also do it when they just want to be left alone.

Both males and females can flatten their bodies and also darken them to absorb more sun or UV rays when they want to warm up. When they get too warm, they will unflatten and move off to a cooler spot. If they are constantly flattened, check your temperatures. It could be their basking spot is not hot enough.

If that's so, here's how to warm it up. Change to a higher wattage heat bulb, or move their basking spot closer to the heat bulb.

DO I NEED TO HELP MY BEARDIE SHED THEIR SKIN?

Beardies will rub their bodies against everything in their vivarium when they're trying to shed.

When they're shedding, they may want to eat less, do less or even spend most of their time in their hides. Mist and bath them to help them feel better. You should never try to pull the old skin off.

Shedding is a natural process, but sometimes things can go wrong. The most frequent shedding problem is when old skin doesn't shed from around the toes or tail tip. Instead, it can bind, becoming too tight and cutting off circulation. When this happens, the tail tip or toes could die.

To prevent this and keep your dragon comfortable as she or he sheds, mist them daily and give them frequent baths two or three times a week. If this doesn't get rid of the dead skin, you can very gently rub it with an old, soft toothbrush.

If your dragon has been trying to bite off the old skin, there may be open wounds. Clean the area and apply an antibiotic ointment such as Neosporin or Betadine. If there is pus, or a bad odour, or swelling, or blackening, then your beardie needs to see the vet.

After shedding, baby and juvenile beardies' colours and patterns change, becoming brighter. They won't have their permanent colours and patterns until they're adults.

WHY ARE THEY TWITCHING?

Twitching is not good. It is most likely caused by a calcium or a Vitamin D3 deficiency. This is the cause of metabolic bone disease (MBD).

If your beardie isn't getting enough calcium, rather than giving them more, cut down on foods with potassium. Some potassium-rich foods are bananas, melons, raisins, sweet potatoes and peas. You can find others you may be feeding too much of by doing an online search for potassium rich foods.

For Vitamin D3 deficiency, start by checking your UVB lighting. It could be you need to replace the tube or bulb. In addition, if possible, let your pet get some direct sun exposure. Glass and plastic filter out natural UVB, so they need to be safely outside for a sunbath.

WHY ARE THEY CHANGING COLOUR?

Beardies' colours become more intense and/or darker as they get older. They don't have their true colours until they are adults, some time between when they're 12 to 18 months old.

They are usually their most colourful as young adults.

Their colour can suddenly darken when they are stressed, cold and want to warm up, threatened, upset or suddenly in a new environment.

Slower darkening can happen when they're ill.

WHY HAS MY PET STOPPED EATING?

Adjusting to a new home, shedding and going into brumation are all normal reasons for a dragon to want to eat less or stop eating completely.

If they're not eating, check that:

- They're happy in their home
- the UV is right
- temperatures are right
- humidity is right
- they aren't shedding, and
- it isn't the cool season or winter.

If all of this is OK, it could be that they have an infection or are overloaded with parasites. If so, it's time to see the vet. Take some of their poop for a fecal exam, which your reptile vet will need to make the correct diagnosis.

WHAT IS BRUMATION?

If you have a dozy, grumpy pet who doesn't want to do anything but rest and sleep, it could be that your beardie has gone into brumation.

This is the lizard form of hibernating. It happens to most beardies, starting after they're a year old.

If you live in a temperate climate, where the temperatures and length of daylight each day doesn't change much throughout the year, your beardie might skip brumation. This is also completely normal.

Brumation is triggered by shorter days and cooler temperatures of late Autumn or Winter (in the Northern Hemisphere) or Spring/Summer in the Southern Hemisphere. It can last for just a week or so, up to a few months. If your pet chooses to brumate for more than a week, wake them up from time to time to give them water.

Otherwise, leave them alone to doze.

Even though brumating beardies usually don't want to eat, they don't lose weight. If your beardie is not eating and is losing weight, this is a sign that something else is going on. Seek your vet's advice.

Brumating dragons that aren't eating at all and aren't pooping don't need their heat lamp on as long as the room they're in never gets colder than 70 degrees F. (21 degrees C.) They also don't need their night heat lamp or their UV light on when brumating.

Younger adult dragons are just dozy and slow during brumation. More mature adults (older than 5 years) could sleep for days, or even months!

Continue to offer them greens. If they do eat, turn the lights back on. They need their heat lights and basking time under the UV light to digest their food.

Give them a warm bath for half an hour or so once a week. Stay with them! A dozy dragon could easily let their head sink below the water and drown. Afterwards, dry them off completely and give them time under their lights.

When they get too warm, they'll go back to their cool hide. If they fall asleep under the lights, just place them back in their hide.

Brumation could last for two or three months. This is totally healthy and normal for beardies. After that, they'll wake up gradually, be very hungry and need their lights back on. This is also when adult males want to mate.

Some owners turn up the heat and the lights, to try to prevent their pets from going into brumation.

Breeders and most experts recommend not doing this. It's also not a good idea to try to wake them up.

It's healthier for dragons to do what comes naturally to them.

Babies and juveniles don't go into brumation.

Usually, the first time your pet will brumate is not long after their first birthday.

WHAT CAUSES DRAGON STRESS?

- Their vivarium is too large (babies and juveniles) or too small (adults).
- Wrong conditions in their vivarium – too much or not enough heat, light, or humidity or they don't like the substrate.
- A dirty vivarium.
- Too much of too much in their home.
- Lack of consistency and routines. They don't know when to expect their next meal or visit from you.
- Loud music, video games, TV, sirens, barking dogs – all loud and unexpected noises are alarming for pets.
- Relocation or travel. New sights, sounds, smells and particularly a new home are stressful for beardies of all ages.
- They're hungry or thirsty.
- They're ill.
- They're bored. Not enough attention from you.
- Vet visits.
- Seeing another dragon (except when mating).
- Other pets (unless they've had a chance to gradually become friends).
- Roommates.

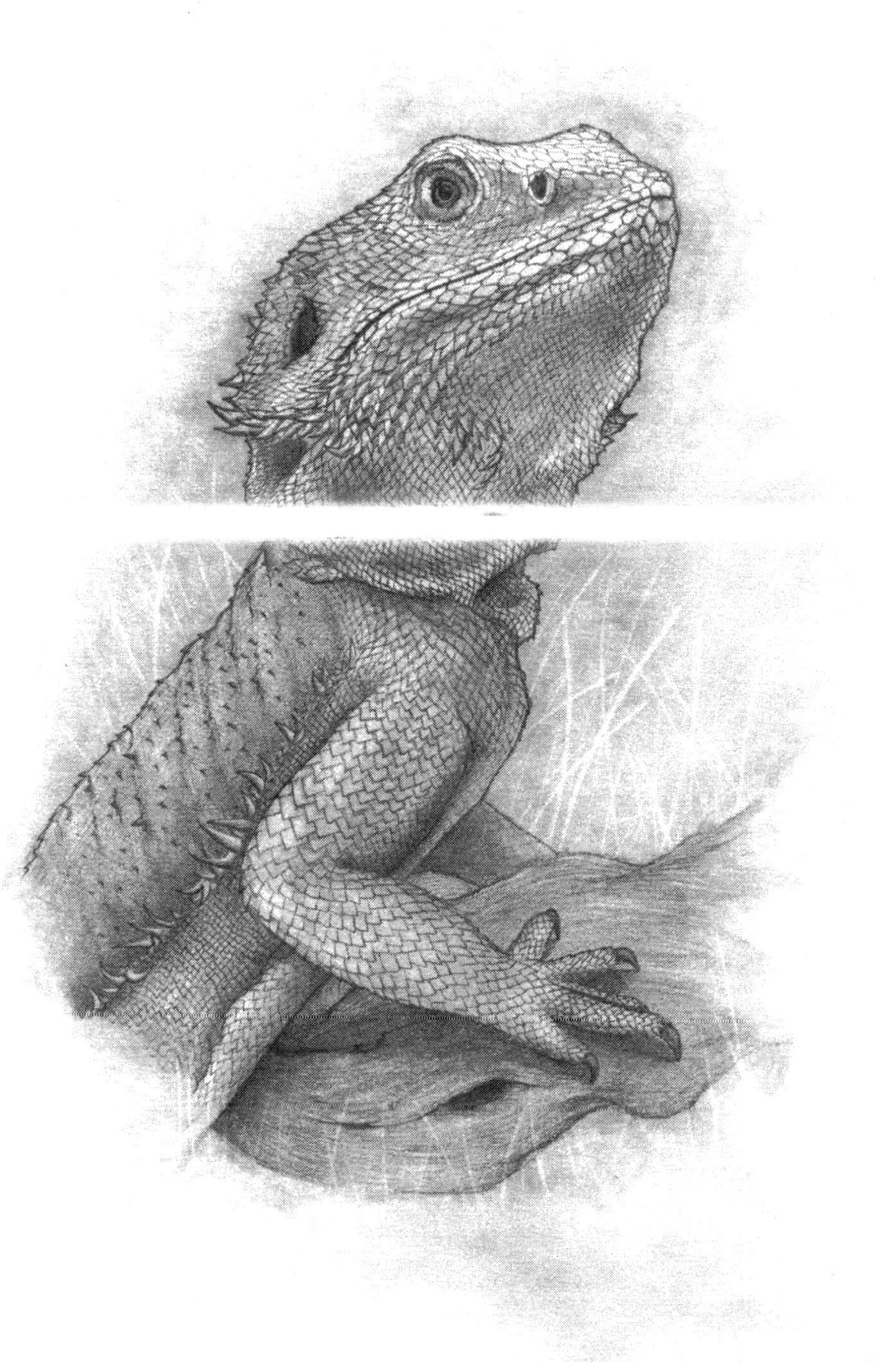

SIX
What Beardies Eat

Beardies, like people, are omnivores. This means they need to eat a variety of foods in the right amounts to stay healthy. There are also some foods they should only get occasionally. And some to avoid.

In the wild, bearded dragons eat leaves, flowers, insects, worms, other lizards (including younger beardies), rodents, snakes and scorpions. They also eat small mammals and birds.

Each dragon has her or his own territory and spends most of their time wandering as they look for food, lick morning dew or rain droplets off leaves and try to avoid confrontations with larger, more powerful lizards or predators.

What you feed your pet beardie needs to be similar to what their wild ancestors evolved, over millions of years, to eat. (Though maybe you won't be serving up the scorpions!)

This means everything you give your dragon to eat must be the same, nutritionally, or close to what they would find to eat in their native territory, which is:

- **Fresh and natural.** Organic is best, because there are no harmful herbicides, pesticides or other chemicals. Thoroughly wash with warm water, rinse and dry any fruit or veg before feeding to your pet.
- **Not cooked**. Beardies only eat raw foods.
- **Not dead**, if it's a worm or insect. Their appetite is stimulated when their food moves. They won't eat dead crickets, no matter how hungry they are.
- **Not canned or processed.** These foods usually have added salt, sugar, preservatives

and other harmful chemicals.

- **Not frozen or heated.** Their food needs to be at room temperature.
- **Not mealworms.** While some experienced owners, breeders and experts claim there is no danger in feeding beardies mealworms, many others say mealworms are off the menu because they cause impaction in their animals. Impaction is serious and can be fatal.
- **Not meant for other types of pets**. They cannot survive on cat food or dog food. Some will eat reptile pellets, for a very short time, if there's nothing else available, but it's not good for them.
- **Not meat**. They can't eat any of the types of poultry, fish or meat that humans eat.
- **Not table scraps**. They can't eat leftovers from the kitchen.
- **Not poisonous to them**. The protein in meat or chicken can kill them. Fireflies (also known as lightning bugs) and some spiders are also certain death for dragons. Anything you catch outside including flies and earthworms is dangerous, since these creatures have probably been exposed to fertilizers, pesticides or herbicides.
- **Not too much of a good thing**. Beardies love fruit, but too much or too often can cause diarrhea. Superworms, butterworms and waxworms are also just an occasional treat, as they are high in fat and can lead to a dragon suffering from fatty liver disease.

To be healthy, beardies must have live insects and raw salads.

The insects pet bearded dragons eat are crickets and insect worms. Insect worms are insects such as beetles in the worm stage of their life cycle.

Bearded dragons are usually good eaters. They're seldom fussy about their food, except when they're ill or brumating.

SAFE AND HEALTHY FOODS FOR DRAGONS

Dubia roaches	Superworms
Crickets	Reptiworms
Waxworms	Pinkie mice (adults only)

GOOD VEG:

Alfalfa	Parsnip	Cabbage
Beans – Green or Snap	Pumpkin	Endive
Bok choy	Watercress	Cassava (Yucca root)
Okra	Sweet potatoes (Yams)	Zucchini
Squash – Acorn, Butternut, Kabocha, Winter		
Bell peppers – all colours		
Herbs – Basil, Cilantro, Mint, Parsley, Chicory		
Greens – Arugula, Kale, Collard, Mustard, Turnip, Chicory, Romaine or Dandelion		

OCCASIONAL FOODS - FRUIT:

Apples	Bananas	Blackberries	Raspberries
Strawberries	Peaches	Pears	Mango
Papaya	Blueberries	Cranberries	Kiwi fruit
Grapes		Tomatoes	
Melons – Cantaloupe, Honeydew		Prickly pear cactus fruit	

OCCASIONAL FOODS - VEGETABLES:

Broccoli	Carrots	Cauliflower	Peas

OCCASIONAL FOODS - FLOWERS:

Dahlia	Hibiscus	Nasturtiums	Clover
Dandelion - leaves, roots and flowers			

Babies need as many feeder insects as they want to eat in 10 minutes, three or four times a day. Let them have a maximum of 50 insects a day. Between the insect meals, get them started on greens when they're a month old. Add morsels of vegetables and fruits, introducing them to a variety of tastes by the time they're six months old. Their diet should be 75 percent insects and 25 percent greens, vegetables and [illegible] where they can see it.

> **INSECT CAFÉ**
>
> www.dubiaroaches.com has plenty of information about feeder insects and also sells and ships them in the USA, except to states where they are not legal (currently Florida and Hawaii). They also sell a range of beardie accessories and supplements.
>
> www.buzzardreptile.co.uk/product/dubia-roaches and www.livefoods.co.uk are two good sources for feeders in Great Britain

Juveniles are hungry all the time, but you should feed them three times a day. After a few days, you'll know how many insects your dragon wants at each meal. Continue offering greens, veg and a bit of fruit.

Don't let them live on only one type of insect. They need variety in their diets!

After they're a year old, they should be fed insects once a day and vegetables once or twice a day. You may need to coax them to eat their veggies. Beardies become adults some time between 12 and 18 months old.

Since Juveniles are growing fast, they can eat a lot. This can get expensive if you're buying your feeder insects from the pet store. To insure a steady supply of healthy insects for your dragon, buy larger numbers online, keep insect colonies or you might also choose to breed your own feeders. It's cheaper, healthier for your pet and more reliable than buying at local pet shops.

If you live in a city, you may have the advantage of being able to buy your insects more

SUPPLEMENT AND VITAMIN STORAGE

It may seem convenient to keep your bottles of vitamins and supplements on top of your beardie's vivarium, out where you can see them and they're a handy reminder to give them to your pet. But this is a mistake. Vitamins and supplements degrade from exposure to light, air or heat. They need to be kept in a cool, dark place and used up, or replaced, every four months.

reliably, for a better price, from a reptile pet store. This is probably your best option if you live in places, such as Florida and Hawaii, that do not allow suppliers to ship live feeder insects.

It's fun to see how excited beardies get when you put a dubia or cricket in their vivarium. They might wave their tails, or even stomp a foot. Just like little kids, they'll try to get you to give them more insects and more fruit while they want to avoid their vegetables.

Young dragons need to learn to eat veggies for the same reason people do, to stay healthy.

Adults more than two years old eat insects two or three times a week. Give them as many insects as they want to eat in 15 to 20 minutes, then remove any uneaten insects from their terrarium. You're doing this to prevent the insects from attacking your pet while he or she is resting or sleeping.

They should get a maximum of 20 insects on a feeding day, or 40 per week. Adults can go without eating for two or three days, occasionally, but they need water every day (See Chapter 7).

All Ages of dragons can have greens and vegetables.

SWEET TREATS FOR BEARDIES

Fresh, washed and cut up:

- 2 or 3 cranberries
- One or two blueberries
- Half an apple slice
- A carrot slice, cut up small.
- One grape.

OFF THE MENU

Beets	Celery	Chocolate	Eggplant
Lettuce	Spinach	Corn	Potatoes
Rhubarb	Parsley	Mushrooms	Meat
Mealworms	Spiders	Ladybugs	Fireflies
Seeds	Onions	Garlic	Avocado
Marijuana or Tobacco		Artificial sweeteners	
Anything cooked		Canned vegetables	
Chicken, Turkey, Duck, or Eggs		Fish or any type of seafood	
Wild-caught bugs or worms		Box Elder Bugs	
Nuts or nut butters		Candy, soda pop or fruit drinks	
Alcoholic drinks (Beer, Wine, Spirits)			
Citrus fruits – Oranges, Limes or Lemons			
Caffeine (it's in Chocolate, Coffee and Tea)			
All dairy products, including Milk, Yogurt, Cheese and Ice cream			
Grains, especially anything made with wheat			
Processed foods such as nacho chips			

THE RULE: Vegetables daily. Fruit occasionally, as a treat.

WHICH BUGS ARE BEST?

For Babies:

- Mini-sized dubia roaches

- Mini-sized crickets

For Juveniles and Adults, appropriately sized:

- Crickets
- Dubia roaches
- Calciworms
- Silkworms
- Phoenix worms (black soldier fly larvae)
- Reptiworms
- Superworms
- Butterworms
- Hornworms

For Adults only, in moderation:

- Waxworms

Smaller crickets are better for your beardie than larger ones, because they have less hard exoskeleton. Eating too many exoskeletons too quickly can cause impaction (severe constipation) for beardies.

It's better for your pet to eat more of the smaller crickets, instead of fewer of the bigger ones.

HOW TO MAKE A BEARDIE SALAD

This recipe is easy and quick to prepare. It keeps well, covered, in the fridge for up to five days.

From the Safe and Healthy list on page 101, choose:

- 2 or 3 types of greens
- 2 or 3 vegetables

Thoroughly wash with warm water. Remove cores, seeds or pits. Cut or tear greens or cut veg into small pieces. If using squashes or carrots, you can grate them. Combine and serve.

For adults, you can top with one fruit (two fresh blueberries, washed and cut in half, for example, or a few small apple chunks) once a week.

You can leave fresh greens in the vivarium with your pet all day. They'll munch away on it when they feel like it. Remove and discard any greens they haven't eaten two hours before lights out in the evening.

That's also a good time to wash their food dish, ready for tomorrow, and give them fresh water.

Don't rely on frozen veg or greens. The freezing process reduces the thiamine [illegible]

WHAT ABOUT SUPPLEMENTS?

Beardies can't get all the nutrients they need from food and water. They need two additional supplements. There are two ways to get these supplements into your dragon.

The first is to simply offer the supplements to them, hoping they'll eat them, which some will. Sometimes.

The second method is to feed or coat your feeder insects or worms with the

WHAT'S IN THE FOOD DISH?

ALL AGES

Fresh greens, every day

Babies up to 3 months old

Mini insects that are smaller than ¼ inch (.6 cm). All they can eat in 10 minutes, four times a day.

Young Juveniles, 3 to 6 months old

Insects that are up to 3/8 inch (1 cm). All they can eat in 15 minutes, three times a day.

Older Juveniles, 6 months to 1 year old

Insects that are a maximum of ½ inch (1.2 cm). All they can eat in 20 minutes two times a day.

Young Adults, ages 1 to 2 years

Insects that are ¾ inch (2 cm). All they can eat in 20 minutes, once a day.

Mature Adults, ages 2 and up

Insects that are 1 inch (2.5 cm), all they can eat in 20 minutes, every other day.

supplements. This requires a bit more effort, but it has big benefits. By doing this method, called *gut-loading*, you know exactly how much supplement you are getting into your dragon.

You can also dust greens with supplements.

Supplements every dragon needs are:

- **Calcium**, daily for babies and five times a week for all other dragons. Buy the type specifically for bearded dragons (at pet stores or online) and follow package directions.

  Calcium is critical because it supports bone growth in babies and juveniles and helps older dragons maintain bone health. It prevents metabolic bone disease (MBD), a crippling disease.

  You don't need to buy Calcium with added vitamin D3. This used to be the recommendation. You will still see this advice in blogs, or possibly hear it from pet store people, other owners and breeders. Recently, it has been proven false.

  Researchers have discovered that bearded dragons can't metabolize the D3 that is added to calcium. It doesn't hurt them, but you are going to pay more for Calcium with D3, without getting any benefit.

- **Reptile vitamin**, containing vitamins: A, D and E. Check the label to be sure it is meant for bearded dragons. Babies and juveniles need their vitamin supplement four or five times a week. Over one year old, three times a week. When they're more than two years old, two or three times a week, or three or four times a week if they're sick.

- **Bee Pollen** adds healthy protein, amino acids, vitamins and minerals. It comes in powder form, convenient for dusting your greens or feeders. Bonus: it tastes a bit

TOXIC PLANTS!

Never feed these common garden plants to your pet:

- Buttercups
- Brachen fern
- Poppy
- Rhododendron
- Foxglove

sweet and even picky eaters like it. You can find it at health food stores or online.

- **Probiotics** may be added to the reptile vitamin. It is also available separately. Some breeders routinely give their animals probiotics only after they've had a course of antibiotics, to regenerate helpful gut bacteria.

Check the label, because probiotics are usually made from a milk product and bearded dragons are lactose-intolerant. There are some brands not made from milk products.

ABOUT BUGS FOR BEARDIES

[illegible] reptiles are loaded with protein and fat. This is exactly what young beardies need to grow strong. For adult beardies, worms are a treat, once or twice a week. Too many worms, and you will have a fat pet that isn't as healthy and won't live as long.

Bearded dragons love insects, especially dubia roaches, grasshoppers and locusts. You can buy them from pet shops or online.

The right size for your beardie is a live insect that is no longer than the space between your pet's eyes. Never let your beardie eat insects

GOING ON VACATION?

If you need to get a pet sitter for your beardie while you go on a vacation, adult beardies can get along for a brief time (no more than a few days) eating reptile pellets instead of live insects, plus their salads.

If you're leaving for a longer break, you may need to find an experienced beardie owner to look after your pet. Failing that, a genuine animal-lover.

Leave them with a good supply of beardie salad in the fridge, plenty of healthy dubias, the contact numbers for you and for your veterinarian and this book!

you catch outside. Wild insects almost always have parasites.

BUYING BUGS

Babies and juveniles can choke on bugs that are too big. Adults will generally ignore crickets they consider to be too small to be worth the effort of chasing.

You might want to form a buying group with another beardie-owning friend or two. You get a lower price when you order, say, 1,000 crickets and pay for half the order and half the shipping fee than when you buy 500 (plus shipping fee) yourself.

A downside of ordering crickets by the thousand is that, after a couple of weeks, the crickets that are left have already grown too large for your pet to eat.

After a few orders, you'll know how many crickets your dragon is eating and how long they last.

WHAT'S SO BAD ABOUT REPTILE PELLETS?

They're easy to find at the pet food store. They're convenient and easy to use. So, what's so wrong with feeding your beardie the pellets instead of live insects and veg?

Here's why:

- Pellets don't give your pet the nutrition they need.
- Most dragons just don't like them. This leads to an underfed pet.
- What they're getting is a processed food that contains fats, dyes and chemical flavouring.
- Reptile pellets also have fillers made from foods dragons don't naturally eat that can upset their stomachs, such as corn, soy and wheat.

CRICKETS

Wild bearded dragons are enthusiastic cricket hunters. Pet beardies are just as happy to consume crickets.

But there's a problem, or possibly a few problems with crickets. Some pet owners say that they don't feed crickets because their pets can get pinworms from the crickets.

Crickets chirp constantly. They can be stinky. They try to escape when you open [illegible] have to be kept warm. And just about every experienced beardie owner has opened a box of crickets, after buying them online or at the pet store, to find a lot of what they paid for is DOA, dead on arrival.

THE TROUBLE WITH MEALWORMS

You may have read, or heard from other beardie owners, that mealworms are a good choice for your pet.

They're widely available in pet stores, easy to keep and convenient. However, there is growing evidence that they aren't healthy for beardies, with many breeders no longer using mealworms because of concerns about impaction.

Mealworms have very hard exoskeletons (chitin) that can clog bearded dragon's short digestive tracts. An impacted bearded dragon usually needs surgery and may not survive.

Mealworms also contain fat, but little nutrition. Other types of insect worms are better choices.

Bearded dragons who never encounter a single cricket can live long and healthy lives. There are other good bug and worm choices to feed your pet. If you do decide to include crickets in their diet, here's what you need to know.

Keep crickets in a critter keeper, available online and at reptile pet shops. Or use a clear plastic storage tub (the kind you might store extra blankets or sweaters in). Cut large holes for air in the top and the sides near the top to provide air. Put aluminum screening over the breathing holes or make a screen top.

> **WARNING – DUBIA ALLERGY**
>
> Some pet owners have developed an allergy to dubias. Early signs that this could also be affecting you are itchy skin, itchy eyes and congestion.
>
> To prevent this, keep your dubias in a well-ventilated room and wear gloves when you handle them. You might also want to wear a mask or respirator. If you do find you're allergic, buying your dubias rather than breeding them is probably a better choice.

Alternatively, crickets can live in a 20 gallon fish tank.

Your cricket home needs to be filled with pieces of egg cartons or egg sheets, to give them places to hide. Without hiding places, crickets go bonkers and start eating each other. If you order them online (they come as 500 or 1,000), they'll come in egg crate layers. Just open the box, flip it over and slide the egg crate/crickets combination into your cricket home. A few might try to escape, but most will want to be deeper in the egg cartons or sheets, away from the light.

You will need to empty out and clean your cricket box once every two weeks. To do this, it helps to have two cricket boxes, so they always live in one and the other is always clean and ready for them to move to.

They do best in a warm room that's at or close to 80 degrees F. (or 27 degrees C). You might want to keep them in the basement or out in the garage, if it's warm enough. Otherwise all that chirping could be annoying!

Feed your crickets apple, sweet potato or carrot slices and dry baby cereal or raw oatmeal. You'll need to replace their food every day.

Cricket water pillows (you can buy these online) make it easy to be sure your crickets get enough water. Or you can give them a water dish with a sponge and add water daily. Or use a cricket waterer.

Crickets don't live for long. Their entire lifespan is only about 9 weeks.

COCKROACHES

Cockroaches aren't welcome when they invade our homes! But they are a good, clean, nutritious food for bearded dragons.

egg cartons for hiding places makes a good home for them. It should be kept in the dark and needs to be 85 degrees F. (29 degrees C.). Your cockroach tank will need an under-pad heater to keep it warm enough for them.

> **HOW TO MAKE ROACH CHOW**
>
> You can buy roach chow at some pet stores and online. Or you could make your own. Here's how.
>
> In a blender, combine equal amounts of:
>
> - Guinea pig pellets
> - Chicken feed
> - Raw rolled oats
> - White corn meal
> - Fish food
> - Oat bran
> - Honey Cheerios
>
> Store in a plastic container. To serve, scoop onto a clean jar lid.

Feed them raw rolled oats or roach chow and slices of bananas, apples, very ripe peaches or plums. Give them some water, using the same methods as you would for Crickets.

REPTIWORMS

High in calcium, low in phosphorous, this is a good choice for adult beardies. They're also convenient. You don't need to feed them. They'll keep for 3 to 4 weeks in a fridge kept at 51 to 55 F (or 10 to 13 C).

Reptiworms can be hard to find, but you can order them online.

WHEN'S DINNER?

Beardies need time to wake up and get active before they eat their first meal of the day. Don't feed them until an hour after they've become active in the morning. They need time to warm up their bodies before they're able to digest their food.

And no evening snacking, either! They need to cool down and stop digesting, so nothing more to eat when it's two hours, or less, till bedtime!

DUBIA ROACHES

With twice the amount of protein crickets have, and a lot less bother to keep, many beardie owners consider dubias the ideal feeder insect.

They live a long time. They don't have the parasites crickets can carry. They're easy for beardies to digest.

Dubias also don't have any of the bad habits of crickets, such as biting, jumping, climbing or being smelly.

Only the males can fly, and that's only a few inches. Another benefit is they produce a LOT of babies.

They can be expensive to buy in pet shops, even though they're easy to breed.

If you choose to breed your own dubias, you'll need two plastic containers (the 30 gallon or 113 litre size works best).

Make a ventilation opening that's at least six inches by six inches (15 cm by 15 cm) on the top and each side near the top.

Cover these with mesh screen and tape or hot-glue in place.

Dubias like to be in the dark, so a dark green or black container is their ideal home.

Fill your dubia home with egg cartons or egg flats (you can buy them online). If you use egg flats, stand them on their ends, with wooden skewers between them to keep them standing upright, like poles and walls inside your dubia keeper and place a strap around the egg flats. Strong twine or an old belt works. This way, you'll be able to lift the egg flats out as one piece and all the dubia poop will fall to the [illegible]

Unless you live in a hot place or keep your home temperature cranked, you'll need a heat lamp or under tank heater at the warmer end of their home. Use a thermostat or lamp dimmer to keep the temperature even and avoid melting their home. They need to be kept at between 90 and 95 F. (or 32 to 35 C.) with humidity at 60 percent.

Put a lid of water crystals and their food at the cooler end.

If all your dubias crowd around the warm end, turn up the temperature. If they spread out through their

MEAL PREP FOR BEARDIES

For veg and fruit, buy organic. Remove labels and twist ties. Wash in warm water, scrubbing thoroughly with a brush.

If you're using frozen fruit or veg, thaw it (but don't cook it) before serving.

Be careful to remove pits and all seeds. Some fruit seeds, such as apple, are poisonous for beardies.

The general rule for beardie servings is never offer a bug or a piece of veg or fruit that is larger than the distance between their eyes.

This means you'll be doing a lot of cutting up of veg and fruit. Also, you'll be buying dubias and other insects by size, depending on how big your dragon is.

The reason for this is that they can easily choke on food that is too large to swallow. They have no ability to chew their food, so this is a real danger, particularly for babies and juveniles!

home, your room and container temps are good.

Dubias moult or shed as they grow. If yours don't, they need more humidity.

Feed them roach chow, insect gutload and apple slices or chunks of orange, beet or sweet potato. They also eat dry fruit, carrot peelings, potato peelings, apple cores or cut up broccoli stalks.

They can not eat dog food, cat food, or meat because dubias turn protein into uric acid, which isn't good for dragons.

Use separate shallow dishes or jar lids for your dubia food and water so the food doesn't get wet and mould.

Remove and replace food every few days, before it can get mouldy. Mould kills roach colonies.

DUBIA CLEANING

You'll need to clean the dubia poop, or frass, from the bottom of their homes about every 10 days or so.

To make this easier, have a spare, clean container ready. Lift the egg crate flats (most of your roaches will be on them) to the clean container. Capture any remaining dubias and transfer them, along with their food and water dishes.

Scoop out frass, leaving about one inch deep on the bottom of their home. Then put the dubias, their egg cartons, fresh food and water back.

HOW TO BREED YOUR DUBIAS

You'll need two dubia containers, one for your breeder colony and the other for feeders.

GETTING THEM TO EAT THEIR VEGGIES

If you're having a hard time getting healthy veggies into your dragon, here are some tricks to try:

1. Put greens on a small jar lid or margarine tub lid and place it where they can see it from their basking spot.
2. Offer veggies before they get insects or worms.
3. Try using reptile salad dressing (you can find it on Amazon).
4. [illegible]
5. Get a veggie clip and hang a small bunch of greens on the side or from the top of the vivarium. It is just a clip, attached to a suction cup. You can usually find them where they sell tropical fish.
6. Beardies want food that moves. If you can arrange hanging greens so that a slight breeze from a fan hits them, they'll be interested in having a taste. Or just hold a small amount of greens or a sliver of squash cut to look like a delicious worm in front of them and wiggle it.

Both are set up the same way.

The breeder colony will need seven or eight weeks to get used to their new home and start making babies. Leave them to it – they're easily disturbed. When you do look inside, what you want to see are dubias that have a red tube extending from their rear ends. That's the egg sac. A frightened dubia female will drop her egg sac, killing the babies.

Ideally, you need three females for every male in your dubia colony. Females become adults at six months and live for two years. Males live for about 18 months.

Females can have 30 to 40 nymphs, born live, each month. New-born nymphs and dubias that have just moulted (shed their skin) are white. It takes them 24 hours to turn black.

Dubia frass (that's the poop) will gather at the bottom of you dubia container. Clean it out when frass gets to be more than an inch deep. You need to keep one inch of frass in the container because that's what baby dubias eat.

PHOENIX WORMS

Rich in calcium, these small white worms, also called Black Soldier Fly larvae, don't need to be fed or given water. They can live at room temperature for up to three weeks, but prefer to stay at about 60 degrees F. (16 degrees C.)

A good choice for beardies, but they can be expensive.

You might notice that some of them will turn black. If so, they'll still be OK to feed to your beardie.

SUPERWORMS

These lively worms are exciting for juveniles to chase and hunt. They're high in fat, so not good for adults. Also high in phosphorous, they must be dusted with calcium right before offering to your pet.

Feed the white ones (they've just shed their outer hard chitlin) to juveniles. If you buy them in the pet store, check that you aren't getting large adult worms.

Feed them cut up potato, acorn squash, carrot or parsnip. They need a thick layer of uncooked old-fashioned oatmeal (not the instant type) at the bottom of their container.

> **SMALL PLATES**
>
> You might see small plates or shallow bowls meant to be food bowls for lizard pets, but you really don't need them. Clean jar lids or plastic tops from the containers margarine, peanut butter or yogurt comes in make great little plates for your pet.
>
> You'll need small tongs, or tweezers, to get worms out of their containers and offer them to your pet.

SILKWORMS

Lower in fat than other worms, silkworms are high in calcium, protein, iron, magnesium and B vitamins.

A good choice for gravid (pregnant) [illegible] because they have about half the fat of waxworms or butterworms, but twice the protein.

High in moisture, silkworms live only on silkworm chow, made from mulberry leaves.

Beardies love them. You can buy them online from reptile pet suppliers.

BUTTERWORMS

Butterworms are bright yellow and are high in calcium.

They come packed in bran. Keep them in the container they come in in the refrigerator until you give them to your pet.

A good choice for dragons that are too thin, gravid, or recovering from an illness.

They last for up to four months when you keep them at about 50 F (10 C).

GUT-LOADING AND DUSTING MADE EASY

You gut-load your insects, or dust them, or both to be sure your pet gets enough:

- calcium, necessary for strong bones
- phosphorus, which helps them convert proteins and fats to energy
- Vitamin D3, which metabolizes the calcium. (Exposure to the sun or UV light also provides D3).

You can also dust your pet's veggies and greens.

Gut-loading

In a blender or food processor mix equal amounts of oatmeal, wheat bran, whole-grain flour, tropical fish food and rabbit food pellets. You can buy all of these at the grocery store, pet store or online. Feed this dry mixture to your feeder insects for the two days before you feed the insects to your beardie. If you don't want to or can't make this dry mix, you can buy it already made up at some reptile stores and online.

Dusting

All worms need to be coated with calcium, just before you feed them to your pet. All insects need to be either dusted, or gut-loaded. To dust, place insects in a small bag. Spoon in powdered calcium or reptile vitamin. Shake gently, so insects are totally covered with the powder. For dusting greens, it's easier if you put your supplement in a clean salt or pepper shaker.

How often?

For babies and juveniles, dust their food with calcium daily and with their multi-vitamin four or five times a week.

For adults, dust their food with calcium five times a week and with multi-vitamin two or three times a week.

TOMATO HORNWORMS

Tomato hornworms bred for reptile feeders are bright green. Keep them in the container they come in from the pet store or buy them online.

They eat hornworm chow.

They'll be fine at normal room temperature.

Tobacco hornworms are blue. They're healthy for beardies to eat, but many beardies refuse to eat them.

Warning - Don't harvest wild hornworms. You may see them on tomato or tobacco plants in your garden. Wild hornworms are toxic for beardies.

WAXWORMS

Waxworms are another type of white caterpillar. They are very high in fat, so only right for a rare treat for your adult beardie.

Feed your waxworms a mixture of glycerin, honey, brewer's yeast and ground oatmeal.

They stay in the container they come in, usually packed in wood shavings and must go in the refrigerator.

PINKIE MICE

Pinkies are newborn mice. You buy them frozen, then feed one at a time (thawed first) to adult beardies. If you find giving pinkies to your pet revolting (many people do) you should know that your bearded dragon can have a long and healthy life without ever tasting a single pinkie.

WHAT ABOUT WATER?

Some beardie owners put a shallow water dish on the cool side of their vivarium, hoping their pets will drink from it. However, most beardies don't like to drink from still water. Instead, they'll walk through it, treating it like a shallow bath.

If you do decide to give them a saucer or shallow dish of water, change the water and clean the dish twice a day.

Here's a better option to get them to drink their water, both for you and your pet. Buy a plant mister. The inexpensive plastic ones work. You can find them in discount or dollar stores (pound shops) everywhere. Fill with drinking water that is room-temperature.

You don't need to buy reptile water conditioner or bottled water. If your drinking water is safe for humans, it's safe for misting pets.

In the morning, an hour or so after daylight, you can lightly mist above their head and around where they're sitting, as if it is very lightly raining.

Wait 20 seconds or so and mist above them again. They'll lick up the water. Also, mist their greens and salads.

Don't mist the walls or the entire vivarium – that's just too wet!

If you live in a heated home or drier climates, like on the Great Plains in the U.S. or the Prairies in Canada, you need to repeat the misting in the afternoon. You'll also need to give your dragon two or three baths a week (See Chapter 7).

SEVEN
Beardie Care Basics

Caring for a bearded dragon isn't any more tricky or difficult than caring for any other kind of pet. Like looking after a dog or a cat, there are some basics you have to give them. The steps to do this are easy. The what-to-do and when and how are all in this book.

What might not be as easy is remembering to do everything.

This is where developing good pet care habits and a good routine really helps. Your routine to deliver the right food and care will make your life simpler and your pet's life happier and healthier. Designing it to fit into your life will make you happier (and maybe even healthier!)

Here's a feeding routine example. Let's say you're a student or you work. You can't get home mid-day to feed your pet. This matters if you have a baby or young juvenile, since they need to eat insects more often. So what to do?

When you can't be at home, perhaps a family member could do the mid-day feeding? Or there are critter feeders (they can't escape) that you can put in your vivarium. Look for these in the larger reptile supplies stores, or online.

WHY HAVE A ROUTINE?

It will save you so much time and worry that it's going to be one of the best things you can do for your lizard friend. Just like us, routines give them comfort and a sense of security.

This care routine is a check-list that you could modify for your own schedule and keep on your phone or laptop. Or you might prefer to have it as a chart on the wall, or written down in a notebook. Choose what works for you and it will make life easier for both you and your pet.

So, what goes on your Beardie Care Routine checklist?

I recommend that you include everything you do for your [illegible] feeding or caring for your feeder insects.

Your feeding care routine and feeder care routine need to be their own checklists, because what you feed your beardie, how much and how often depends on their size and age. Feeder care also differs, by type of insect. (See Chapter 6).

Everything in the Care Routine is there to make your beardie comfortable in their home and keep him or her healthy.

It's a short list (compared to, say, what routines and good habits it takes to keep *you* comfortable and healthy) but it's all important.

NIGHT, NIGHT LITTLE BEARDIE

Bearded dragons need to have their last meal (or snack) at least two hours before lights out to give them time to warm up enough to digest it. They cool down at night, meaning undigested food could sit in their gut. Not good.

Your evening routine is to spot clean, remove any uneaten food including the [illegible] dish.

Check the night temperatures in the vivarium. They should never go below 65 F (18 C). If they do (this can happen even in summer if you have the AC running) you need a night heat lamp.

BEARDED DRAGON CARE ROUTINE

Do this TWICE every day:

1. **Clean their water dish**.

   Remember that beardies poop everywhere, all the time (if they don't, they could be suffering from impaction, which can be serious).

   They poop on everything in their vivarium, including on their food and in their water dishes. Twice a day is usually often enough to clean the water dish (if you use one) and change their water, except for babies and very young juvenile beardies. For them, three times a day is better.

2. **Give them fresh water to drink**.

   City and town (municipal) water is treated with chemicals, including chlorine and may have additives such as fluoride meant to prevent disease or otherwise improve human health. Some people argue that these additives aren't very healthy for people or pets.

   Instead, you could use spring water or bottled water for their drinking water. If this isn't possible, your next best option is to put tap water in a pan and let it sit overnight. Most of the added chemicals will evaporate out of water left standing for several hours, making it safer for pets to drink (or bath in).

   Some beardie owners don't put a water dish in the vivarium because they find it makes it harder to control tank humidity. Instead, they mist the vegetables their pets eat and the plants in the vivarium. Beardies lick the water drops off their food and the plants, just as they would in the wild. The problem is that this, too, can raise humidity. You'll have to try out both methods to see what works best for you.

   Adult beardies can go a few days without food. No beardie can survive even one day without fresh drinking water.

Do this ONCE every day:

1. **Spot clean** all the surfaces in their vivarium every afternoon or evening before lights out. Wipe down the inside of the vivarium. Remove any uneaten food. Never leave insects or worms in the tank because they could attack your pet.
2. **Check the temperatures** in the three sections of the vivarium.
3. **Mist above your beardie's head once a day,** or twice a day for babies.
4. For babies or juveniles, **replace the paper towel substrate**.
5. **Play** with your juvenile or adult beardie for at least one hour (but first, give them an hour to digest their most recent meal. Handling them too soon after they eat

Do this two or three times a week:

Bath Time!

Your juvenile or adult beardie would love a good soak in his or her own bath! Use a plastic box, the kind you might get to keep a large salad in, just a bit longer than they are. Never use the kitchen sink or family bathtub, because of the danger of cross-contamination.

Fill your beardie bath hip deep with mildly warm (never hot or cold!) water. Don't add any soap or anything else to the water. Put them in their bath and stay with them. Just like with little children, it isn't safe to leave beardies in the bath without supervision. Baths can last 15 or 20 minutes.

If your beardie is trying to jump out, they want the water to be warmer.

Most beardies love a soak in still water. They can swim, but most would rather not.

Two or three baths a week isn't too often (plus daily misting).

Beardies who are shedding may need more frequent baths and help from you to very gently rub away the old dead skin, especially on the tip of their tail and around their claws.

Do this ONCE every week:

1. Cleaning

Find a safe spot for your beardie to relax while you do his or her housekeeping. An empty fish tank that is bigger than they are or even a clean cardboard box is OK for their chill-out zone. They probably won't like it, but they won't be there for too long.

Next, remove everything from their home. Discard or clean the substrate. Clean everything else, using a solution that is one part regular chlorine bleach to nine parts water. If you have super-bleach, it should be one part super-bleach to 18 parts water. Don't use repti-cleaning products. These are designed primarily for snakes.

Wearing protective gloves, clean everything in the vivarium. Thoroughly rinse the inside of the tank and everything that will go back into it with warm water.

Clean the outside of the vivarium glass with vinegar water (mix a generous splash of white vinegar in a spray bottle, then fill to the top with tap water.) Dry the inside of the glass tank wall with newspaper or paper towel (kitchen roll). Allow everything to dry.

Put the vivarium back together with fresh (or just-cleaned) substrate.

An alternative to bleach cleaning is steam cleaning. If your beardie is sick or has been sick, steam cleaning is the better choice. Buy or rent a steam cleaner and follow the directions that come with it.

2. **Check the temperatures** in the three vivarium zones.
3. **Adjust timers** for lighting to match the day/night cycle.
4. **Check the humidity level** and make any needed adjustments.
5. **Weigh your beardie**. Weight loss is a sign that something is wrong and you need the vet.
6. **Check the lights**! Be sure that all lights are working and remind yourself when bulbs need to be replaced.

Do this every few months:

Change the vivarium layout and décor.

Wild bearded dragons wander around their range. While our pets are many generations away from life in the wild, adult beardies still get tired of the same old tank.

Change it up with a different arrangement. Their basking branch or platform still needs to be under the heat lamp, but beyond this, there's lots you could do to make their vivarium more interesting.

Add a background mural panel on the back wall. Give them a different hide. Change their plants around. Give them a ping-pong ball.

File or Trim their nails

Wild bearded dragons naturally wear down their claws as they walk over rocks or stony ground. Your beardie can't do this, so they need your help to keep their nails from growing uncomfortably long and sharp.

You'll need pet nail clippers. The kind made for trimming cats' claws works well. Or you could use a cuticle clipper.

Be careful to only cut off the clear nail tip. If you cut more than that their toe will bleed and cause them pain.

Beardies usually are pretty laid back about getting a pedicure. But if you aren't quite sure how to do it, ask your vet to show you how. Or you could look on YouTube where breeders and experienced pet owners demonstrate safe nail clipping.

Do this in summer, or the warm season where you live:

Your beardie would love some time outside to catch some rays. They can do this in a kiddie pool that is partly in the sun and partly in the shade, but be careful, because plastic can overheat, burning their feet.

Some pet owners build outdoor enclosures for their beardies with plastic mesh or wire mesh sides. The danger with wire is they could cut their feet. Another danger with outdoor enclosures is you must be sure snakes (if there are snakes where you live) and other small wild animals can't possibly get in.

Never leave them alone outside. And never put them out in a glass tank. Sun will quickly heat the glass. Even on a mild day, the temperature inside the tank will soon overheat and could kill your pet.

Do this ONCE a year:

Visit the veterinarian for an annual check-up. Take a stool sample (some of their poop) in a clean, small plastic container so the vet can do a fecal sample test for parasites.

YOU NEED AN EMERGENCY PLAN!

Imagine that you wake up tomorrow and discover that the power is out. You have no electricity, no heat and no hot water. And, even worse, you don't have any running water.

That's exactly what happened to a lot of families in Texas in early 2021, when a freak winter storm knocked out all their services. And in California and Australia, in the 2020 fires. And in parts of England that flooded in 2019 and 2020. And in many other parts of the world.

Whether it's caused by snow, ice storms, tornadoes, hurricanes, volcanoes or fire, it's an emergency for people and for their pets. What would you do, if this happened where you live?

Do you have an escape plan? A survival plan? Do you also have an emergency plan for your pets?

If not, you need these. Now is a better time to create your Emergency Plan than in the midst and chaos of a crisis!

Your Pet Emergency Plan

Imagine in the middle of the night there's a pounding at the door. At the same time, your phone pings with a message and, somewhere, you hear sirens.

Still half asleep you stumble to the door. It's one of a group of emergency response officers door-knocking your street. Their message: everyone has to evacuate. You have 10 minutes to get out.

EMERGENCY!

If there is no heat, do not feed your beardie, because they won't be able to digest their food. They will still need water.

If they get colder than 65 F (18 C) and they are an adult, they could go into brumation.

A pet that has endured cold, smoke, fasting or dehydration (not getting enough water) will need to see the vet.

You're stunned. Frozen with shock.

They explain you have to gather what you need, get in your car and join everyone else driving to – where?

There's no time to ask. The officer has already moved on to your neighbour's door.

All you want to do is head back to bed. That's not an option. On TV, on the radio, texts coming to your phone – they're all saying the same thing. Get out. Now!

The reason could be a hurricane. Flooding. Drought. Fire. It doesn't really matter why you have to leave. There's no time at all to think about any of this. You have to move. Shove a few things into a bag. Get yourself and your family into your car. Get going.

Maybe this nightmare scenario has already happened to you. Maybe it's happened more than once. If so, you know how terrifying it is to suddenly face losing your home. What you can't do, at such a time, is make rational choices about what to pack and what to leave behind.

This is why you need to keep the car gassed up. You need a go-bag containing everything you will need to survive for at least three days, for every family member. This means drinking water, food, basic clothing and grooming products and any medications you take. You won't forget keys, wallet with cards, phone and charger, books to read or games to pass the time, wherever it is you end up till it's safe to come home again.

But what about your pet?

An adult bearded dragon could get along for a few days or so, as long as the power wasn't knocked out so they still had the right amount of heat and light. This would be with a feeder and drip water arrangement set up for them.

However, in an emergency, you can't know that you'll be able to return in just a few days. After massive flooding, a hurricane or having your entire town destroyed by fire, it could be weeks before you are allowed to come home to find whatever is left of your home. No pet could survive that long without you.

So, you need a plan for what could happen, including worst case scenario. You need to know what you'll do:

> **If the power is knocked out**. It could be you need a back-up generator.
>
> **If you have to evacuate**. You need a warm, comfortable pet carrier. Your adult beardie can get along for a few days without food or lights, but not without water or the warmth they're used to. Beyond then, you'll need to find a way to get them into a terrarium. This is one more time when having a network of beardie-loving friends can help you. Or you can help them.
>
> **After trauma**, such as surviving cold, smoke, dehydration, fasting or other threats to their health, your pet will need a full health check-up with his or her vet.

CAN BEARDED DRAGONS SWIM?

Yes, if they have to. They don't seem to enjoy it. They'd much rather relax in a warm bath.

EIGHT
Staying Healthy

HANDS OFF!

Remember to never handle pet poop. Use a scoop, or rubber gloves. There are diseases, transferred in body waste, that can jump from pets to their owners.

Bearded dragons start life as incredibly nervous and nimble yet fragile hatchlings.

They are born hungry and soon scramble from the nest to find insects, moisture and shelter. They must do this quickly, before hungry predators find them.

The lucky ones remain babies for the first four months or so of their lives. That's when they've grown into juveniles. Juveniles are voracious eaters and very active.

When a dragon is able to mate and have babies they have reached sexual maturity. This happens when they are somewhere between 12 and 18 months old. Exactly when this happens depends on heredity, food supply, climate, heat and possibly other growth factors we don't know about.

Sexual maturity is when beardies are considered to be adults. That's when females have eggs and males have the ability to fertilize those eggs.

Unlike when they're younger, adult bearded dragons are very hardy. This means that although they can become ill or injured, they tend to be and stay healthy. As wild animals, they probably have short lives. As pets, they tend to live longer. Bearded dragons can be hurt or become sick, but it isn't nearly as common as for some other types of pets.

BEARDIE SOAKS

For a beardie with dehydration, constipation, impaction or who isn't eating or is shedding, mist them and give them two warm baths a day, once in the morning (at least an hour after they wake up) and again in the evening (at least an hour before bedtime).

All reptiles have a slower metabolism than mammals, so reptiles generally get sick slower than other pets (or people). This also means that it generally takes reptiles longer to recover from illness.

This chapter starts with the most common but less serious beardie illnesses and then goes on to ones that are rarer, but worse. To people who love animals, it is distressing to read about them suffering. Even though it is troubling to read about what might go wrong with your pet's health, every owner needs to be aware of what could happen. For your own peace of mind and your beardie's good health over a long life, arm yourself with information!

Just remember, beardies are survivors. They're fairly tough little creatures. You might see some of these health challenges over the life of your pet. You certainly won't see all of them or even most of them, not even if you become a breeder or veterinarian yourself.

This book, and particularly the information in this chapter, is not meant to present medical guidance or replace expert help from a reptile veterinarian. Find a vet who is experienced in reptile health who is skilled, compassionate, kind and thorough. This is who you can rely upon if – when – you and your pet urgently need them.

You might need to be vigilant to know when this is.

As adults, bearded dragons, like many animals, are very good at hiding illness. In the wild, this ability helps protect weakened animals from attack. Looking healthy and strong is a survival strategy. It's a law of nature that only the healthiest and strongest get the best food, shelter and mates.

This instinctive need and ability to disguise illness can have the opposite effect when beardies are pets. A sick pet will do everything they can to hide their problem. As an aware, responsible and caring pet owner, you need to be on the look-out, always, for any health problems your beardie would rather you not find out about.

Most health problems, if caught early, can be treated and even cured. Here are the main things to pay attention to:

1. Their weight. Weigh your pet a couple of times a week, using a gram scale. Record their weight. Weight loss can be a sign of parasites, or something more serious. Weight gain can lead to illnesses such as fatty liver disease. For all of these, you need the vet.

2. Is your pet eating normally? Getting water? Pooping normally? Behaving normally? Not stressed?

3. Are they having healthy sheds?

4. Are they mostly a bright-eyed, happy pet? If they're grumpy all the time, they're either going into brumation, or they're sick.

5. Do they sleep 8 to 12 hours at night?

6. Are they basking?

In general, the most frequent **causes for injury** are fighting with another beardie, falling, escaping or being burnt in their vivarium by a heated rock, under-tank heating pad or getting too close to their heat or UV lamp.

Causes for illness are fungal infections, mites or parasites caught from the insects or greens they eat. Poor or wrong food and vivarium conditions cause or contribute to gut or respiratory issues, eye problems, dehydration (not enough water), metabolic bone disease (MBD), mouth rot, and other diseases that can be fatal.

The good news is that good nutrition, the right vivarium conditions and regular care can prevent most of what can go wrong with your pet's health. If they do get sick, early intervention could save their life.

HEALTH BASICS

If you want to reduce the risk of having a sick beardie, here's what you must do:

- Always be sure their home is warmer than 65 F (18 C) overall and never hotter at the warm end than 110 F (43 C).
- Always be sure their UV light is working properly and they can safely get close enough to their light.
- Don't feed too many insects (even though almost every beardie would love you to do this) or not enough thoroughly-washed fresh greens and vegetables.
- Be sure they have clean water, either by misting or giving them a shallow water dish.
- Use a humidity gauge and check it daily.
- Just one animal per vivarium. They are always healthier living alone.
- Watch out for a pet that is twitching, restless, depressed or not interested in eating.
- If they're standing with one leg or foot extended, it may look odd. It's also a sign of trouble. So is hunching their body, with their belly tucked up, or when they won't lie down, even in their favourite spots.
- A beardie that is very moody and has become aggressive, not wanting to be touched at all, is ill.

CALL THE VET!

WHEN TO CALL YOUR VET

- Low or no energy (unless it's brumation or they're about to shed).
- Makes jerky movements.
- Won't eat.
- Is limping.
- Is constipated (not pooping).

Signs that you need the vet immediately are:

- Runny or bloody poop.
- They suddenly smell bad.
- They refuse to eat.
- They seem depressed.
- An unusual lump.

Choose the reptile vet who asks questions, listens and checks carefully, taking all the time needed to help you and your pet.

Find a good vet by getting referrals from other beardie owners in your area. If you don't know anyone like that yet, join the local Herp club.

There are vets who just seem to prescribe antibiotics, no matter what, and send you on your way. This is not the vet you want.

When you go to the vet, expect your pet to not like it much (no pet ever does). An annoyed beardie is apt to poop and might bite, so be prepared.

Put them in a cardboard box with holes for air circulation, or better, a small pet carrier. Place shredded newspaper on the bottom. If it's cold out, warm up the car first. If hot, turn on the AC.

Take a small sample of their most recent poop for the vet to do a fecal exam.

Unlike other types of pets such as dogs or cats, reptiles don't get shots (vaccines).

REPTILE EXAM

Here's what happens at a reptile vet exam. It generally begins with the vet asking a lot of questions about what's normal for your beardie and what's been going on recently. Then they'll do a thorough physical examination.

The vet will look first for the most obvious signs of dehydration or malnutrition.

They'll look in the mouth for infection and do the fecal test for parasites.

They may do a blood test.

There might be x-rays needed to find abnormalities in size, shape or position of body organs. This will also reveal a mass or tumour, joint damage or broken bones.

BEARDED DRAGON POOP

Bearded dragons poop a lot, especially when they're younger and eating more protein. Two or three times a day is normal for babies. This decreases to two or three times a week in adults.

When they're brumating, they might poop only once a week, or not at all if they aren't eating. All of this is normal.

Bearded dragon poop is usually greenish, long and solid, with yellowish or whiteish urine. There might also be a bit of clear liquid. This is just a sign your pet is getting enough water.

Their poop can be green, yellow, red or black. This usually depends on what they've been eating or a medicine they're taking.

Poop that is runny and constipation (not being able to poop) are signs of a sick beardie.

DIARRHEA

A day or two of diarrhea, or frequent, runny poop, isn't usually a problem for your dragon, but it may be for you because it stinks! It could just be caused by something they ate.

If it goes on for longer than two days, or there's also pus or blood in their poop and if they don't want to eat, or seem to have no energy or are losing weight, you need the vet.

The usual cause of diarrhea is parasites, but it can also be a sign that they're stressed, there's been a change in their diet or they're eating too much fruit. Other reasons could be they're getting tap water with high levels of chlorine or heavy metals (if so, give them spring water).

CONSTIPATION

Constipation is common in dragons. It could simply be that they need more water. Another cause is stress. Or getting too many insects and not enough greens and veg.

For some adults, only pooping once a week is normal. Any dragon that goes longer than that is in trouble and needs the vet. Prolonged constipation can cause intestinal polyps or tears that cause internal bleeding.

Give them a warm bath, then a very gentle tummy massage. If this doesn't work, see the vet.

SAFE SHEDDING

All bearded dragons shed old skin as they grow. Unlike people and other mammals, reptiles' skin doesn't stretch. It sheds.

Babies and juveniles are growing rapidly, so they shed often. By adulthood, beardies shed twice a year.

Beardies getting ready to shed might be less active, wanting to stay in their hide and eat less. Their colour will also change to a duller, grayish version of what it usually is.

The skin will come off in large pieces, usually within a couple of [illegible] scratch against. Egg cartons, or a plastic hide meant to look like a cave are great shedding scratchers.

Never try to pull off the shedding skin, because it is easy to damage the tender new skin underneath. It also is not a good idea to put hand lotion or oils on your pet.

Misting and more frequent warm water soaks help get rid of old skin. Watch for a retained shed. This happens when the old skin fails to shed around toes and tail tip, cutting off circulation. If not caught in time, a retained shed could cause a dragon to lose a toe or the tip of his or her tail.

BEARDIE REVIVER

This will help hydrate your constipated, dehydrated, not-eating or generally unwell juvenile or adult dragon. Do NOT use this for babies.

Method:

Stir reptile electrolytes or Pedialyte into a tablespoon of strained baby food (chicken or beef flavour). It should be as thick as pudding.

Use an eyedropper or oral syringe to put a bit on your pet's lips, being careful not to get it in their nostrils. They'll lick it off. Repeat, until they've eaten it all. Do this two or three times a day, for two days. Add just a sprinkling of calcium and their vitamin supplements once a day.

This should get your dragon back to his or her regular eating (and pooping) routine. It also works for new pets, stressed pets or when you're travelling.

After shedding, their colour, appearance and behaviour will be brighter as they return to feeling like their normal selves.

DEHYDRATION

Dehydration means they're not getting enough water or moisture in their food. A dehydrated dragon will have no appetite or energy. They'll soon also have sunken eyes and wrinkled skin. If you gently pinch some of their skin between your thumb and second finger and it doesn't immediately relax back to where it was, this is a fast test of dehydration (it also works for humans – try it!).

Chronic dehydration leads to a more serious condition, kidney disease.

You need to get them into some liquid (a warm bath) and get some liquid into them. You could try making them a smoothie (slurry) of greens, fruit and water and giving it to them with an eyedropper or syringe. If you still can't get some liquid into your dragon, call the vet!

NOT EATING

There are times when not eating much or at all are normal. These are when they are going into brumation, during brumation, for the first couple of days after coming to a new home or getting a new vivarium, and when starting to shed.

If none of these is true and you have a skinny dragon that is a picky eater or doesn't want to eat at all, they're probably ill.

Start by checking these things, in this order:

- are your vivarium temperatures too cool?
- Is it time to change the UV bulb?

- Are the insects you're offering the wrong size (or they just don't like that particular insect – it happens)?
- Are they getting enough variety in their meals and snacks?

You can tempt an under-eater with tidbits of fruit or live insects or worms, but be careful with worms. They're fatty and high in calcium.

No animal will intentionally starve itself. If your beardie isn't eating for more than two days (babies), go to the vet. If not eating for more than four days (juveniles) or more than a week (adults), try beardie reviver to get them eating again.

If this doesn't get them eating, go to the vet. It could just be they have parasites, both common and treatable. Or it could be more serious, such as an infection. Either way, you

VOMITING

If your pet is throwing up, check the temperatures in his or her vivarium and the lights. If these are OK, you need to see the vet. Take a sample of the most recent vomit for the vet to test.

SAND TRAP!

If you use sand as a substrate, your pet may develop eye problems from sand dust. Calcium sand is especially likely to cause this problem. Switch to paper towel or newspaper for your substrate and you'll probably need to give your pet reptile eyedrops two or three times a day.

IMPACTION

It used to be believed that reptiles just naturally eat some sand, If their vivarium substrate is sand, in their eagerness to gobble insects. Noticing this, pet supply manufacturers began putting calcium in the sand they sold for reptile substrate, reasoning that it would be a benefit to get pets to eat 'nutritious' sand.

Then owners and breeders began to suspect that impaction, that's a dragon with a gut full of sand that can kill them, was a common result of using sand for vivarium substrate.

In the gut, sand tends to compact and harden into something like cement. It feels like what it is, a rock in the belly of your pet.

The thinking on this has evolved, with many breeders and owners now declaring that sand substrate is generally safe for adult beardies, but not the younger ones. But sand floors have another health problem because sand easily traps waste and uneaten food. This creates an ideal place for harmful bacteria to multiply.

It's also become clear that it's not only sand that causes impaction. It might be what they're eating. Impaction can be caused by your dragon eating mealworms or reptile food pellets.

A dragon that has impaction will stop eating, stop pooping and may stop using their hind legs. These are signs of severe impaction.

If your dragon has mild impaction, treat it like constipation. If that doesn't help you need to see the vet!

OBESITY

An overweight beardie is a problem, because obesity can lead to some serious health issues and will shorten their life.

The usual cause is too many fatty worms. Change their diet to just dubias, greens, salads and veg, with fruit as a once-a-week-only treat. Be sure they're getting enough water.

ABOUT THEIR TEETH

Dragons' front teeth fall out and new ones grow in throughout their lives. Their side teeth are permanent.

EYES AND EYESIGHT

Beardies have good eyesight and they see in colour. However, because their eyes are on the sides of their heads, not on a flatter face (as humans have), they don't have good depth perception.

Droopy eyes can be a sign that they have parasites, an infection or kidney problems, [illegible]

Sunken eyes are a sign of dehydration.

Swollen eyes can be the first sign of shedding. But it could also mean they have an eye infection, parasites or are getting too much Vitamin A.

STRESS

Almost every pet owner knows what stress is, for humans.

Generally, the cause is not getting what we need, particularly when it's beyond our control. For pets, this is not enough healthy food, not the climate they need (heat, sunshine, coolness, humidity), not enough fresh water, no shelter from enemies, a home that isn't clean or not enough space (not living in crowded conditions) and variety in their lives to avoid boredom.

Pets need an abundance of the basics of life (air, water, food, shelter, space,) and they also have emotional needs for routine, human companionship at times and protection from harm. You promise to provide all of these when you take on pet parenting.

Here's what bearded dragons find particularly stressful:

- Being too hot or too cold.
- Too dry or too wet.
- Bad food/no food or water.
- Sharing their vivarium.
- Seeing other bearded dragons (even in other vivariums).
- Other, larger family pets they haven't met yet.
- Loud noises (TV, video games).
- Moving to a new vivarium or home.
- Their enclosure or basking spot is too small.
- No cool hide.
- Rough handling.
- Neglect.
- A dirty vivarium.
- Night lights.

SIGNS OF A STRESSED BEARDIE

- Not eating.
- Not basking.
- Hiding.
- Refusing to leave a cool hide (unless they're brumating).
- Bearding.
- Darkening their skin colour (also a sign they're too cold).
- Stress marks.
- Biting.
- Glass surfing.

Stress marks are ovals or dark lines that appear on your pet's chin or belly. These lines, usually brownish, make patterns that look something like snakeskin.

Stress marks are natural during stress, such as when you first bring your pet home. They can also appear when your beardie is very interested in something, annoyed by something and sometimes, it might seem, for no reason at all.

When all is well in a beardie's world, stress marks naturally fade away in a few days.

BREATHING PROBLEMS

Gaping is normal for beardies when they are under their basking light. This is a sign that you have the tank temperatures just right.

If they seem to be gaping and staying at the cool end of their vivarium most of the time, it could be that it's too hot.

A dragon that seems to have his or her mouth open all the time and is making a popping sound or sounds like they're choking or is panting or wheezing needs to see the vet. These behaviours could be due to an upper respiratory infection (URI), parasites or pneumonia.

URI is a bacterial infection caused by too much humidity in their vivarium. It is usually curable. Pneumonia is also caused by too much humidity. All this dampness means that mould grows in their vivarium substrate.

Pneumonia is more serious, but also usually curable if you catch it early. In addition to following the vet's advice, you will need to adjust the humidity in your vivarium and steam clean it.

SALMONELLA

All reptiles carry salmonella. They get it from the greens, vegetables and insects they eat. Usually, it's not a problem unless they walk through their poop and then through their

BEARDIE POISONS!

All of these can kill your pet:

- Fireflies (lightning bugs)
- Some spiders
- Evergreen wood – cedar, yew, spruce, pine
- Citrus fruits
- Avocado

food or water dish, or they poop in their bath water and you let them stay there a while longer. Salmonella is in the poop. If it gets from there to their mouth, they will get sick.

If you kiss your pet, don't wash your hands before and after you handle them, or aren't careful about their housekeeping, salmonella could also spread from them to you.

Humans also can carry some salmonella without being overwhelmed by it and becoming ill. There can be salmonella in eggs and raw or under-cooked chicken, turkey or duck. Eating foods that have salmonella is a much more common way for humans to get ill than by catching it from their pets. In people, salmonella mimics food poisoning, causing fever, nausea, vomiting, cramps and diarrhea. It's rarely serious. Almost always, people recover from salmonella in a few days without needing to see the doctor.

The usual treatment for salmonella, for both people and pets, is antibiotics.

PARASITES

Having a parasite overload is the most common health problem among pet bearded dragons. Fortunately, it's also almost always curable.

Parasites make their home in the digestive system. Most animals, including humans, have gut parasites. Some of these parasites are critical for our digestion and good health. Others aren't so desirable.

The different types of parasites are only visible under a microscope. Your dragon may have small amounts of bad parasites and never be troubled by them. Stress, such as when a dragon is shipped to a new owner and must adjust to a new home or when they are in a vivarium that is too small, too cold or dirty, can cause parasites to rapidly multiply. When overwhelmed by parasites, a bearded dragon will not be able to hide the signs.

A dragon with a high parasite load will be:

- Slow-moving or sluggish.
- Have low or no energy.
- Not eating.
- Vomiting.
- Diarrhea.
- [illegible]
- Sunken eyes.

The three most common types of parasites bearded dragons become overloaded with are pinworms, coccidia and amebiasis. They can also get tapeworms and giardia.

Usually, with good care, dragons are able to lower their own parasite levels. If they don't seem to be better in a few days (or two days for babies or juveniles) take them to the vet along with a sample of your pet's most recent poop and vomit, if they're throwing up.

A fecal exam will reveal the type of parasite, which will determine the treatment. For coccidia, it is a sulfa drug. For pinworms, it's a de-wormer, usually pills you need to get into your pet once a day for three to five days, repeated 10 days later with another fecal test to check for results in three weeks. For amebiasis, the treatment that is recommended by vets and breeders is Metronidazole, an antibiotic.

Tapeworms look like small, white grains of rice in their poop. The usual drug given to eliminate tapeworms is Droncit, given once and repeated two weeks later.

Mites and ticks live on an animal's skin. They are uncommon in bearded dragons, through if you also have pet snakes, snake mites can spread to your dragon.

To recover from a bad bout of parasites, a dragon will need prescribed medication and also reptile probiotics and electrolytes.

If you have a pet with too many parasites, in addition to them getting their meds, reduce all your vivarium furniture and décor to the minimum and clean everything with bleach-water. Switch to paper towels for substrate.

If they have had coccidia, you will need to steam-clean the vivarium and everything in it except the lights, plus anything you use for your pet. Bleach-water will not kill coccidia.

For a recovering pet, spot clean their home twice a day. Give them clean water and food twice a day.

A pet can take several weeks, and possibly two or three visits to the vet, to overcome a serious parasite overload.

Be aware that most parasites can easily travel to people. This is another reason to always wash your hands, with soap and warm water, before and after handling your pet or cleaning anything that is theirs.

MOUTH ROT

Mouth rot, or Infectious Stomatitis, is when an infection, caused by bacteria, fungus or a virus, overwhelms your pet's immune system.

A beardie with mouth rot has a red, inflamed mouth and will stop eating. There will be yellowish or grayish skin around their mouth. They may drool. In the most severe cases, their head will swell, a painful condition for your pet.

Causes are the usual list of what makes dragons ill or ends their lives prematurely. These are: wrong vivarium temperatures or humidity levels, poor diet and stress.

This very common illness is easy to spot if you pay attention to your pet. Catch it early, and your vet will prescribe antibiotics, flush their mouth with antiseptic and, possibly, give them stronger injections of antibiotics or other drugs. It is usually curable if caught and treated early.

Later intervention can mean surgery to remove dead tissue, so a bigger vet bill. Even then, your pet might not survive.

SHAKING OR QUIVERING

A bearded dragon that is often shaking or quivering isn't showing that they're too cold or they're anxious.

Here's what could be the problem: they have low blood sugar.

Another cause for tremors, twitching or muscle spasms is they're getting too much or not enough calcium or phosphorus or not enough Vitamin D3.

TAIL ROT

This nasty infection will do what the name says, lead to your pet's tail [illegible] that happens, it has spread through their body, leading to organ failure, which isn't something they can survive.

Early attention means your pet will keep part, maybe most of his or her tail and be in as little pain as possible. Early treatment is critical. Tail rot is treated with antibiotics.

YELLOW FUNGUS

If your pet develops a yellow or brown crust on the scales of their head, back or tail and they are eating less or not at all, it could mean they have yellow fungus. Also called CANV, it is an easily-spread infection.

The causes are a dirty vivarium, living with others in a crowded tank or chronic stress. You will need your vet's help to treat yellow fungus.

METABOLIC BONE DISEASE

Metabolic Bone Disease, or MBD, causes a bearded dragon to become paralyzed. It is most often diagnosed in juveniles or very young adult dragons. Gravid females can also develop MBD because egg-laying means they need more calcium than normally, when they're not pregnant.

This same disease in humans, also caused by not getting enough calcium, is called rickets.

MBD is completely preventable, but there is no cure. Dragons with untreated MBD usually die as they become too weak to catch their food, move to their basking spot or get to their cool hide.

The causes of MBD are not getting enough calcium, Vitamin D3 or UV-B light.

The earliest signs of MBD are their lower jaw or legs swell. Their toes, tails or joints could become twisted or crooked. They might develop an overbite or an underbite. They could have constipation and bloating. They may refuse to eat, grow slowly or not at all, seem to be awkward and get lumps along their legs or backbone. As the disease advances, they will have tremors and their bones will break, seemingly for no reason.

MBD is a disease that develops over time, so it can be easy to miss in the earlier stages, particularly by new pet owners. This is another reason to be a vigilant owner, weighing and taking a close look at your pet regularly and keeping notes about their health.

A pet with MBD will need more calcium supplements, water or rehydration medicine, injections of Vitamin D3 and of calcitonin (calcium injected into their bones). Their diet will need to be changed and their UV-B light checked frequently.

Caught early enough and with treatment, they can partly recover but may need ongoing calcium shots.

> **STEAM CLEAN!**
>
> If your pet has parasites, any type of infection or virus, you need to take everything out of his or her vivarium and either discard or steam clean the tank and everything that goes back in it.
>
> Regular bleach-water or vinegar-water cleaning is NOT enough to kill these threats to your pet's recovery and health.
>
> If it isn't possible to steam clean something in the vivarium (for example, you can't steam clean the light fixtures) thoroughly clean with disinfectant solution.
>
> If there are live plants in their vivarium, discard them.
>
> Remember to clean and disinfect everything they come in contact with. Stay extra-vigilant about your cleaning to help them recover.

PARALYSIS

Serious impaction can also cause a bearded dragon to become paralyzed.

The first sign is a dragon that seems to be dragging a [illegible] sitting in a way that seems strange.

If you see this behaviour, you need the vet immediately.

ADENOVIRUS

Adenovirus is common in juveniles and young adults.

The signs are weakness, not eating and they may become paralyzed. There is no cure.

Dragons with this illness almost always die.

ABSCESSES

An abscess looks like a lump, bump or tumour, but it is not a cancer. It forms when white blood cells become trapped in the body, usually after infection. In humans, these used white blood cells that have died after fighting infection are broken down into a liquid (such as in a pimple).

Reptiles don't have this ability to break down and get rid of old white blood cells, so they can develop abscesses to store the old cells, turning them into a pus that is semi-solid, like cheese.

An abscess can develop anywhere in a bearded dragon's body. It could be very visible, such as a golf-ball sized growth on a leg that makes them lame. Or it could be more hidden, such as in their jaw or brain.

Common signs that your pet has a hidden abscess are not eating, breathing problems, blood in their poop, or seizures. Adult males are prone to hemipenal abscesses.

Having to share their vivarium, stress, wrong temperatures, too much humidity, not getting enough Vitamin A and being injured are the risk factors for abscesses.

Another cause is having an overload of the Salmonella bacteria, which all reptiles carry some of.

Your vet will take a blood sample to test and probably also biopsy (take a sample of) the abscess. They may also suggest an ultrasound to see the internal extent of an abscess or x-rays to show internal damage to bones. The usual treatment is surgery to remove the abscess, followed by antibiotics you will need to give your pet at home.

Early, aggressive treatment can usually save your pet's life if they develop an abscess.

GOUT

The main cause of gout in dragons is eating too many of only one kind of high-protein bug, such as cockroaches.

They can survive this illness, usually, with the help of a vet, though you should know that treatment can be expensive.

Better to avoid the discomfort and pain by feeding your pet a healthy, varied diet.

FATTY LIVER DISEASE

Like gout, fatty liver disease is the result of too much high-protein and high-fat food, such as worms and insects, along with not eating enough greens and vegetables.

Like some little children and candy, your pet might try almost anything to get you to give them more insects and less veg. You, as the parent, can't let this happen.

KIDNEY DISEASE

Beardies need their moist veggies and water to drink or misting to avoid dehydration, a cause of kidney disease. Kidney failure is also possibly caused by too much calcium and Vitamin D3, however there isn't enough research yet to be certain about this.

TUMOURS AND CANCER

A dragon that develops odd dark spots or a lump or growth may have cancer. Not all odd spots, bumps or lumps turn out to be cancer. You'll need the help of a vet to know exactly what's going on with your pet, and what to do next.

Cancer is a group of diseases. In all types of cancer, cells mutate and divide in a way that isn't normal. These abnormal cells do not work in the way that healthy cells do. Without treatment, the rogue cells can quickly outnumber healthy ones, severely weakening the animal. Finally, an infection kills them. Odd dark spots may be melanoma, one of the types of cancer that is increasing in pet dragons, particularly in the US.

Cancers can be hard to detect in lizards, but caught early, they might survive. Watch their weight and how much they're eating. Gently feel for lumps and anything that isn't normal, especially in their chest, belly and legs.

Your vet will do an X-ray to look for internal tumours. Surgery may be a part of the treatment. You'll need to do a bleach/water cleaning of everything in your pet's vivarium, then use paper towel for substrate.

Gastic neuroendocrine carcinoma, or GNT, has increased among pet bearded dragons in the past decade. It starts in the stomach, but quickly spreads to the liver, pancreas and kidneys, intestines and heart. The cause is unknown.

So far, no wild dragons have been found with GNT. It mostly affects juveniles and young adults. The first signs are vomiting, not eating and generally seeming unwell. It is diagnosed by vets using blood tests, X-rays and, sometimes, biopsies. This might be followed by surgery to remove the tumour, but there is usually no cure.

All you can do is keep your dragon as comfortable as possible, for as long as possible.

REPRODUCTIVE HEALTH

Adult females can become egg-bound. This can happen even if they haven't been with a male recently. An egg-bound female may be able to lay a few eggs, but then stop, with an enlarged, lumpy belly full of unlaid eggs.

She might resume laying after a relaxing warm bath.

If not, do not try to massage her belly in hopes that she will resume laying. More likely what will happen is some of the eggs will break inside her body, which will cause pain, possible infection and internal damage from the egg shards.

If you have an egg-bound female, you need the vet. If they can't see you immediately, put her in a nesting box with sand or vermiculite and keep her in it until your vet appointment.

Male bearded dragons can have a similar problem when their femoral pores become blocked. This condition is called a hemipenile plug, seminal plug or sperm plug. Males can also get a prolapsed hemipene, when a part of the hemipene moves outside the body. Either is serious and usually requires help from your vet.

If your pet has one of these conditions, there will be something that isn't poop coming from their vent and the vent will be swollen. A seminal plug will be hard and yellowish-amber coloured.

Hemipenes are delicate. Attempting to remove sperm plugs can cause serious damage. To ease your pet's discomfort if you can't get to the vet immediately, let them soak in warm water. Usually, this doesn't remove the seminal plug or cause a prolapsed hemipene to move back into the body. Your vet may try to free the seminal plug by massaging their lower body with antibiotic cream. Most often, this doesn't work and the next best option is surgery. Surgery is also the solution for a hemipenile prolapse.

VET BILLS

To avoid vet bill shock, start a health savings plan as soon as you get your pet. This could be as simple as tossing pocket change (if you still use paper money and coins) into a jar.

Another way to avoid financial pain on top of the worry of having a sick pet is this. Take a small amount from each paycheque (such as $25 or £25) and tuck it away in a 'rainy day' savings account specifically for your pet.

[illegible] available where you live.

NINE
Babies And Seniors

Bearded dragons become adults, and able to breed, when they're about one year old, though for some it can take another six months to be fully mature adults. Healthy adults will want to breed a few weeks after they come out of brumation as the days are becoming longer and warmer.

He will puff out and blacken his beard and begin a mating dance of bobbing his head and stomping.

She will bob her head, wave to him and move closer.

He will circle around her, keeping an eye out for other males while getting close enough to bite the back of her neck. Then he moves on top of her. He'll scratch her with his hind legs to get her into the proper position, then insert his hemipenis into her vent. They will remain together for several minutes and sometimes until both are exhausted. Then they go their separate ways.

She will dig several test burrows before choosing a nesting place she likes and laying her eggs. This nest needs to be deep enough that she can get all of her body into it, leaving only her snout visible.

A gravid female who is spending more time basking, putting on weight and becoming swollen with a lumpy belly is almost ready to lay her eggs. She'll also poop less often.

If she's not happy with her nest, she will pace and try to escape. If she can't get to a place she considers suitable for her nest, she may become egg-bound, which means she's unable to lay her eggs.

Egg laying is usually four to six weeks after mating, but it can be as long as 100 days.

While you might want to watch the egg laying, she will want some privacy. Once she's laid her eggs, usually over several hours, she will fill in the hole of her nest, as if tucking the eggs in to protect them from too much heat or predators.

If the egg laying goes on for longer than a day, she will be exhausted and in trouble. This is when you need the vet.

Once she's finished egg laying, she'll have lost a third of her weight and look very thin. This is normal. She needs water, food and extra calcium plus time in the sun, or, if that's not possible, under her UVB lamp to recover.

She may produce as few as seven eggs, or as many as 45. 20 to 30 is average. After laying her eggs, she will be ravenous, eating up to 100 bugs or worms a day. She needs this protein and fat to regain her strength.

She'll also be thirsty. Not long after laying her eggs, she'll leave the nest partly covered and go in search of food and water. She may check back on the nest a few times, but at this point, she's had enough of mothering and goes back to her usual routine. Hatchlings are completely on their own, reliant on instinct for survival.

The eggs left behind look like marshmallows, with a tough, leathery shell that has a pink dot on it. 55 to 90 days or so after they're laid, bearded dragon eggs start to hatch. It is temperature that determines hatch timing. Cooler conditions make a longer time between egg laying and hatching.

For about a day before they are ready to hatch, the eggs will sweat. Eggs become soft, like a deflated balloon, 12 hours before the babies emerge. The babies cut their way through their shells with egg teeth at the end of their snouts. They are born with their eyes closed, but after they absorb their egg sacs they will start to move around and open their eyes.

Hatchlings emerge from their eggs with an orange stripe near their eyes. It will fade away by the time they are juveniles.

They are born with a pinkish mass that looks like a small tumour on their bellies. This is the egg sac. It will be reabsorbed into their bodies within a few days.

The world is a dangerous place for a new baby dragon. The first to be born can easily trample their later brothers and sisters. They must quickly find shelter, water and insects to eat, while avoiding predators just waiting for new dragons to hatch.

A STRANGE FACT ABOUT FEMALE BEARDIES

You could have a female pet beardie who becomes gravid, or pregnant, without ever having been with a male. She will make a nest and lay these eggs, but because they aren't fertile, there will be no babies.

If this happens, you should remove the eggs and destroy them. You do this by freezing them and then discarding.

Afterwards, your pet will need extra calcium and extra insects and water to get back to her normal healthy weight.

Babies born to be pets are luckier. Breeders usually remove eggs from the nest to incubating boxes that are carefully controlled for heat and humidity. Once a baby is active, it is removed for safety. Larger dragons will attack smaller ones. Adults, including their own parents, will eat the babies if they're kept together.

Babies are usually 3 to 4 inches (7.6 to 10 cm) long at birth. In the first four months, they grow fast – as much as ½ inch (1 cm) per week.

Baby dragons are twitchy, nervous animals, with good reason. By instinct, they know their world is full of danger. They will try to jump away if you pick them up and could easily fall and be injured. Until they are five months old, you should handle them as little as possible, or not at all.

FEEDING BABIES

You need to give babies the smallest-sized roaches or other insects (these are usually sold as "minis") to avoid choking. Choking is common in babies and juveniles who try to eat food that is too large for them. You'll also need to cut up or tear up greens into small pieces. For babies 1/2 inch to 3/4 inch (or 1 to 2 cm) is fine.

New babies eat only bugs until they are about one month old. Then they eat a diet made up of 75 percent bugs and 25 percent greens as older babies and juveniles.

Some owners who feed crickets remove the back legs of the feeder bugs, but this isn't necessary.

COMMON MISTAKES WITH BABY BEARDIES

If you have a pet that has dull eyes, seems to have no energy or isn't growing, or if you have two or more babies in the same tank or vivarium and they are trying to eat each other, you need to act fast to save them.

You should never have more than one beardie per enclosure. The larger one will always harass the smaller or younger one. Fingers, toes and tail tips could be damaged (or eaten!) Hungry beardies do become cannibals.

Don't make these mistakes with your baby dragon:

- Offering too many greens and not enough insects
- Insects are too large – longer than the space between your beardie's eyes
- Feeding them nothing but bearded dragon pellets or commercial pet foods
- They're too cold or too hot, with no cool hide
- They get no or not enough UV light
- They get no water
- They get no supplements and vitamins – either gut-loaded or dusted insects
- Too much humidity or too dry

Babies and juveniles love to chase bugs. Seeing them and chasing them is what stimulates their appetites.

All babies would love to eat bugs and nothing but bugs. To be healthy, and get a broad range of nutrition, they need to learn to eat their greens. If you have a baby or juvenile who refuses to eat anything but bugs, take the bugs off their plate for a day or two and offer only greens.

You could start off with collard, mustard or turnip greens. Each week, mix in something different to make it interesting and tempt your baby to eat a variety of foods. This could be any of the following cut into small chunks:

- Acorn or Butternut squash
- Red or yellow Bell pepper
- Parsnip
- Fennel
- Alfalfa
- Bok choy

A baby that won't eat is a concern. Babies are far less hardy than adult dragons. The babies can fade fast and die in just a few days. The problem for a dragon that won't eat is usually that their vivarium isn't warm enough or they aren't able to get close enough to their UV light.

WHAT WILL MY BEARDIE LOOK LIKE?

All bearded dragons change colour, and sometimes their stripes or patterns, as they get older. Their colours also become brighter after each shed, until they are seniors.

SHOULD YOU BREED YOUR BEARDIE?

Breeding beardies is something many experienced pet owners look forward to doing. But is it right for you? Here's how to tell if you're ready for babies:

1. **Experience** – You've had more than one bearded dragon, for a number of years, and know a lot about them including the basics of feeding and care routines. You are totally in control of heating, lighting, humidity and feeders.
2. **You have the space** – You have space for incubators and to keep babies in their own enclosures.
3. **You have the time** – Babies need a lot more frequent care than adults. They need to be fed four or five times a day and misted once or twice a day. You need to check on them almost constantly.
4. **You have the insects** – Babies, as well as gravid and post-gravid mothers, are big eaters. You have a steady, guaranteed supply of insects.
5. **You have the money** – It costs more to feed a baby or juvenile than an adult, because they eat more insects. Multiply that by the many babies you might have from a clutch of eggs.
6. **You have a reliable reptile vet**, in case of any problems.
7. **You have a network** for advice and support.
8. **Know your 'why'** – Don't have babies simply for the experience or because you might make some cash. Breeding animals isn't simply a side-hustle. It requires 24/7 attention, space and investment which all adds up to a big commitment. Also, it will be difficult to find good homes for pets you don't choose to keep, unless you're a recognized breeder and these babies are 'something special' in their colours or markings.

The only way to know what your baby or juvenile bearded dragon will look like when they grow up is to meet or see photos of their parents. This is one reason why it is an advantage to buy your pet from a reputable breeder. These breeders stake their reputations on producing quality animals and keep careful records.

GOOD CARE FOR SENIORS

From about age six, bearded dragons breed less often, then not at all. The females will have smaller clutches of eggs, perhaps for a couple of years.

Few animals reach their senior years in the wild. Pet beardies, with good care, can live to age 12 and sometimes beyond then. Average life expectancy for a pet beardie is 8 to 10 years. This means that caring pet owners may have a senior citizen beardie for several years.

By this time, you and your beardie know each other very well. You also know what he or she likes and what they don't really care for.

You know each other's routines. You fit into each other's lives. A senior will want more of

HOW TO RE-HOME YOUR PET

Here's what to do instead. You can offer your pet to a loving new home on a herps forum. You can let friends at your local herp society know you have a pet that needs to be rehomed. Get the word out among people who care about reptile pets to find a good new owner for your pet.

If your pet is very old or very sick, the humane thing to do may be euthanasia, which means putting them to sleep. A vet will do this with the minimal amount of fear and pain for your pet. If you are concerned about the cost, it is about the same as what you would pay for a regular vet visit.

what they've always liked. They tend to slow down, content to bask or rest in their hide for hours. Senior beardies like their home comforts.

If they want to eat a bit less than when they were younger and laze around most of the time, this is normal. If they stop eating, stop pooping and it isn't time to brumate, just like younger dragons, they may be ill.

Offer senior dragons the same foods and do the same supplements you would do with an adult who isn't gravid (See Chapter 6). As they relax into old age, seniors' colours can darken or seem duller than when they were young adults.

Elderly dragons can suffer from gout and failing eyesight. Late in life, they may become feeble or disabled. If so, you will need to hand-feed them and mist them so they get enough water. They could need help getting to their basking spot and back to their hide. They'll also appreciate baths.

Most dragons end their lives naturally, but if they are in pain, your vet might recommend euthanasia, or being put to sleep. This is fast and painless for your pet as they drift off with a painkiller.

THE LAST GOOD-BYE

The heartbreaking fact about pets is that they experience time differently than we do. Their lives are lived out fully much faster than our own. Only a very few pets, such as parrots, commonly outlive their human companions.

This is an easy thing to ignore when you get a new pet. You're excited about all the good times you'll share and how much fun you'll have, getting to really know each other. If you adopt a baby or juvenile, unless you are careless or you are both unlucky, there will be many good years before you must part.

Even though we know our pets will eventually die, as owners it is so much easier to ignore this until it's happening. When it does, it comes as a shock. It can be wrenchingly painful.

Thoughtless people may tell you "they were just a pet," or "that's what happens. You'll get another one," but this is missing the point. The animal friend you want is the one that, until so recently, was your everyday normal. You want normal back.

Possibly, mixed in with the grief, there is also guilt. Did you do all you could to give your pet an excellent life? Always? Every single day of their time with you?

Or there's anger: why didn't they live longer? You've heard of other beardies that do. Why was it your pet that got sick?

Or possibly regret: maybe you shouldn't have ever gotten a pet at all. If so, you wouldn't have to go through this pain of losing them now.

Or you could be bargaining. If you could just do it over, it would be so much better. You'd be so much better, as a pet owner and a friend.

Most likely, you'll feel all these emotions, over and over. That's what grieving is.

No, you will never forget them. In time, it will hurt less. It will be easier to remember all the good times you had with your pet. You'll be able to look at your photos of them. It will feel OK to talk about them. Eventually, the sharp edge of loss will soften.

In the meantime, look after yourself. Own your feelings, because they are real and important. They honour the value of life and the gift of having a close, intimate friendship with a living being so different than ourselves. That's a very special thing.

Maybe, in time, you'll feel ready to form that same kind of relationship with someone new. Or not.

It's your choice, in your own time.

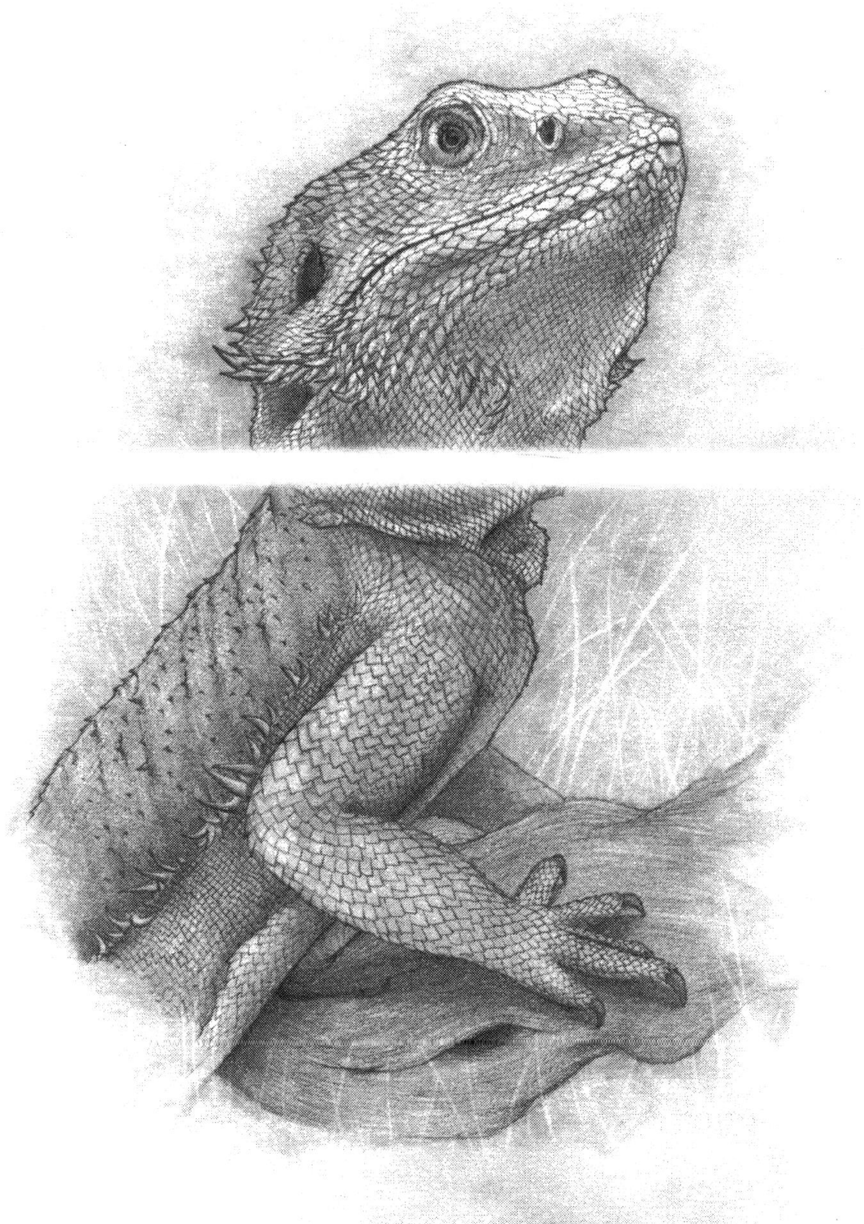

TEN

You & Your Beardie, Happily Ever After

GO PLAY OUTSIDE!

For their own comfort, protection from enemies and safety, pet bearded dragons spend a lot of time in their terrariums. It will amount to almost all of their lives.

But no matter how comforting home routines are, life can get a bit boring at times when all you do is stay inside in your room. That's as true for pets as it is for people.

What your pet really wants is time with you doing something interesting. This can be as simple as going outside, in warm weather. Some outside play with you can be a happy time for both you and your pet.

HAVE FUN WITH YOUR BEARDIE:

1. Play safely outside.
2. Go for a car ride.
3. Grow a beardie garden.
4. Take a dip.
5. Join a herp group.
6. Keep learning and sharing your pet parenting knowledge.

Before you head out, think about how you can give your beardie a fun experience that is also safe for them and worry-free for you.

This means, never leave them on their own.

Never leave them in a glass container outside. A larger plastic or wood box is a safer choice.

Some pet owners like to sit outside, with their beardie in a pet enclosure, the type suitable for a cat or rabbit. This is fine, but only if there is nothing harmful in the pet playpen, including any wild insects.

Others build a sort of enclosure, above ground, something like a rabbit hutch only larger. If you decide to do this, it needs mesh sides that doesn't allow other creatures to get in. Your pet-pen also needs to be placed so that your beardie can catch some rays, but also get into cooling shade.

Some owners leave their pets outside for hours at a time on mild days, in their enclosure but on their own. I think it's risky to ever leave a beardie (or any pet) unattended outside, but that's a personal choice. Do what you think is best for your pet.

CAR RIDES!

Every beardie I've ever met just loves going for car rides. They'll sit up, alert and looking around, enjoying the passing scenery.

Though they'd surely enjoy it, don't allow them to free-roam in your car. Or ride a reptile hammock strung up in a car window. Or expect them to just sit quietly in something they can easily get out of, like an open tote bag or doggie-carrier bag.

For car rides, pets need to be restrained (it's the law in many places, probably including where you live). For larger animals, this means a harness and possibly also a car-seat. For little lizards, it means a pet crate. The type designed for cats or medium-sized dogs is the one you want.

Even if you and your pet don't plan any car outings, an emergency could mean a road trip is in your future. As a part of your Go Bag for your beardie, you're going to need a pet

CAN MY BEARDIE DO ANY TRICKS?

While some owners claim they've trained their pet to come when their name is called, or play with a ping pong ball, or do other wondrous feats, the truth is your beardie probably can't do any tricks.

Or maybe they can. A researcher at University of Lincoln in England did train a bearded dragon to open a little door to get food. Not exactly a trick, but still, pretty smart, remembering that there is food hiding behind a door.

You could try teaching your dragon a trick, like jumping up on your chest when they want to come out of their vivarium for some quality time together. With patience, they might do it.

Are bearded dragons smart? Yes and no. They have a reptile brain, which means they're smart about and very focussed on getting everything a small reptile needs to survive. However, they can't make and use a tool to get their food (like a crow can) or find their way through a maze (any rodent can do this).

They're exactly smart enough to be a small lizard, living on scrubland, enjoying life in the sun.

carrier.

They're widely available in discount stores and online. If you decide to buy a used pet carrier, it will need a steam clean before it's safe for your pet.

GROW A BEARDIE GARDEN!

If you have a back yard or garden, an allotment or plot in a community garden, some containers on your patio or balcony or just a sunny spot in a window, you've got space to grow nutritious food for your pet!

It's easy, it's fun to do and you know the food you grow for your pet is healthy and organic (no pesticides or herbicides or other nasty chemicals).

So what will you grow? There are so many choices:

- **Dandelions** for the leaves.
- **Almost any herb** – try mint, thyme, basil. They all have tasty leaves.
- **Edible flowers** – there's a long list of healthy edible flowers, but I suggest you start with the three that are most widely available as seeds or starters and easiest to grow. They are nasturtium, petunias and geraniums.

ODD FACT

Adult females are able to store sperm in their bodies for up to a year after mating. They may use only some of the sperm to fertilize eggs immediately. This means a female could have several clutches of eggs in the warm season, all the result of breeding just once.

It's interesting to wonder why nature allowed dragons to develop this ability. Perhaps it is because two animals that are mating are distracted. Enemies could easily attack. Hatchlings are also very vulnerable. They're easy pickings for feral cats, foxes, large birds and other reptiles. Efficiency in mating and laying a lot of eggs increases the chance of enough hatchlings surviving to continue the species.

These are all annuals, so they grow fast. They're bright and colourful as well as easy to grow. They grow outside in summer, but you can also grow them inside, with gro-lights, year-round. Beardies (and people) can eat both leaves and flowers of these cheery plants in salads.

I recommend growing your salads in containers. Containers are easier to move to spots with more sun or more shade or more protection from the wind, as necessary.

All you need is a plant pot with holes in the bottom. You can buy these, or just use any metal or plastic container you happen to have.

Add the few holes in the bottom for drainage, a plant saucer (purchased, or the plastic bowls and lids from store-bought salads work), some organic potting soil and plants or seeds. Water generously, place in a sunny spot, and watch your salads bloom!

Don't use fertilizer or spray with anything.

Also great for beadies and easy to grow: clover, carrots, spinach, and greens such as turnip tops, beet tops, collard greens, mustard greens or kale.

TAKE A DIP!

On a warm day, place a kiddie pool mostly in the shade. Fill to no more than hip-deep for your pet. Make sure the water is neither cooler or warmer than the air outside.

Put a smooth, flat rock in the pool that can be his or her private island.

Stay with them when they're in the pool. Beardies like a cooling dip and they can swim, though they aren't fond of it.

Unattended, they could doze off on a hot day and drown.

JOIN A HERP GROUP!

If your live in a city or larger town, chances are there's a herp group near you. Look in free newspapers or online to find them. Or ask the people who work at your nearest pet store that specialises in reptiles. They're probably members.

There's lots of great things about meeting some new lizard-loving friends.

You'll already have plenty in common to talk about. You can share information and resources.

Having a few friends who have beardies or other insect-eating lizards means you can order together, split the costs, and save money.

You'll also have someone nearby to call, if you need a beardie-sitter, for example, or help finding a reptile vet.

KEEP LEARNING!

BOOKS, NATURE SHOWS, HERP GROUPS, ONLINE

No one ever can learn absolutely everything there is to know about pets, but it's fun trying to! And, who knows, you might also be the one who discovers something astonishingly new, previously unsuspected by any expert or the millions around the world who love these animals!

Places to learn include reading books, talking to people at herp and nature shows, and joining herp groups or starting one if there isn't already a good one in your area.

If you look online, you'll also find you can connect with other beardie lovers on forums. Three good ones I recommend are:

- www.beardeddragon.org/forums
- www.beardeddragonforum.com
- www.reptileforums.co.uk/forums/lizards

COULD MY PET GO WILD?

No. Creatures bred to be pets may be able to survive, briefly, in the wild, but everything is against them. Chances are they won't live for more than a day or so.

Even if they do survive, find another of their kind and mate successfully, there will not be a happy end to this story.

You only need to look at the long list of animals that should never have been introduced to a place that is not their native home to see why.

PROTECT YOUR BEARDIE!

You cannot feed your pet any insects you catch in a field or in your backyard.

When you're outside, don't let your beardie eat ladybugs (ladybirds), mosquitos, butterflies, moths, bees, wasps, centipedes or any other wild creature out there.

Don't give them wild and roadside plants to eat.

Wild eating could make your beardie seriously ill. Wild plants could have insects, been sprayed with chemicals or have taken in car exhaust. Wild insects could be full of gardening or farm field chemicals like weed-killer. The wild insects might also carry parasites.

Never let a beardie eat a firefly. Even eating just one firefly can kill a bearded dragon!

The gray squirrel, brought to Great Britain as a curiosity a few centuries ago, has now almost completely crowded out the native red squirrel, which is now either extinct or severely endangered almost everywhere in UK.

The (introduced in the last century) moose of Newfoundland have become a highway menace, responsible for many serious road accidents annually.

And we've all heard the horror stories of other invasive species including the Common

HOW TO COPE WITH CLIMATE ANXIETY

We live in the era of climate anxiety. This is the term given by the American Psychological Association for the "anxiety or worry about climate change and its effects." Perhaps you've also heard it called eco-anxiety.

The distress at seeing what is happening to our beautiful world is a real feeling. Never allow anyone to tell you that you are worrying needlessly, that the world will simply right itself, or that "everything will be OK."

It won't be, unless we take these feelings and use them to power effective actions to save our home planet. We must shift the focus from worry, anxiety, and grieving to taking meaningful action.

How can you, or I, or anyone do this? After all, it is a global problem, far beyond any one person's ability to solve this problem. Feeling overwhelmed by the scale of this problem makes us the victims of our own polluting ways. It's not the path forward. Instead, both for your own health and for the health of all who share our world, find a community of like-minded people engaged in solving one part of the climate change crisis.

Look online and you will find groups such as For Our Kids, a national Canadian network of parents and grandparents who are finding many ways to fight climate change. Another group to look at is Parents4Climate. If there is no such group where you live, or that you have online access to, perhaps you are the person to start such a group?

European rabbits in Australia, the Burmese pythons in Florida, the snakehead fish, the killer bees, the Asian black rats...

To protect our natural wildlife and our ecosystems, don't release pets, or anything else that doesn't naturally belong there, into the wild. If you truly can no longer keep your pet, for any reason, the humane thing to do is to responsibly re-house them.

Don't give your pet to someone who has never had a bearded dragon before and has no idea how to care for them, or any desire to put in the effort to learn how.

Don't advertise that you have a pet to give away on the free online sites like Kejiji and Craigslist. That is another way to attract an irresponsible new owner for your pet.

B.C. IS BURNING!

As I write this final chapter, the skies are gray on a warm summer day. The sun, as round and intensely orange as a tangerine, is the only thing that shows through the haze. The air is full of the smell of smoke. This is not caused by local fires, but fires burning in British Columbia, on the other side of the country, 5,600 km (or about 3,500 miles) away from where I sit writing now.

It's fire season out West. Happens every year, just as it does in Australia. But this year, in both these places as well as in California and other hot-spots, the fires are worse than in anyone's living memory. That follows last year, which was also a record-breaking year for fire destruction.

Plants, animals and people are losing their homes, and many, their lives.

The reason is climate change and, specifically, what we, the humans, have done to our world. We've soiled our own terrarium, our beautiful Blue Planet.

If we don't change our ways, and quickly, we could find there is nowhere to run to and nowhere to hide from hellish lives of near-constant emergency, seeking shelter from the

SMALL ACTS, BIG REWARDS

So what can we all do to save the blue planet we all call home, and everything that lives here? Small acts, by many, can add up to universal rescue

- Plant a pollinator garden – or plan one for next summer. If it's currently winter or the cool season, you could start seedlings indoors.
- Take public transportation, ride-share or walk rather than drive.
- Write to your local and federal (national) politicians about the importance of legislation that will help reduce greenhouse gasses and other pollutants.
- Speak up! Advocate for real change in banishing coal production, saving old-growth forests, endangered species at home and abroad and the pollinators world-wide.
- Turn off lights or AC when you're not in the room.
- If you live in a city, be on the look-out for places that need or could support a tree. Call the responsible city or town office to recommend they plant that tree. Take responsibility for watering the sapling.
- Plant a boulevard garden and care for it.
- Start a community garden or support the local allotments scheme.
- Start an environment club at school or your workplace. Challenge each other – what are more practical ways you and your friends and colleagues can save our home?

storms.

While the plants, the creatures and we continue to suffer.

There are some who will say that there's really not much that one person can do about these threats. Some even dismiss it as merely "bad weather." Others say they need only live their own lives, and that people in so-called fire zones, or ice-storm zones, or hurricane zones, or places that have flooded should simply move "somewhere else."

We all make our own choices, but few have that option to move somewhere else that may possibly be safer. We don't have that luxury of only caring about our own lives.

As a part of that life, you can choose to have a close and loving relationship with one small creature. Special as that is, it's not enough to help save their species. Or all the species, including our own.

I don't know what you will do to help save the creatures and us all, but I urge you to do something, mindfully and with passion and commitment. Some one, possibly small but purposeful thing. By each of us doing our small somethings, we can join the world community to achieve great things. We can each take steps to save ourselves and every living plant and creature that shares our planet by simply saving our planet.

There is still time for the dragons, the whales, the red squirrels, and the millions more plants, species and humans, to survive and to thrive.

It is still possible to do what we must do to win many more happy and healthy years together, which is my wish for you and yours and for all the world's people and creatures, great and small.

Thank you for reading this book, caring about pets and all animals and doing your part to protect their world and our own.

Fondly,

Jacquelyn

MORE READING

Looking for a shorter, simpler book about bearded dragon pet care suitable for children or new readers? Or are you interested in learning [illegible] about other types of pets?

You'll find all these and more at **Crimson Hill Books** (**www.crimsonhillbooks.com**). To discover your next interesting read, have a look!

ACKNOWLEDGEMENTS

Special thanks to these pet owners, researchers, veterinarians, breeders and suppliers who have been generous with information and insights:

Joe Cattey, SouthTexasDragons.com
Melissa Kaplan, anapsid.org/bearded.html
Dubiaroaches.com
Russ Case, reptilesmagazine.com
Bush Heritage Australia, bushheritage.org.au
Brian Resnick, Umair Irfan and Sigal Samuel, vox.com
Kathleen R. Smith, Viviana Cadena, John A. Endler, Warren P. Porter, Michael R. Kearney and Devi Stuart-Fox, in *Proceedings of the Royal Society Biological Sciences*, royalsocietypublishing.org
Andrew Trounson, University of Melbourne
Beautifuldragons.com
Adrienne Kruzer, thesprucepets.com
Australian Museum, Australian.museum/learn
CDC, Centers for Disease Control and Prevention, USA
South Australia Department of Environment and Water, environment.sa.gov.au
Dr. Brad Lock, vertinarypartner.vin.com
Dr. Rick Axelson and Dr. Laurie Hess, vcahospitals.com
Members of Beardeddragonforum.com
Members of Beardeddragon.org/forums
Members of Reptileforums.co.uk/forums/lizards
Stacey, reptile.guide
Fern, pedpad.com
The Pulsifer family: Doug, Debbie, Tristan and Delaney

For their beautiful work thank you to cover photographer Raphael Kaiser (Snap_it) and wildlife artist Kaitlyn Bauer

And to my Crimson Hill Books partners:

Wayne Johnson and Jesse Johnson

ABOUT THE AUTHOR

Jacquelyn Elnor Johnson started telling stories to entertain her younger sisters, discovering in the telling what it takes to engage your audience! By age 15, she was a correspondent for the local newspaper and had written her first book. She went on to have careers in writing for and editing newspapers and magazines and teaching journalism.

In 2014, she moved with her family to Nova Scotia, drawn by the opportunity to live near the ocean. With the move came a change of focus to creating compelling books for adult readers and fun books for kids ages 9 to 12. A life-long pet lover, she is the bestselling author of 11 books about caring for and enjoying pets and animals, including **I Want A Bearded Dragon** and **Fun Bearded Dragon & Leopard Gecko Facts.**

In addition to writing practical, helpful and entertaining non-fiction, she writes novels including the Morley Stories series for girls ages 10 to 13.

Find all these books and more at www.CrimsonHillBooks.com

ABOUT THE ARTIST

Drawing, and especially drawing birds and animals, "always feels like coming home," says Canadian wildlife artist, advocate and art educator Kaitlin Bauer. A West-coast native, she spent every summer hiking and camping, a family tradition that sparked her love of encountering animals in their natural surroundings. She recalls her desire to show their intelligence, wit and resilience in her art starting almost from the time she learnt how to hold a drawing pencil.

Attending an elementary school where students had the advantage of learning First Nations cultures is where she first came to understand her own spiritual connection to the animals she was drawing. That sense of connection and love for animals has become her favourite aspect of wildlife art.

Her commitment to her art increased with a move to rural Nova Scotia in 2013, where she was able to establish her studio in the home she shares with her husband and beloved dogs. Crows, foxes, owls and wolves now feature in the works it excites her to share with her students and collectors of her art.

To see more, please visit her website at www.KaitlinBauer.com

Printed in Great Britain
by Amazon

35645644R00101

COLLECTION IMAGINÉE ET CRÉÉE PAR **PIERRE MARCHAND**

Directeur
Frédérique de Buron

Directeur de projet
Fabrice Le Jean

Directeur d'ouvrage
Yves Cohat

Édition
Sandra Berthe

Directrice artistique
Isabelle Roller

Ont collaboré à cet ouvrage
Charlotte Bourgeois, Briq, Céline et Laurent Hindryckx, J.-P. Leblan, Erich Lessing, Bertrand Loquet, Sylvie Michel

ISBN 201291984-7 – Imprimé et relié en Malaisie par TWP – Dépôt légal 49546 – Mars 2005 – EAN 9782012919846/01 – Nuart 29/1984/3.
Loi n° 49-956 du 16 juillet 1949 sur les publications destinées à la jeunesse –

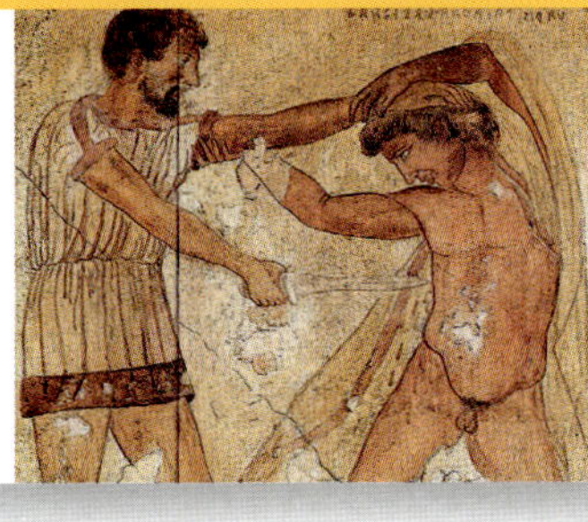

BIGB@NG

Rome

LA GLOIRE D'UN EMPIRE

Agnès Bérenger-Badel *Maître de conférences d'histoire romaine, université de Paris-Sorbonne (Paris IV)*
Christophe Badel *Professeur d'histoire romaine, université de Rennes II*

HACHETTE
Jeunesse

Mode d'emploi du livre

Un système de bandeaux en haut de chaque page vous propose des liens complémentaires vers les autres thèmes de la collection grâce à un code-couleur.

La Lune, l'unique **satellite naturel de la Terre,** est sans doute née après la collision de notre planète avec un énorme corps céleste. Ce choc colossal aurait projeté en orbite des matériaux fondus et vaporisés qui, après avoir formé un anneau, se seraient agglomérés.

Ce bandeau rouge signale un lien vers des informations concernant le thème **Sciences et technologies.**

Ce bandeau vert signale un lien vers des informations concernant le thème **Terre et Univers.**

Ce bandeau bleu signale un lien vers des informations concernant le thème **Le monde vivant.**

Ce bandeau jaune signale un lien vers des informations concernant le thème **Histoire et civilisations.**

Ce logo vous indique que cette image est proposée dans le CD-Rom en **animation** (rubrique « Panoramas et documents »).

La fondation de Rome

La ville qui allait un jour dominer le monde est à son origine une petite cité du Latium. Elle aurait été fondée par Romulus, enfant recueilli et allaité par une louve. Les fouilles archéologiques ont montré que cette légende avait un fond de vérité.

■ *Le site primitif de Rome* est situé sur la rive gauche du Tibre, fleuve qui relie la ville à la Méditerranée, distante d'environ 25 km.

Selon la légende, la ville de Rome a été fondée par Romulus, le 21 avril 753 av. J.-C. Romulus et Rémus, son frère jumeau, sont les enfants de Rhéa Silvia, la fille du roi d'Albe, Numitor. Ce roi a été détrôné par son frère, Amulius. Craignant que sa nièce n'enfante des garçons qui viendront un jour réclamer l'héritage de leur grand-père, il contraint Rhéa Silvia à devenir une vestale, prêtresse qui doit rester vierge sous peine d'être enterrée vivante. Mais Mars, le dieu de la guerre, séduit la jeune femme, qui donne naissance à deux jumeaux. Furieux, Amulius ordonne d'abandonner les enfants sur les rives du Tibre, à la merci des bêtes sauvages. Quelques jours plus tard un berger, Faustulus, est intrigué par le manège d'une louve qu'il voit aller au même endroit quotidiennement. Il la suit et constate qu'elle allaite deux nourrissons. Faustulus et sa femme les recueillent et les élèvent. Devenus adultes, ils découvrent leur noble origine et rétablissent leur grand-père sur le trône d'Albe. Ils décident ensuite de fonder leur propre cité, à l'emplacement où la louve les avait allaités.

■ *Au cours d'une fête* à laquelle ils ont convié leurs voisins, les Sabins, les cavaliers romains enlèvent les jeunes Sabines pour en faire leurs épouses.

■ *La statue de la louve* est d'origine étrusque et date du Ve siècle av. J.-C. Les jumeaux, œuvre d'un artiste anonyme de la Renaissance, ont été ajoutés vers 1471.

■ *Cette urne* qui contenait les cendres et os des défunts reproduit la forme des cabanes primitives du Palatin.

L'observation du vol des oiseaux, signe de la volonté divine, indique que Romulus sera le fondateur officiel. Il trace un sillon avec une charrue, afin de délimiter l'enceinte sacrée de la ville, autour de la colline du Palatin. Mais Rémus, furieux, saute de chaque côté du sillon en se moquant de son frère. Au cours de la bataille qui éclate entre les partisans des deux frères, Rémus trouve la mort. Romulus règne pendant quarante ans, et disparaît mystérieusement. Les Romains lui rendent alors un culte, sous le nom de Quirinus.

Cette tradition, longtemps considérée comme purement légendaire, a été revalorisée par des fouilles archéologiques. Les restes de trois cabanes et des tessons de céramique datant du VIIIe siècle av. J.-C. ont été dégagés sur le Palatin. Au pied de cette colline, les archéologues ont retrouvé les traces d'un mur très ancien, remontant aux années 730-720 av. J.-C., et d'une palissade en bois. Ces découvertes prouvent qu'une installation humaine a existé sur le Palatin à la date donnée par la légende. Mais il s'agit encore d'un peuplement assez lâche, et non d'une vraie ville, telle que la présentent les récits de fondation.

Ce logo vous indique que cette image est proposée dans le CD-Rom en **impression** (rubrique « Espace découverte »).

Sommaire

Les **premiers êtres vivants** à avoir colonisé notre planète sont des organismes unicellulaires. Parmi eux, les stromatolithes, des algues bleues qui vivaient il y a 3,4 milliards d'années, ont formé des récifs fossiles en Australie et aux Bahamas.

C'est en 1992 que la **recherche spatiale** est parvenue à apporter une preuve d'un début de l'univers. Cette année-là, le satellite *Cobe* est parvenu à photographier le rayonnement fossile du big bang, émis il y a 15 milliards d'années.

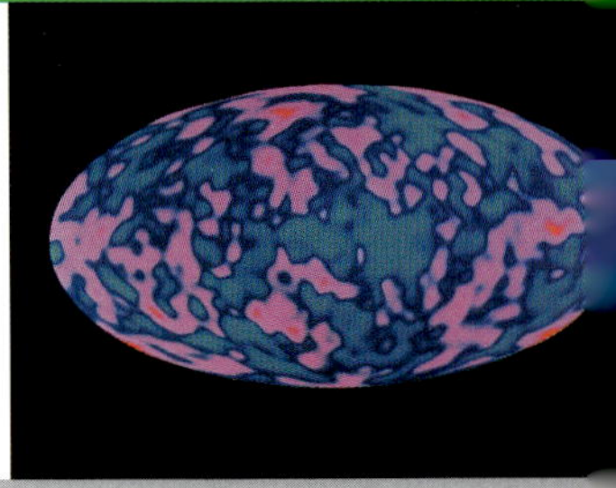

La ville qui allait un jour dominer le monde est à son origine une petite cité du Latium. Elle aurait été fondée par Romulus, enfant recueilli et allaité par une louve. Les fouilles archéologiques ont montré que cette légende avait un fond de vérité.

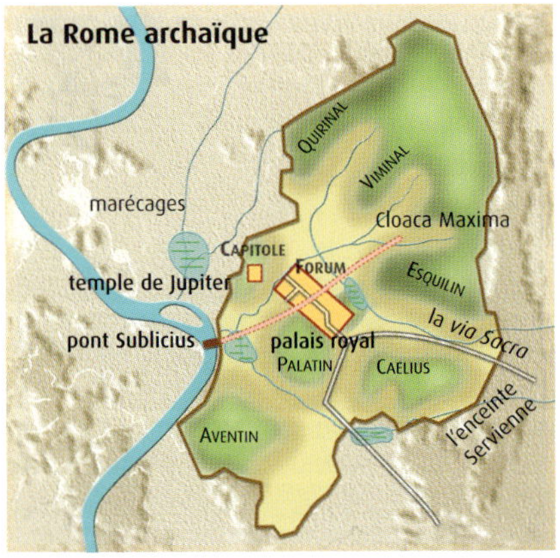

■ *Le site primitif de Rome est situé sur la rive gauche du Tibre, fleuve qui relie la ville à la Méditerranée, distante d'environ 25 km.*

> **Selon la légende, la ville de Rome a été fondée par Romulus, le 21 avril 753 av. J.-C.** Romulus et Remus, son frère jumeau, sont les enfants de Rhea Silvia, la fille du roi d'Albe, Numitor. Ce roi a été détrôné par son frère, Amulius. Craignant que sa nièce n'enfante des garçons qui viendront un jour réclamer l'héritage de leur grand-père, il contraint Rhea Silvia à devenir une vestale, prêtresse qui doit rester vierge sous peine d'être enterrée vivante. Mais Mars, le dieu de la Guerre, séduit la jeune femme, qui donne naissance à des jumeaux. Furieux, Amulius ordonne d'abandonner les enfants sur les rives du Tibre, à la merci des bêtes sauvages. Quelques jours plus tard, un berger, Faustulus, est intrigué par le manège d'une louve qu'il voit aller au même endroit quotidiennement. Il la suit et constate qu'elle allaite deux nourrissons. Faustulus et sa femme les recueillent et les élèvent. Devenus adultes, ils découvrent leur noble origine et rétablissent leur grand-père sur le trône d'Albe. Ils décident ensuite de fonder leur propre cité, à l'emplacement où la louve les avait allaités.

■ *Au cours d'une fête à laquelle ils ont convié leurs voisins, les Sabins, les cavaliers romains enlèvent les jeunes Sabines pour en faire leurs épouses.*

À Héliopolis, les anciens **Égyptiens** vénéraient le dieu solaire sous plusieurs formes dont Atoum/Rê. Créateur de l'univers, père de Tefnout, l'humidité, et de Chou, l'air, il est toujours représenté coiffé de la double couronne symbolisant la Haute et la Basse-Égypte.

La Lune, l'unique **satellite naturel de la Terre,** est sans doute née après la collision de notre planète avec un énorme corps céleste. Ce choc colossal aurait projeté en orbite des matériaux fondus et vaporisés qui, après avoir formé un anneau, se seraient agglomérés.

5

La fondation de Rome

■ *Cette urne qui contenait les cendres et os des défunts reproduit la forme des cabanes primitives du Palatin.*

■ *La statue de la louve est d'origine étrusque et date du ve siècle av. J.-C. Les jumeaux, œuvre d'un artiste anonyme de la Renaissance, ont été ajoutés vers 1471.*

L'observation du vol des oiseaux, signe de la volonté divine, indique que Romulus sera le fondateur officiel. Il trace un sillon avec une charrue, afin de délimiter l'enceinte sacrée de la ville, autour de la colline du Palatin. Mais Remus, furieux, saute de chaque côté du sillon en se moquant de son frère. Au cours de la bataille qui éclate entre les partisans des deux frères, Remus trouve la mort. Romulus règne pendant quarante ans et disparaît mystérieusement. Les Romains lui rendent alors un culte, sous le nom de Quirinus.

Cette tradition, longtemps considérée comme purement légendaire, a été revalorisée par des fouilles archéologiques. Les restes de trois cabanes et des tessons de céramique datant du VIIIe siècle av. J.-C. ont été dégagés sur le Palatin. Au pied de cette colline, les archéologues ont retrouvé les traces d'un mur très ancien, remontant aux années 730-720, et d'une palissade en bois. Ces découvertes prouvent qu'une installation humaine a existé sur le Palatin à la date donnée par la légende. Mais il s'agit encore d'un peuplement assez lâche, et non d'une vraie ville telle que la présentent les récits de fondation.

Les **éléphants** d'Afrique vivent en groupes familiaux composés de jeunes immatures et de femelles d'âges divers dont la plus expérimentée joue le rôle de chef. Les mâles qui sont plutôt solitaires ne rejoignent ces groupes qu'à l'époque des amours, pour se reproduire.

Les sociétés humaines ne sont pas les seules à être structurées. Chez des **insectes** sociaux comme les abeilles, chaque individu est doté d'une spécialisation comportementale qui permet à la collectivité de subsister, c'est-à-dire d'organiser son habitat, d'élever les jeunes, d'exploiter les ressources de nourriture et d'assurer sa défense.

Le citoyen à l'apogée de la

Le régime républicain, instauré à partir de 509, durera jusqu'en 27 av. J.-C. Il présente des caractéristiques originales. Plusieurs organes participent à la gestion de l'État et sont dotés de pouvoirs fondamentaux.

▪ *Lorsque l'orateur prononce un discours, il souligne ses paroles avec des gestes amples de son bras droit, laissé libre par le drapé de sa toge.*

> **La tyrannie des successeurs de Romulus entraîne le renversement de la royauté en 509 et l'instauration de la République.** Dans ce régime, le Sénat, assemblée des anciens magistrats, est chargé de la politique extérieure : il reçoit les ambassadeurs et décide de la levée des troupes en cas de guerre. À Rome, il s'occupe surtout des finances et fixe le montant de l'impôt. Les décisions votées par les sénateurs sont appelées « sénatus-consultes ». Leur liste, l'album, est révisée tous les cinq ans par les censeurs, qui peuvent exclure les sénateurs dont la moralité est jugée indigne.

▪ *Une scène de recensement. Le citoyen romain, debout, en toge, déclare son nom et ses biens que le scribe, assis sur la gauche, inscrit sur un registre.*

Les magistrats sont élus par les citoyens, en général pour un mandat d'un an. Les candidats doivent posséder un capital de 400 000 sesterces*. Une hiérarchie des magistratures s'est peu à peu fixée et il

L'Althing islandais est la plus ancienne assemblée parlementaire connue au monde. Réunie pour la première fois en 930, elle se tenait une fois par an dans le site de Thingvellir. Les chefs **vikings** et les hommes libres de l'île y siégeaient pendant plusieurs jours pour légiférer et rendre la justice.

Le 10 août 1792, le roi Louis XVI, qui, après sa tentative de fuite, a perdu tout crédit auprès de la population, est déchu et mis en prison avec sa famille. Le 22 septembre, la nouvelle Assemblée, la Convention, proclame « l'an premier de la **République française** ».

République

■ *Cette fresque d'une tombe étrusque,* dite « Tombe François », édifiée vers 350 av. J.-C., représente un épisode de la lutte entre Étrusques et Romains.

faut en principe les revêtir dans un ordre précis. Ce parcours est appelé *cursus honorum* (la « course des honneurs ») et commence par les magistratures inférieures : les questeurs* sont chargés des affaires financières, les édiles s'occupent de la surveillance des marchés et de l'approvisionnement et organisent certains jeux. Les magistrats supérieurs détiennent un pouvoir appelé *imperium**, qui leur donne le droit de commander les armées et condamner à mort. Les préteurs rendent la justice à Rome. Les consuls* sont les magistrats les plus importants et commandent les armées. Les tribuns de la plèbe* ont été créés au ve siècle av. J.-C. et doivent protéger les plébéiens. Ils disposent pour cela d'un pouvoir particulier, la sacro-sainteté : personne ne peut les agresser sous peine de mort.

Les assemblées des citoyens sont nommées « les comices ». Elles se réunissent sur convocation des consuls et sont chargées de voter les lois et d'élire les magistrats. Les comices* sont structurés en classes, groupes censitaires regroupant les citoyens selon leur fortune. Il existe cinq classes, mais les plus pauvres, que l'on appelle « prolétaires » (ceux qui ont leurs enfants pour unique richesse), en sont exclus. Le rôle de la fortune est fondamental dans ce système, car les plus riches, qui sont regroupés dans la première classe, votent les premiers et les opérations de vote s'arrêtent quand la majorité est atteinte.

La campagne électorale est très animée : les candidats, vêtus d'une toge blanchie à la craie et accompagnés de leurs amis, se rendent sur la place centrale, le Forum*, et viennent supplier les électeurs de leur donner leur voix. Des affiches électorales, peintes en rouge sur les murs de la ville, appellent à voter pour tel ou tel candidat. Des agents électoraux sont chargés de distribuer des cadeaux, mais cette pratique finit par dégénérer en corruption des électeurs, malgré les lois qui tentent de juguler ces abus.

LES ROIS ÉTRUSQUES, VÉRITABLES FONDATEURS DE ROME ?

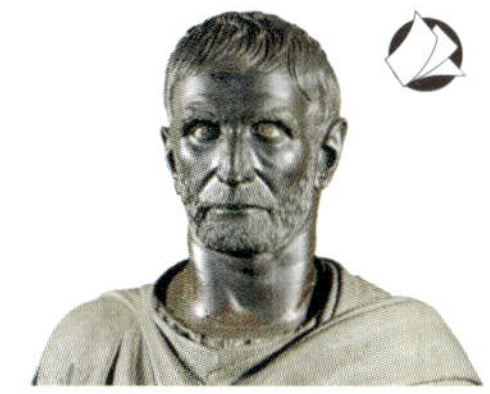

Brutus, le fondateur de la République.

Selon les historiens romains, les rois latins héritiers de Romulus furent supplantés en 616 av. J.-C. par une dynastie de condottieres étrusques, fondée par Tarquin l'Ancien. Vivant dans la Toscane actuelle, les Étrusques possédaient la civilisation la plus brillante dans l'Italie centrale de l'époque. Ils réformèrent le système civique et militaire sur le modèle grec et procédèrent à des grands travaux d'urbanisme, donnant à Rome un grand éclat, même s'il est peut-être exagéré de les considérer comme les véritables fondateurs de la cité romaine. Rome leur doit son premier égout et le temple à Jupiter Capitolin. Mais la tyrannie de Tarquin le Superbe dressa les sénateurs contre lui et une révolution aristocratique, conduite par Brutus, le chassa et instaura la République.

■ *La construction de la* via Appia*, qui mène de Rome à Brindisi, sur la côte adriatique, commença en 312 av. J.-C., durant la censure d'Appius Claudius Caecus.*

Le 23 janvier 1960, le physicien suisse Jacques Piccard et l'Américain Don Walsh établissent un **record de plongée** qui fait d'eux des conquérants des abysses. À bord du bathyscaphe *Trieste* 2, ils atteignent dans la fosse des Mariannes, à l'est des Philippines, la profondeur incroyable de 10 916 m.

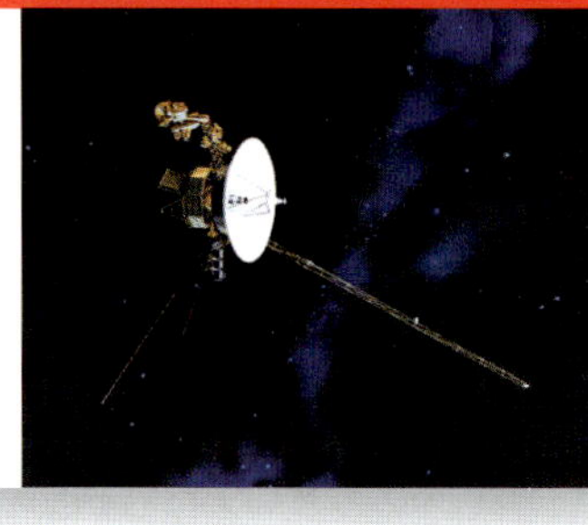

Après un voyage de 25 années dans l'espace durant lequel elles ont survolé Jupiter et Saturne et, pour l'une d'entre elles, Uranus et Neptune, les **sondes américaines** *Voyager* 1 et 2 approchent de la frontière de notre système solaire tout en continuant à transmettre des données.

À la conquête du monde

Grâce à la supériorité de ses légions, Rome conquiert en deux siècles tout le bassin méditerranéen. En annexant la Gaule, César lui ouvre le cœur du continent européen.

■ ***Le général romain Scipion l'Africain*** *remporta sur Carthage la victoire décisive de Zama (202 av. J.-C.). Son buste est entouré de monnaies grecques et gauloises, dépouilles des conquêtes.*

■ ***Représentant un Galate blessé*** *lors d'un combat, cette sculpture témoigne de la peur des Grecs et des Romains face aux Gaulois. Les Galates étaient un peuple celtique installé en Anatolie.*

■ ***Grand général carthaginois, Hannibal*** *voulait utiliser les éléphants comme force de frappe contre les Romains mais un seul d'entre eux survécut au passage des Alpes (218 av. J.-C.).*

Le 3 août 1492, au lever du soleil, une flottille de trois bateaux sous les ordres de **Christophe Colomb** quittait le port de Palos pour un extraordinaire voyage vers l'inconnu. Après une traversée de 36 jours, elle touchait terre et faisait une découverte qui allait bouleverser le monde : l'Amérique.

Si, pendant l'ère secondaire, les continents sont dominés par les **dinosaures**, d'autres reptiles colonisent l'air et l'eau. Les ptérosaures dont les plus grands ont une envergure de 11 m sont les maîtres des cieux, alors que dans l'océan rôdent de terribles fauves comme le *Kronosaurus* ou d'élégants élasmosaures à la silhouette élancée.

En 168 av. J.-C., le roi Antiochos IV de Syrie envahit l'Égypte et marche sur sa capitale, Alexandrie, en suivant la côte. La route de la ville lui semble ouverte lorsqu'un ambassadeur romain, Laenas, se présente devant lui, sur une plage, et lui ordonne d'évacuer le pays. Avec insolence, le Romain trace un cercle sur le sable autour du roi et lui intime de ne pas en sortir avant de lui avoir donné une réponse. Impressionné, Antiochos fait retraite, tant la puissance de Rome effraye déjà les souverains de l'Orient.

Un siècle plus tôt, Rome n'est qu'une puissance régionale, dont les horizons se bornent à l'Italie centrale. Mais une première poussée l'amène à conquérir l'Italie du Sud et la met en contact avec Carthage, maîtresse de la Sicile. Grande cité d'Afrique du Nord fondée par les Phéniciens, Carthage domine la Méditerranée occidentale du détroit de Gibraltar aux côtes de la Tunisie actuelle. Deux conflits dramatiques, les guerres puniques (264-241, 218-201), opposent les deux cités et Hannibal, le meilleur général carthaginois, menace un moment Rome.

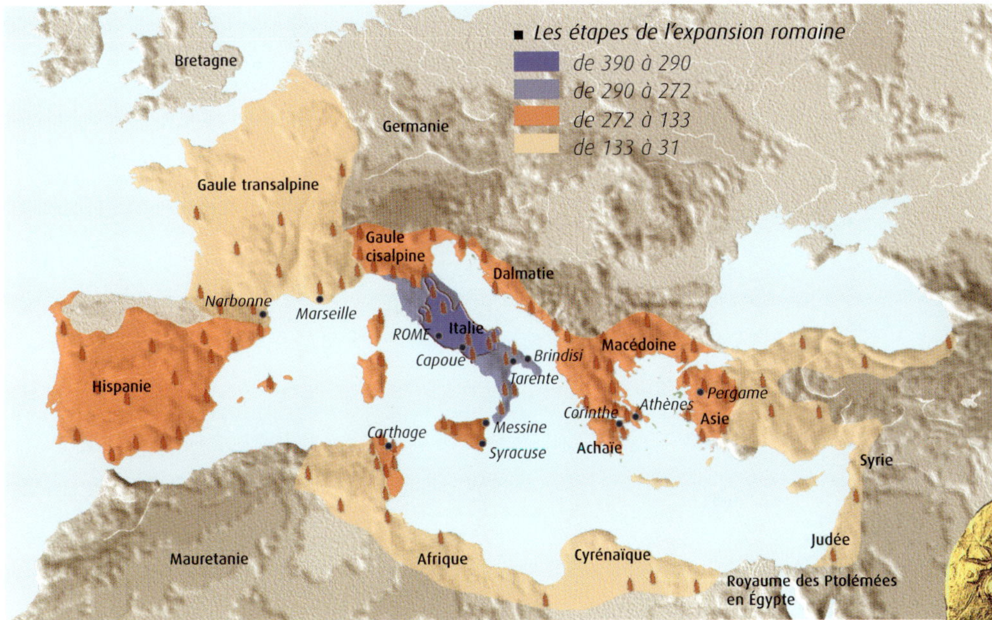

Mais l'armée des soldats-citoyens romains se révèle à la longue plus solide que les troupes de mercenaires puniques, offrant ainsi à Rome la victoire et la suprématie sur la Méditerranée occidentale. Une troisième guerre punique (149-146) parachève son triomphe car Carthage est détruite par Rome, qui sème du sel sur son sol pour y interdire toute vie.

Mais la conquête de l'Orient grec, dirigé par des souverains héritiers de l'empire d'Alexandre le Grand, a déjà commencé. La phalange grecque, composée d'une ligne rigide de fantassins lourdement armés, se révèle inefficace face à des légions romaines plus souples et plus mobiles. Vassalisant d'abord les royaumes pour les conquérir ensuite, Rome met la main sur la Grèce en 146, l'Asie Mineure en 133, la Syrie en 64. Profitant du jour du sabbat, Pompée enlève le Temple de Jérusalem en 63 av. J.-C. Rome domine l'ensemble de la Méditerranée et commence même à mordre sur l'Europe continentale à la fin de la République. Profitant de la division des peuples celtiques, César soumet assez facilement la Gaule (58-51), en dépit d'une ultime révolte menée par le jeune chef arverne, Vercingétorix. Chaque soldat romain reçoit un prisonnier gaulois comme esclave et Vercingétorix périt étranglé dans sa prison lors du triomphe de César en 45 av. J.-C. Pour la première fois, les frontières du monde romain atteignent la Manche et le Rhin.

Le navire de combat classique de l'Antiquité est la **trière grecque** dont les Romains s'inspirèrent pour construire leurs propres navires. Cependant, comme ils n'accordaient pas une importance capitale à la vitesse, leurs bateaux étaient plus massifs pour emporter un plus grand nombre de combattants.

Alexandrie fut l'une des villes les plus brillantes du monde grec. Elle était célèbre à la fois pour sa Bibliothèque fréquentée par les plus grands savants de l'époque et par son Phare qui passait pour l'une des Sept Merveilles du monde.

Le temps des guerres civiles

Le 2 septembre 31 av. J.-C., le sort du monde romain se joue sur mer, à Actium, sur la côte adriatique de la Grèce. Les deux généraux rivaux Octave et Antoine confient leurs espoirs à la flotte et le second compte beaucoup sur l'aide de son alliée et épouse, la reine d'Égypte, Cléopâtre. Mais la flotte d'Antoine se trouve prise au piège dans le golfe et Cléopâtre, paniquée, fuit dans le soleil couchant, suivie par son mari désemparé. Octave se retrouve seul maître du monde romain. Ainsi finit un siècle de troubles et de guerres.

■ *Petits-fils de Scipion l'Africain, les frères Gracchus, « les Gracques », tribuns de la plèbe, tentèrent de démocratiser la République par des distributions de terres et des ventes de blé à bon marché.*

Ce ne sont que les symptômes d'une crise générale du régime républicain, dépassé par ses propres victoires. La conquête du monde méditerranéen a provoqué de graves problèmes pour les paysans-soldats romains car les guerres continuelles les tiennent éloignés de leurs champs et favorisent la mainmise des grands propriétaires sur leurs terres. Par ailleurs, leurs victoires éclatantes enivrent les généraux, les *imperatores**, qui rêvent d'établir leur pouvoir personnel à Rome. Deux frères, Tiberius et Caius Gracchus, tentent de résoudre la crise sociale en proposant de diviser entre les pauvres des lots de terre du domaine public pour renforcer le groupe des citoyens-paysans. L'opposition du Sénat fait échouer leur projet et les deux frères périssent au cours d'émeutes organisées par leurs opposants (133 et 121).

Les ambitions des généraux peuvent alors se déchaîner au cours de guerres civiles sanglantes. Vainqueur de la première (88-82), Sylla instaure sa dictature et fait publier des listes de proscriptions, condamnant à mort ses adversaires. Des têtes de proscrits décorent le Forum. Mais ce personnage énigmatique cherche aussi à réformer les institutions républicaines et abdique son pouvoir de son plein gré pour se retirer dans une villa* près de Naples (79 av. J.-C.).

■ *Datant de sa dictature (49-44), cette monnaie de César révèle un ambitieux fiévreux au cou décharné, coiffé de la couronne de laurier, insigne du triomphateur, qui lui permettait de cacher sa calvitie.*

Provisoirement restaurée, la République doit bientôt faire face aux ambitions de deux nouveaux *imperatores*, Pompée, conquérant de l'Orient, et César, vainqueur de la Gaule. Après une courte guerre (49-48), César l'emporte et rétablit la dictature (49-44). Portant sans cesse le costume du triomphateur – couronne de laurier et toge de pourpre – il rêve du titre de roi et se fait adorer comme un demi-dieu, le « divin Jules ». Épouvantés, des conjurés républicains le percent en plein Sénat d'une trentaine de coups de poignard (44 av. J.-C.). Meurtre inutile ! Son fils adoptif, Octave, et son principal lieutenant, Antoine, se partagent alors le pouvoir et le monde : au premier l'Occident, au second l'Orient (il va y rencontrer Cléopâtre) – la République est bien morte. Il ne reste plus qu'à savoir qui sera le maître : à Actium, le sort des armes désigne Octave.

Alexandrie sur laquelle règne Cléopâtre est plus une ville grecque qu'une cité égyptienne. Elle a été fondée par Ptolémée, un des généraux d'**Alexandre le Grand**, qui, à sa mort en 323 av. J.-C., se sont affrontés pour se partager son empire.

C'est sans doute par un cobra d'Égypte, symbole de la déesse protectrice du royaume du Sud, Ouadjet, que se fit mordre **Cléopâtre**. Ce serpent, qui a la faculté de déployer les côtés de sa nuque en une sorte de capuchon, possède un venin extrêmement puissant qui rend sa morsure fatale pour l'homme.

Minée par la crise de la petite paysannerie et les ambitions des généraux, la République sombre dans les guerres civiles à partir de 88 av. J.-C. César échoue à restaurer la royauté mais son fils Octave recueille son héritage.

■ *À Actium, les trières de la flotte d'Octave, légères et mobiles, s'attaquent aux lourds vaisseaux égyptiens. Grâce aux passerelles, les légionnaires se battent sur les navires comme sur terre.*

Depuis Charlemagne, l'empereur du **Saint Empire romain germanique** est à la fois un personnage religieux qui représente le Christ sur Terre et le premier de tous les rois de la chrétienté. L'un d'eux, Otton III (996-1002), rêve de rétablir la puissance de l'antique Empire romain.

Pour affirmer sa légitimité et son pouvoir qu'il estime lui être conférés par la Nation et non pas par Dieu, **Napoléon** multiplie les gestes symboliques : il se couronne lui-même, puis l'impératrice, et choisit comme emblème impérial l'aigle des anciennes légions romaines.

■ *L'empereur Marc Aurèle fait son entrée solennelle dans Rome, monté sur un char triomphal, après ses victoires sur le front danubien.*

L'Empire des Césars :

Conçu comme un principat libéral ou une monarchie despotique, le régime impérial peine à trouver son équilibre au Iᵉʳ siècle. Grâce au système de l'adoption, les Antonins fournissent au IIᵉ siècle une série d'empereurs remarquables qui assurent la Paix romaine.

> **Au printemps 99 ap. J.-C., le nouvel empereur, Trajan, de retour de la province rhénane de Germanie, fait une entrée triomphale à Rome.** Les toits sont couverts de monde et même les malades se sont traînés sur place pour acclamer l'empereur. Au contraire de ses prédécesseurs, qui se déplaçaient sur un char, il marche à pied et embrasse chaque sénateur venu le saluer. Cette simplicité affichée fait figure de programme politique.

Depuis ses débuts, le régime impérial peine en effet à trouver son équilibre. Le fondateur, Auguste* (27 av. J.-C. – 14 ap. J.-C.), qui a commencé sa carrière sous le nom d'Octave, met en place une monarchie libérale, le principat, qui garde des apparences républicaines. Avec lui, fils adoptif de César, ce nom familial devient un titre impérial. Il vit dans une maison simple et ne porte que des vêtements tissés par sa femme.

■ *L'Auguste dit « de Prima Porta » montre l'empereur en chef militaire.*

■ *Portrait de Néron.*

■ *Portrait de Trajan.*

Mais il n'a pas prévu de règle successorale claire : ce qui ouvre la voie aux ambitions des soldats. Les gardes impériaux, les prétoriens*, portent ainsi Claude au pouvoir parce qu'ils l'ont repéré caché derrière une tenture en 41 ap. J.-C. D'autre part, certains empereurs cherchent à imiter les souverains orientaux, despotiques et sacrés. À la suite d'un incendie qui ravage le centre de Rome en 64, Néron y construit un splendide palais, la Maison Dorée, dont l'entrée est ornée par une statue colossale de l'empereur représenté en dieu-Soleil. Il finit renversé par une révolte des légions d'Espagne en 68.

Avec Trajan, l'Empire revient à la formule du principat et trouve enfin un système successoral efficace, le « choix du meilleur ». Le souverain choisit pour successeur le sénateur

L'empereur aztèque portait deux titres : *tlacateruchtli,* qui signifiait « chef des guerriers » et le désignait comme chef suprême des armées, et *tlatolli,* qui voulait dire « celui qui parle » car, même s'il succédait à son père, il devait convaincre les autres seigneurs de le désigner pour accéder à cet honneur.

Pour affirmer la puissance de leur pouvoir, les hommes à l'instar des empereurs ont souvent besoin d'insignes comme une couronne ou un sceptre. Certains animaux comme le **mandrill** mâle, avec son nez rouge encadré de bourrelets bleus, affichent leur dominance sur leur propre corps.

une dynastie de paix

■ *Marc Aurèle jeune.*

■ *L'empereur Commode est représenté sous les traits du dieu Hercule, avec une massue et la peau du lion de Némée.*

■ *Camée représentant l'empereur Claude avec le front ceint d'une couronne laurée.*

le plus méritant et l'adopte comme son fils pour lui préparer la voie. L'hérédité directe est rejetée même si la plupart des empereurs ont des liens de parenté éloignée entre eux. Par le moyen de l'adoption se construit ainsi une remarquable dynastie, les Antonins (96-192), qui apporte au monde la Paix romaine. Par d'incessants voyages dans tout l'Empire, Hadrien (117-138) améliore l'administration provinciale : il en rassemble les souvenirs dans sa luxueuse villa de Tivoli aux portes de Rome. Empereur-philosophe, Marc Aurèle (161-180) est le plus vertueux des Césars* mais il prend une décision néfaste en léguant le pouvoir à son fils, Commode. S'identifiant au dieu Hercule, le jeune prince se bat dans l'arène comme un gladiateur et se montre si tyrannique que ses propres familiers finissent par l'étrangler dans son bain en 192. Le siècle d'or de l'Empire finit ainsi tragiquement.

Chaque année au printemps, l'**éléphant de mer** mâle remet en cause son statut de reproducteur. Il lui faut affronter ses congénères pour conquérir un territoire suffisamment vaste pour accueillir la vingtaine de femelles qui composeront son « harem ».

Avant d'être monté et utilisé pour combattre et se déplacer, le **cheval** a, dans un premier temps, été chassé pour sa viande. C'est seulement il y a environ 5 500 ans qu'il aurait été domestiqué dans les plaines d'Ukraine d'abord, pour être mangé puis pour être attelé à des chars de combat.

■ *L'arc de triomphe de Titus, édifié sur le forum de Rome, célèbre la victoire remportée sur les Juifs et la prise de Jérusalem en 70 ap. J.-C.*

Un Empire universel

L'étendue territoriale de l'Empire romain s'est accrue durant le régime impérial, mais ne progresse plus guère après les conquêtes de Trajan. La citoyenneté romaine et le culte impérial sont deux facteurs essentiels qui assurent la cohésion de ce vaste ensemble.

> **Le règne de Trajan voit les dernières conquêtes territoriales importantes.** De 101 à 106, les légions romaines guerroient en Dacie (actuelle Roumanie) contre le roi Décébale, qui a conclu des alliances menaçant les intérêts romains. Le roi vaincu se suicide et son royaume devient une nouvelle province. Les mines d'or de Dacie sont désormais sous le contrôle de Rome et le butin servira à édifier l'imposant forum de Trajan à Rome. La célèbre colonne Trajane y relate, sous la forme d'une frise en spirale, les épisodes de la conquête.

En revanche, les tentatives romaines de conquête en Orient s'avèrent moins fructueuses. Certes, Trajan occupe en 106 le royaume des Nabatéens, qui devient la province d'Arabie, mais l'ennemi séculaire de Rome, les Parthes qui occupent un vaste territoire (Iran et Irak), reste un adversaire redoutable. Si Trajan remporte plusieurs victoires sur eux et crée une éphémère province de Mésopotamie, son successeur Hadrien abandonne toutes les conquêtes au-delà de l'Euphrate, car il estime impossible de les conserver. Les nouvelles expéditions contre les Parthes, sous Septime Sévère et son fils Caracalla, n'aboutissent pas non plus à des conquêtes durables. Les victoires remportées sont toutefois célébrées sur un arc de triomphe élevé sur le Forum, en plein centre de Rome, et Septime Sévère arbore désormais le surnom de victoire « Très Grand Parthique ».

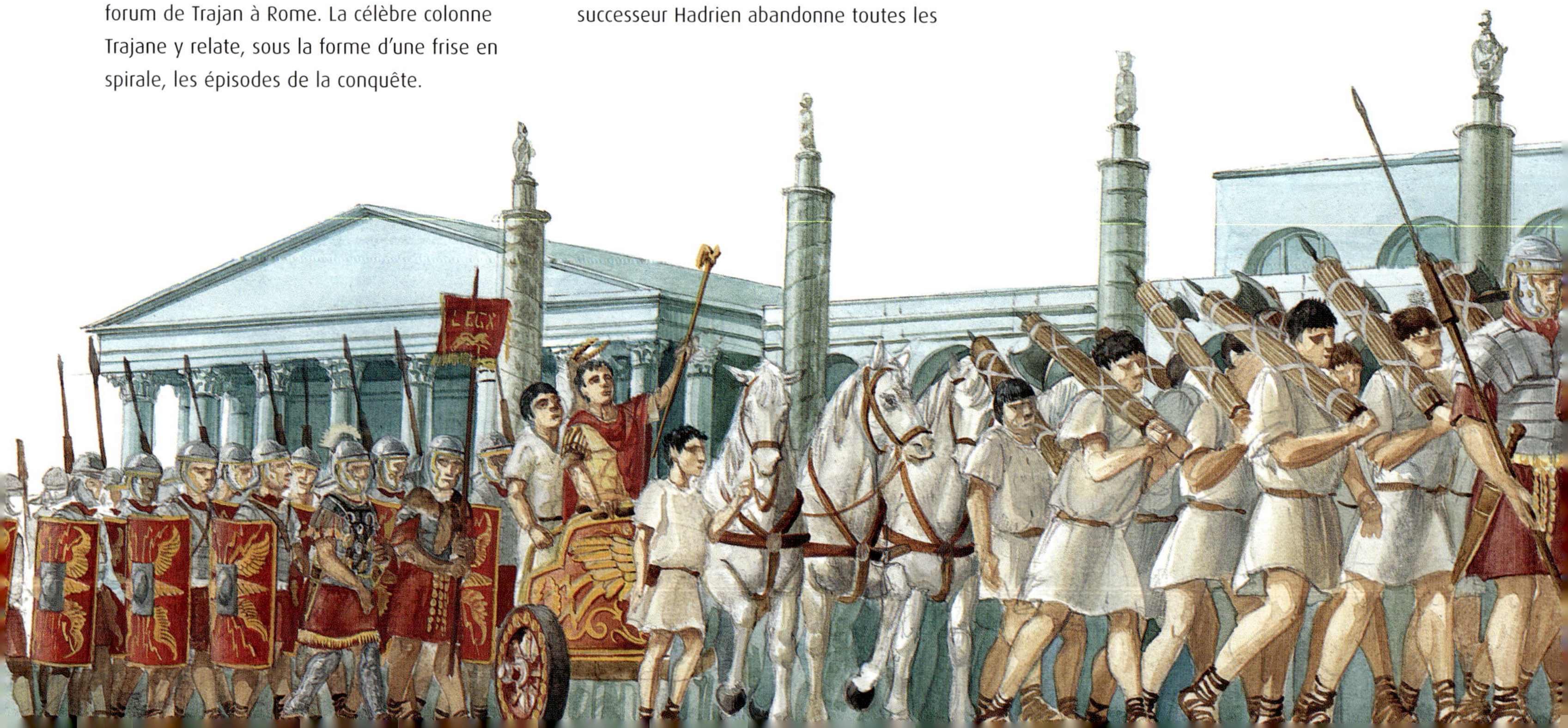

Le **pharaon** détient tous les pouvoirs politiques, militaires et religieux. À la fois dieu et homme, il n'agit pourtant pas uniquement selon son bon plaisir. Il doit en effet se conformer aux principes de justice et d'ordre qui régissent la société égyptienne.

L'arc de triomphe du Carrousel, à Paris, a été commandé par **Napoléon Ier** en 1806 à Vivant Denon. Il s'inspire de celui de Septime Sévère à Rome, et comportait initialement les chevaux du temple du Soleil à Corinthe, que Bonaparte alors général de la jeune République française avait volés à la cathédrale Saint-Marc de Venise.

Dans cet Empire aux dimensions gigantesques coexistent des hommes aux statuts juridiques très variés. À côté des citoyens romains, qui bénéficient de privilèges juridiques étendus, on rencontre des pérégrins*, hommes libres mais qui n'ont pas la citoyenneté romaine, et des esclaves. La différence des statuts est abolie par Caracalla en 212. Cet empereur décide en effet d'accorder la citoyenneté romaine à tous les habitants libres de l'Empire, et justifie cette mesure sans précédent par la volonté de faire participer les pérégrins au culte des dieux romains et d'unifier juridiquement le monde romain.

L'un des éléments assurant la cohésion de tous les peuples de l'Empire est le culte impérial. Les empereurs, après leur mort, peuvent être divinisés au cours de la cérémonie de la *consecratio**, si le Sénat en a donné l'autorisation. Dans la plupart des cités de l'Empire, un temple est consacré au culte des empereurs et un prêtre, le flamine*, en est le responsable. Des cérémonies en leur honneur ont également lieu dans les capitales des provinces. À Lugdunum (Lyon), le grand prêtre célèbre le culte tous les ans, le 1er août, à l'Autel du Confluent.

■ *Trajan a orné son forum avec des statues de prisonniers daces en marbre et porphyre. Certaines ont été ensuite réutilisées pour l'arc de triomphe de Constantin.*

■ *Lors de la cérémonie du triomphe*, le général vainqueur défile à la tête de ses troupes et exhibe le butin et les prisonniers faits pendant la campagne.*

Au **Moyen Âge**, le contrat qui lie un seigneur et son vassal se noue non par écrit mais au cours d'un rituel. Le vassal s'agenouille devant son seigneur et place ses mains jointes à l'intérieur des siennes : c'est l'*hommage*.

Dès la **plus haute Antiquité**, les villes phéniciennes de Tyr et de Sidon en Méditerranée devinrent les cités les plus florissantes de la région. Elles devaient cette richesse à un coquillage, le murex, qui fournissait un colorant pourpre très prisé pour teindre les étoffes et faisait d'elles des étapes incontournables sur la Route de la Soie.

Des sénateurs

■ *Ce sarcophage du IIIe siècle ap. J.-C., représentant une procession de sénateurs, met en valeur la majesté des plis des toges, un des insignes de l'ordre.*

> **Clarissime, c'est-à-dire « très éclatant » : tel est le titre officiel des sénateurs sous l'Empire,** qui proclame bien leur prééminence sociale. Comme beaucoup de sociétés traditionnelles, la société romaine est une société d'ordres*, où les groupes sociaux se définissent par des critères juridiques et non pas économiques. Un ordre est un groupe chargé d'une mission au service de la cité, bénéficiant de privilèges particuliers, et l'ordre clarissime* trône au sommet de la hiérarchie des ordres romains.

Son rôle consiste à fournir les membres du Sénat (300 sous la République, 600 sous l'Empire), les magistrats et les hauts fonctionnaires sous l'Empire. Principal organe dirigeant de la République, le Sénat garde une place importante sous le principat car il vote les pouvoirs de l'empereur et le conseille. Tout Romain peut reconnaître un sénateur à sa tenue : tunique barrée d'une large bande de pourpre (le laticlave*) et bottines de cuir rouge ou noir décorées d'un croissant d'ivoire. Lors des grands

■ *Dans les séances du Sénat, l'éloquence jouait un rôle important, comme le montre ce discours du consul Cicéron (à gauche) dénonçant la conjuration de Catilina contre la République en 63 av. J.-C. (à droite).*

De tous les pigments utilisés au **Moyen Âge** pour teinter les encres qui servaient aux moines à copier et à enluminer les manuscrits, l'un des plus précieux était une pierre importée d'Afghanistan à grands frais : le lapis-lazuli. Réduite en poudre, elle permettait d'obtenir un bleu autrement plus pur et profond que celui que fournissaient des végétaux comme l'indigo ou la guède.

En **Égypte**, après le pharaon, le vizir est le personnage qui détient le plus de pouvoir. Il est responsable de l'administration du territoire, promulgue les décrets royaux, surveille la crue du Nil et les cultures, et dirige enfin la police et la justice.

« éclatants »

Les sénateurs constituent un ordre chargé de servir la cité et de fournir le vivier des magistrats et des fonctionnaires. Leur richesse foncière, leur réseau de clients et l'orgueil de leurs ancêtres assurent leur prestige social.

▪ *Construite par César, la curie Julia remplaça un bâtiment plus ancien disparu dans un incendie (52 av. J.-C.), pour abriter les séances du Sénat. Elle fait face aux Rostres, la tribune aux harangues.*

votes, les sénateurs votent avec les pieds, en se regroupant dans un coin de la curie, leur bâtiment de réunion, selon leur opinion. Tous les efforts d'un sénateur sont tendus vers l'ascension de la hiérarchie des magistratures, le *cursus honorum**, dont le consulat constitue le sommet. Sous l'Empire, les souverains multiplient les postes administratifs et militaires confiés aux sénateurs pour gérer le monde romain. Le rêve d'un sénateur est alors de finir comme préfet de la ville, chargé d'administrer Rome.

Le prestige social des sénateurs ne tient pas seulement à leurs fonctions politiques. La fortune est tout aussi essentielle car un capital minimal (un million de sesterces sous l'Empire) est indispensable pour entrer au Sénat. De nature terrienne, elle se compose de grands domaines centrés autour de luxueuses villas. Afin de contrôler la plèbe, les sénateurs y tissent des réseaux de clientèle, basés sur l'aide matérielle et l'échange de services. Tous les matins, les clients viennent saluer le sénateur dans sa maison, reçoivent alors de lui une petite somme d'argent pour la journée puis l'accompagnent sur le Forum.

Plus le cortège des clients est imposant, plus le prestige du sénateur est grand. Au sein des clarissimes, les nobles jouissent d'une aura particulière, due à leur naissance. Ils descendent de consuls et gardent le souvenir de leurs ancêtres sous la forme de masques de cire moulés sur le visage des défunts, les « images* ». Lors des funérailles d'un noble, celles-ci suivent son cercueil, portées par des acteurs : c'est comme si ses ancêtres ressuscitaient pour l'accompagner dans la mort.

▪ *Ce noble romain porte les masques de cire de son père (à droite) et de son grand-père (à gauche). La dénivellation entre les deux images marque la différence des générations.*

Les animaux occupent depuis fort longtemps une place importante sur les champs de bataille. Aujourd'hui, on les utilise même pour accomplir des missions trop difficiles ou dangereuses pour des hommes. L'armée américaine emploie ainsi des **dauphins** pour repérer des mines grâce à leur exceptionnelle capacité d'écholocalisation.

La construction de la Grande Muraille de **Chine** s'étale sur plusieurs siècles. C'est d'abord l'empereur Quin Shi Huangdi qui deux siècles avant J.-C. fit relier par des remparts des fortins pour se protéger des invasions turco-mongoles. Puis au XVe siècle, la dynastie Ming édifia une nouvelle Muraille au sud de l'ancienne.

Une armée en mutation

Composée de soldats-citoyens à l'origine, l'armée romaine se professionnalise à partir de la fin de la République. Les légions, unités de fantassins lourds, se fixent sur la frontière sous l'Empire, mais ce *limes* est une zone-tampon, non une barrière linéaire.

Ce légionnaire, fantassin lourd, porte la cuirasse articulée de l'époque de Trajan (98-117). Il tient à la main droite son pilum, javelot destiné à être lancé au début du combat.

> **À la mort de l'empereur Auguste, en 14 ap. J.-C., les légions du Rhin et du Danube se soulèvent** car les soldats ne supportent plus leurs conditions de vie et la sévérité de la discipline. Agressant leurs sous-officiers, les centurions, ils massacrent l'un d'entre eux surnommé « Encore », car il ne cessait de frapper les soldats à coups de cep de vigne. Le nouvel empereur Tibère doit envoyer ses fils calmer les troupes. Ce tableau misérable ne correspond pas à l'image glorieuse de l'armée romaine.

Depuis un siècle, cette armée a en fait connu une mutation considérable. À l'apogée de la République (IIIe-IIe siècle), le service militaire fait partie des devoirs du citoyen et seuls les plus pauvres en sont dispensés car le légionnaire doit payer son équipement. Cette armée de soldats-citoyens est à l'origine des victoires sur Carthage et les rois d'Orient mais se révèle inadaptée face à la multiplication des expéditions. Le besoin d'effectifs amène l'*imperator* Marius à ouvrir les légions aux prolétaires (107 av. J.-C.), entraînant à terme

En Orient, le limes *s'appuyait sur une multitude de petits forts, abritant une cohorte (500 hommes) au maximum, permettant de quadriller le désert.*

Si la Première Guerre mondiale est encore un combat de fantassins et d'artillerie, elle marque néanmoins un tournant dans l'**évolution des armées.** L'aviation fait son apparition et la cavalerie est remplacée par les blindés dont les premiers exemplaires sont engagés en 1917.

L'utilisation militaire des matières inflammables est très ancienne, mais ce sont les Byzantins qui perfectionnèrent cette **technique de combat.** Grâce au feu grégeois, ils projetaient à l'aide de tubes métalliques un mélange d'hydrocarbures et de soufre qui, propulsé par réaction comme une fusée, incendiait les navires ennemis.

sa professionnalisation puisque ces pauvres s'engagent pour gagner leur vie. Sous l'Empire, l'armée romaine s'est muée en armée professionnelle, basée sur le volontariat et un service de longue durée (25 ans). Si la discipline est dure, le soldat peut compter sur une solde régulière, augmentée de cadeaux ponctuels de l'empereur, et une retraite lui permettant d'acheter un lopin de terre après sa sortie du service.

Le fer de lance en est la légion, unité de 5 000 hommes, composée de fantassins lourdement armés. Sa subdivision en manipules (160 hommes) et en cohortes (500 hommes) lui permet de s'adapter avec souplesse à toutes les situations et à tous les terrains. Signe du pragmatisme romain, l'armement en est emprunté aux peuples vaincus, tel le glaive d'origine espagnole. Cotte de mailles sous César, la cuirasse est composée de lames de métal « articulées » entre elles à l'époque de l'empereur Trajan (98-117). Des unités auxiliaires, recrutées chez les anciens peuples vaincus, fournissent les cavaliers et les fantassins légers absents des légions. Mobiles et provisoires à l'époque républicaine, les légions se stabilisent sous l'Empire et se fixent sur les frontières à la fin du Ier siècle ap. J.-C. Jalonnée de camps légionnaires, la frontière, le *limes**, présente rarement l'image d'une barrière linéaire comme le mur d'Hadrien en Bretagne (Angleterre). Zone-tampon appuyée sur un réseau de routes et de fortins, le *limes* permet une défense en profondeur autant qu'il peut servir de base à une nouvelle offensive.

■ *Destinée surtout à la reconnaissance et à la poursuite, la cavalerie disposait d'un équipement plus léger que l'infanterie. Ce cavalier porte une cotte de cuir et non une cuirasse articulée.*

■ *La colonne Trajane célèbre la conquête de la Dacie par Trajan (101-107). Sur ce panneau, l'empereur franchit le Danube sur un pont de bateaux, précédé par les porteurs d'enseignes.*

■ *Ce casque de cavalier romain, décoré d'un masque, servait sans doute plus à la parade qu'au combat.*

À Rome, s'il existe à partir d'Auguste un service rapide de messages administratifs, ce n'est que sous Henri IV qu'est initié un service public de communication du courrier. Puis Louis XIV accorde à la Ferme générale des Postes le monopole de la **communication** des lettres et paquets, qui sont ainsi acheminés dans les malles-poste jusqu'au XIXe siècle.

Depuis la mise en orbite du premier satellite de télécommunication géostationnaire en 1964, les applications de ces engins ne cessent de se diversifier. D'abord utilisés pour la téléphonie à longue distance, ils permettent désormais de communiquer à partir de téléphones fixes et mobiles, de diffuser des chaînes de télévision ou de transmettre toutes sortes de données.

Comment gouverner l'Empire

Au fur et à mesure qu'elle conquiert de nouveaux territoires, une question se pose à Rome avec de plus en plus d'insistance : comment organiser et exploiter ces vastes étendues qu'elle domine ? C'est ainsi qu'est élaboré le système provincial.

1 *Bateau transportant des barriques de vin*
2 *Le mur d'Hadrien au nord de la Bretagne*
3 *Enfant portant un cucullus, manteau gaulois*
4 *Maquette d'un camp romain*
5 *Bibliothèque de Celsus à Éphèse*
6 *Tombeau de Palmyre*
7 *La grande colonnade à Palmyre*
8 *Portrait funéraire d'une momie du Fayoum*
9 *Chasse d'animaux exotiques*

Certaines **fourmis** se regroupent pour former d'immenses colonies comprenant plusieurs centaines de fourmilières abritant à elles toutes plus de 150 millions d'individus. Elles forment alors de véritables empires qui conquièrent des territoires de plus en plus vastes en éliminant toutes les fourmis indigènes qui peuvent s'y trouver.

Les **Égyptiens** imposent aux peuples qu'ils soumettent un tribut. C'est un excellent moyen de se procurer certaines denrées rares ou inconnues en Égypte. Les Syriens leur fournissent des chevaux ; les Nubiens, de l'or, du bétail et des animaux exotiques ; enfin les envoyés de Pount leur apportent l'encens qu'ils utilisent pour le culte des dieux.

Le terme de « province » désigne un territoire soumis à Rome, dont les habitants ne sont pas citoyens romains. La première province est la Sicile, conquise à l'issue de la première guerre punique, en 241 av. J.-C. L'Empire territorial de Rome connaît son extension maximale au IIe siècle ap. J.-C. mais une telle mosaïque de peuples n'est pas aisée à gouverner, ne serait-ce qu'en raison de la diversité des langues, des cultures et des pratiques. L'habileté de Rome va consister à ne pas imposer autoritairement le droit romain, mais à concilier l'héritage antérieur et ses propres principes.

Ces provinces sont administrées par un gouverneur envoyé par Rome. Il peut s'agir d'un ancien préteur ou d'un ancien consul, pour les provinces les plus riches et les plus prestigieuses, comme l'Afrique (actuelle Tunisie) et l'Asie. Le système est réformé par Auguste en 27 av. J.-C. Il opère un partage des provinces avec le Sénat. Cette assemblée garde la responsabilité des territoires les plus anciennement romanisés et les plus calmes. Lui-même se réserve les provinces les plus récentes et les plus proches des frontières, où la présence d'une garnison est souvent nécessaire. Mais il conserve aussi la riche Égypte, qui vient d'être annexée et qui est devenue le grenier à blé de Rome. Elle sera confiée à un chevalier* en lequel l'empereur a toute confiance, car il craint un soulèvement orchestré par un sénateur ambitieux.

Le gouverneur est le représentant de Rome, mais certains voient surtout dans ce poste un moyen de s'enrichir. Des procès pour corruption viennent parfois frapper les plus avides d'entre eux. Ainsi Verrès, gouverneur de Sicile de 73 à 71, fut accusé par les provinciaux en 70 pour avoir pillé l'île et arraché d'innombrables richesses artistiques aux nobles siciliens. Le grand avocat Cicéron défend les Siciliens et prononce plusieurs discours où il relate en détail les forfaits commis par Verrès. Ce dernier s'enfuit de Rome avant sa condamnation. Auguste met en place une législation plus sévère, mais cela ne suffira pas à éviter à l'avenir toute dérive.

D'autres représentants de Rome sont envoyés pour s'occuper des questions financières, en particulier des impôts. Dans les provinces sénatoriales cette fonction est dévolue à un jeune magistrat, le questeur, alors qu'un chevalier, le procurateur*, en est chargé dans les provinces impériales.

■ *Le chevalier Caius Julius Pacatianus, originaire de Vienne en Narbonnaise, gouverna la Maurétanie et la Mésopotamie. Ses concitoyens l'honorèrent avec une statue en bronze.*

Le **commerce équitable** est une nouvelle organisation des marchés qui veut mettre fin à l'exploitation des petits paysans des pays du « Sud » en les considérant non plus comme des subordonnés mais comme des partenaires.

L'ambre, que les Romains vont chercher en mer Baltique, est une résine fossilisée. Elle provient de conifères qui vivaient à l'ère tertiaire. Des insectes ou des feuilles se sont souvent englués dans cette pâte visqueuse et collante qui s'est ensuite solidifiée autour d'eux.

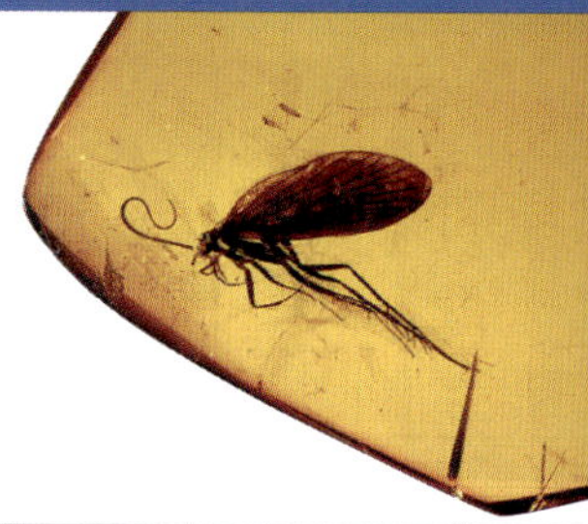

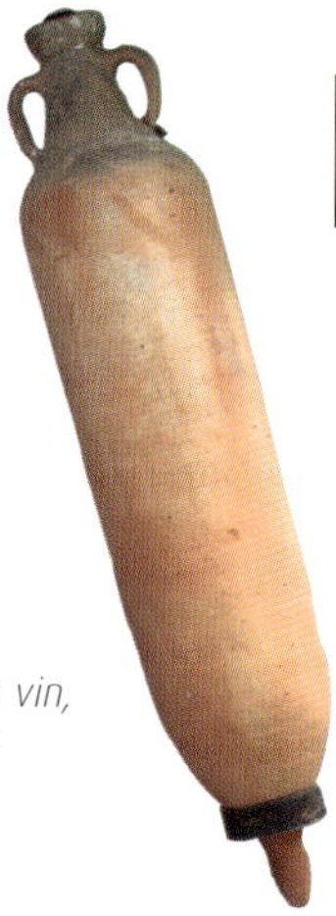

■ *Ce type d'amphore était surtout utilisé pour transporter du vin, plus rarement du garum.*

Le commerce : maritime et dynamique

De nombreuses marchandises sont transportées d'un bout à l'autre de l'Empire, essentiellement par voie d'eau. Il s'agit aussi bien de produits agricoles que de marchandises manufacturées. Le commerce de détail, au cœur des villes, contribue à l'animation des rues.

Le blé est la base de l'alimentation et il est consommé sous la forme de bouillie ou de pain. La seule ville de Rome, avec son million d'habitants, a besoin chaque année de 350 000 tonnes de blé. Elle l'importe des provinces productrices : la Sicile, l'Afrique et l'Égypte. L'huile représente aussi une denrée indispensable, car elle est utilisée dans la cuisine, mais aussi pour l'éclairage (lampes à huile). La Bétique (au sud de l'Espagne) et l'Afrique en sont les principales productrices. Le vin produit en Gaule et en Italie se diffuse dans tout l'Empire.

■ *Dans cette boulangerie de Pompéi, le pistor vend de grosses miches de pain rondes.*

Ces deux produits sont transportés dans des amphores. Des millions de fragments (tessons) d'amphores accumulés au cours des siècles ont formé à Rome une véritable colline artificielle, le Testaccio, qui subsiste encore aujourd'hui. Les gourmets n'hésitent pas à se procurer à prix d'or les mets les plus raffinés, comme les huîtres du lac Lucrin, en Italie, ou des loirs engraissés, que l'on sert saupoudrés de miel et de pavot. Le meilleur *garum*, une sauce à base de morceaux de poisson macérés et décomposés, est à base de maquereau et vient d'Espagne.

Rome est un grand centre d'artisanat de consommation et exporte des lampes à huile et des sarcophages en marbre. Des lampes et de la céramique sigillée (vernissée) rouge fabriquées en Italie se retrouvent dans tout l'Empire et même en dehors de ses frontières.

Les Romains achètent à prix d'or les magnifiques **étoffes en soie** venues de Chine jusqu'à Alexandrie ou Byzance, chargées sur des chameaux. Ils n'imaginent pas que le fil qui a servi à les fabriquer provient du cocon d'un papillon, mais plutôt d'une sorte de laine mystérieuse qui pousse sur certains arbres.

L'unique moyen pour les Européens d'atteindre l'océan Indien pour conquérir les **routes maritimes** de l'Orient dominées par les commerçants arabes était de contourner l'Afrique par le Sud. Ce que fit le premier Vasco de Gama (1469-1524) en atteignant Calicut, le 22 mai 1498.

Les produits de luxe, destinés à une clientèle fortunée (les perles et pierres précieuses, les ivoires et la soie), proviennent aussi du commerce lointain avec des pays comme l'Inde ou l'Arabie Heureuse (le Yémen), ou la Baltique pour l'ambre.

Le transport par voie d'eau, fleuves ou mer, est préféré car moins coûteux et plus rapide que la voie terrestre. Les navires de commerce qui sillonnent la Méditerranée ne le font qu'à la belle saison. En effet, par peur des tempêtes durant l'hiver, la mer est décrétée « fermée » d'octobre à mars. Lorsqu'ils s'embarquent, les marins invoquent la protection du dieu de la Mer, Neptune, et lui offrent un sacrifice une fois arrivés à bon port.

Le commerce de détail, dans les villes, a lieu dans des boutiques appelées *tabernae*, situées au rez-de-chaussée des immeubles. Elles ouvrent de plain-pied sur la rue et les boutiquiers ont tendance à empiéter sur les trottoirs en y installant leurs marchandises – ce qui provoque des encombrements dont se plaignent les Romains. Dans l'Antiquité, les marchands n'ont pas bonne réputation. On les soupçonne d'être prêts à tout pour obtenir des gains et de ne pas hésiter à tromper leurs clients en vendant des marchandises de médiocre qualité à un prix élevé.

▪ *Ces deux reliefs représentent des boutiques. En haut, celle d'un marchand de coussins. En bas, l'étal d'un charcutier.*

▪ *Des portefaix apportent des sacs de blé et les vident dans un récipient qui sert à contrôler les quantités.*

Au **Moyen Âge,** les paysans les plus pauvres sont des serfs. Ils ne peuvent disposer ni d'eux-mêmes, ni de leurs biens, ni de leurs enfants. Attachés à la terre, ils sont vendus avec elle lorsque le seigneur remodèle son domaine foncier.

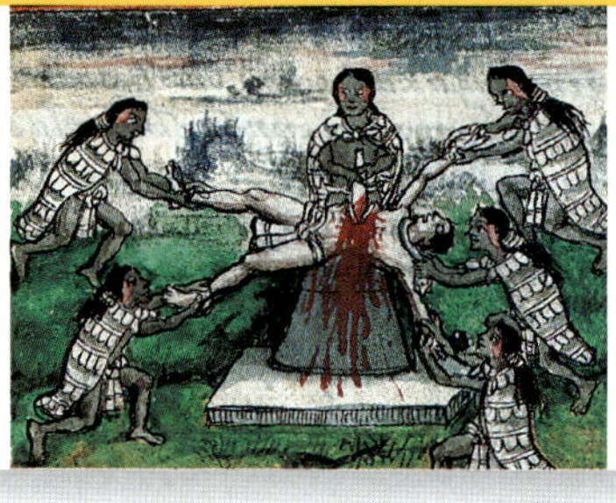

Pour les **Aztèques,** la guerre était le moyen le plus commode de se procurer des prisonniers. Les guerriers ennemis capturés sur le champ de bataille étaient ramenés dans la capitale Tenochtitlan où on les traitait avec de grands égards jusqu'à leur mise à mort au sommet du temple-pyramide.

D'esclave à

> **En mars 71 av. J.-C., 6 000 esclaves suppliciés sur des croix jalonnent la voie Appienne**, route reliant Rome à Capoue, et ce spectacle macabre proclame la victoire de Rome sur la révolte de Spartacus. Pendant deux ans en effet (73-71), ce gladiateur thrace a dirigé une vaste révolte des esclaves d'Italie du Sud, détruit plusieurs armées romaines et même menacé Rome : il fallut lever six légions pour l'écraser. Devenues légendaires, les grandes révoltes serviles n'en furent pas moins rares à Rome.

■ *Cette scène du film* Spartacus *montre à tort le Thrace mourant sur la croix. Il périt en fait dans son ultime combat contre Rome.*

■ *Servant lors d'un banquet, ce jeune esclave porte la tunique courte, vêtement servile par excellence. Choisis pour leur beauté, ces esclaves pouvaient espérer un affranchissement rapide.*

En **Égypte,** la plupart des esclaves étaient des prisonniers de guerre et les besoins en main-d'œuvre tellement importants que de nombreuses campagnes militaires entreprises par les pharaons n'avaient pas d'autres buts que de razzier des travailleurs pour effectuer les tâches pénibles et dangereuses.

En Méditerranée pour manœuvrer sa flotte de **galères,** Louis XIV recrute de force dans ses prisons 12 000 forçats qui sont traités comme des esclaves ; on les marque au fer rouge sur l'épaule avec les lettres GAL pour « galérien ».

affranchi

Procuré par les conquêtes, l'esclavage fournit aussi bien la main-d'œuvre des grandes villas que le personnel domestique. Grâce à l'affranchissement, l'esclave peut espérer monter dans l'échelle sociale.

Limité à l'origine, l'esclavage devient un phénomène massif à Rome à partir du IIe siècle av. J.-C., sous l'impulsion des conquêtes et du développement de l'agriculture spéculative. D'énormes masses de prisonniers de guerre s'écoulent sur le marché, tel le million de Gaulois vendus après la victoire de César sur Vercingétorix en 52 av. J.-C. Les grandes villas, domaines ruraux tournés vers la production de vin et d'huile, en font leur main-d'œuvre privilégiée, mais l'esclavage fournit aussi bien la domesticité des grandes maisons. Seul le statut juridique unifie ce groupe qui présente par ailleurs des situations sociales très différentes. Aux yeux du droit, l'esclave n'est qu'une chose et le maître a le droit de le tuer et de le battre. La condition des esclaves ruraux est assez dure : ils travaillent parfois enchaînés et les maîtres les empêchent d'avoir des relations amoureuses car elles gêneraient leur activité. En revanche, les esclaves citadins jouissent souvent des avantages apportés par la proximité quotidienne du maître et beaucoup vivent en couple.

■ *Lors des ventes d'esclaves, les marchands ne devaient rien cacher de leur corps, car leur prix dépendait de leur état physique, ainsi que de leurs compétences techniques ou culturelles.*

■ *La laideur et les traits négroïdes de cette statuette représentant un esclave témoignent du mépris attaché à l'esclavage.*

Les esclaves urbains ont aussi plus de chances d'obtenir l'affranchissement, qui est couramment pratiqué à Rome. Selon un principe qui surprend beaucoup les Grecs, un esclave affranchi* devient non seulement libre mais obtient aussi les droits du citoyen romain (à l'exception du droit aux magistratures). Très nombreux parmi la plèbe urbaine, les affranchis dominent les métiers du commerce et de l'artisanat, méprisés par les aristocrates. Sous l'Empire, ils fournissent le personnel de la bureaucratie centrale et la domesticité du palais – ce qui leur confère une grande influence politique. À l'époque de Néron (54-68), l'affranchi Pallas joue le rôle d'un ministre des Finances, amasse une énorme fortune et devient même l'amant de l'impératrice Agrippine, mère de l'empereur. Au début du IIe siècle ap. J.-C., l'historien Tacite note amèrement que beaucoup de sénateurs descendent d'affranchis enrichis. Si l'esclavage est un instrument d'oppression, il représente aussi un facteur d'ascension sociale.

Il y a environ 10 000 ans au Proche-Orient, l'Homme est parvenu à domestiquer les premières **plantes**, après les avoir cueillies, cultivées et sélectionnées. Parmi elles, l'engrain sauvage, l'ancêtre du blé, pousse encore à l'état naturel dans les vallées d'Anatolie.

Dans les années 1930 aux États-Unis, le surpâturage et de mauvaises méthodes agricoles ajoutés à une longue période de sécheresse provoquèrent d'immenses **tempêtes de sable**, appelées *Dust Bowls*. Elles forcèrent des milliers de fermiers réduits à la famine à aller chercher du travail dans les villes.

Terre et paysans : un monde

Malgré des évolutions incontestables au cours des siècles, le monde paysan reste très divers et comprend aussi bien de riches domaines que des lopins misérables. Mais certains problèmes, comme l'insécurité, touchent tous les habitants et persistent.

> **Les campagnes sont divisées en villages,** les *uici*, qui regroupent des paysans libres, petits propriétaires, et dépendent de la cité sur le territoire de laquelle ils se trouvent. On y trouve aussi un habitat dispersé, avec des villas* rurales. Ces dernières, de taille très variable, comprennent une partie réservée aux quartiers d'habitation, la *pars urbana*, et une partie regroupant les locaux d'exploitation, comme les granges, les étables et les celliers, appelée *pars rustica*. Les villas dites « suburbaines » (dans la proximité immédiate d'une ville) sont en général spécialisées dans des productions intensives de haut rapport, destinées à la consommation urbaine (fruits, légumes, volailles). Un petit élevage de luxe s'est ainsi développé, tel celui des paons, très recherchés sur les tables des gourmets.

Les exploitations rurales sont de taille très variable. Les petits propriétaires pratiquent une agriculture vivrière et un modeste élevage. Outre le blé, l'orge, les fèves, le chou et les lentilles sont également cultivés, car ils constituent la base d'une alimentation frugale. Sur les exploitations plus importantes, une partie du domaine est cultivée par des esclaves, alors qu'une autre part est divisée en parcelles confiées à des petits paysans, les colons, dont un contrat fixe le loyer, souvent versé en nature.

À la fin du IIe siècle av. J.-C., l'arrivée massive de prisonniers de guerre réduits en esclavage bouleverse l'agriculture italienne. Les propriétaires

Les conquistadores ne rapportèrent pas que de l'or des Amériques, mais aussi de nombreuses plantes que les **Indiens** étaient parvenus à domestiquer. Parmi elles figurent des espèces qui constituent une part importante de notre alimentation comme la pomme de terre, la tomate, le maïs, le haricot ou la courge.

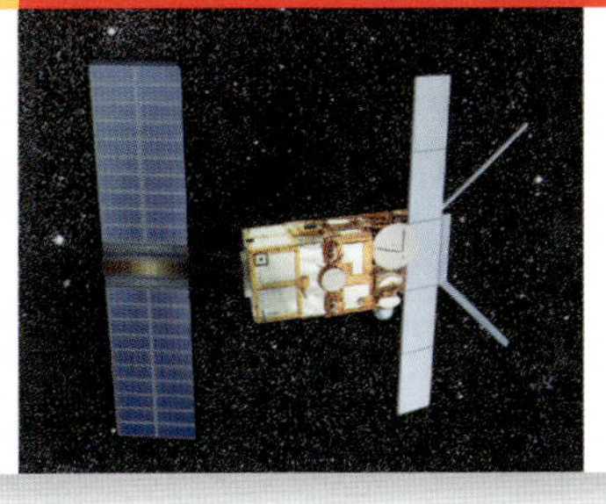

Désormais les **satellites** constituent un outil essentiel pour ausculter la planète et détecter les éventuels maux dont elle souffre. Capables de « voir » la nuit et à travers les nuages grâce à leur radar, ils permettent de surveiller les déforestations, d'estimer la biomasse ou de détecter des feux de forêts.

très divers

des *latifundia*, grandes propriétés, emploient des centaines d'esclaves, les préférant aux hommes libres, qui ont le défaut d'être mobilisables. Ils résident le plus souvent à la ville et confient leurs domaines à un intendant, le *vilicus**. Ils privilégient sur leurs exploitations des cultures rentables, comme la vigne et l'olivier. Parmi les crus, certains sont très réputés, comme le *falerne* de Campanie. L'élevage transhumant se développe, avec de grands troupeaux sous la conduite de bergers esclaves. L'agriculture demeure routinière et peu productive. La terre reste en jachère une année sur deux. Quelques innovations se font toutefois jour, comme la moissonneuse, constituée d'une caisse dentée poussée par un mulet, qui apparaît dans le Nord-Est de la Gaule au IIIe siècle ap. J.-C.

Les paysans ont à se plaindre d'exactions, en particulier de la part des soldats de passage qui exigent d'être logés. Les zones rurales sont parfois infestées de brigands qui attaquent et rançonnent les voyageurs imprudents. Les esclaves ruraux, souvent mal traités par leurs maîtres, n'hésitent pas à se révolter. Ainsi, des milliers d'entre eux rejoignent le gladiateur Spartacus quand celui-ci se soulève (73 av. J.-C.) et met sur pied une véritable armée contre Rome.

■ *Lors de la fondation d'une cité romaine,* le fondateur délimite une enceinte sacrée, le pomerium*, en traçant un sillon avec une charrue attelée de deux bœufs. Il reproduit ainsi les gestes du laboureur.

■ *Les scènes sur ces mosaïques symbolisent les quatre saisons.*
printemps : les semailles ;
été : la récolte du chaume ;
automne : la cueillette du raisin sous une treille ;
hiver : le tressage de paniers.

C'est durant le haut **Moyen Âge,** à partir du XIe siècle, que les villes se réorganisent grâce à la croissance démographique et à l'expansion du commerce. Progressivement leurs habitants, les bourgeois, vont s'associer et remettre en cause le pouvoir seigneurial.

À l'époque de la conquête espagnole, la ville de Mexico était une des plus grandes métropoles de son temps. Protégée par une digue, elle était construite sur un marécage. Entourée de jardins flottants, elle comptait de nombreux palais et en son centre un immense sanctuaire où les **Aztèques** pratiquaient des sacrifices humains.

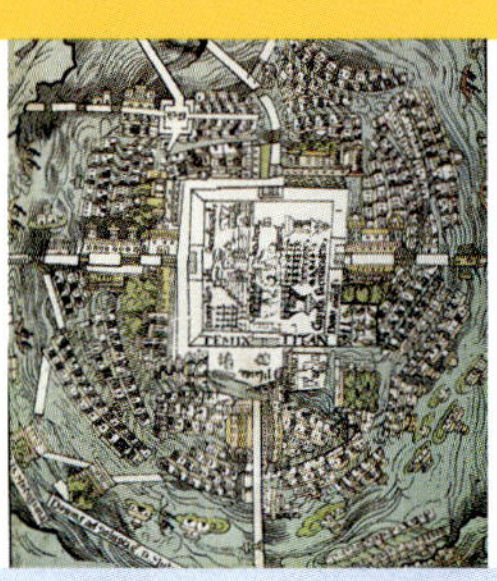

■ ***La ville de Timgad,*** *fondée sous le règne de Trajan, en 100 ap. J.-C., représente le modèle idéal de la ville romaine, avec son plan orthogonal et ses rues se coupant à angle droit.*

Le monde des cités

Le modèle romain va se diffuser à travers l'Empire par le biais de la civilisation urbaine et du modèle de la cité. Certains bâtiments et pratiques se retrouvent, avec parfois quelques adaptations, de la Bretagne au désert de Judée.

Si les progrès techniques ne permettent pas encore la construction de villes ou d'usines sur d'autres planètes du système solaire, l'Homme ne renonce pas à coloniser l'**espace**. Dans les prochaines années, six spationautes devraient séjourner en permanence dans une Station spatiale internationale, alimentée en énergie par 400 m² de panneaux solaires.

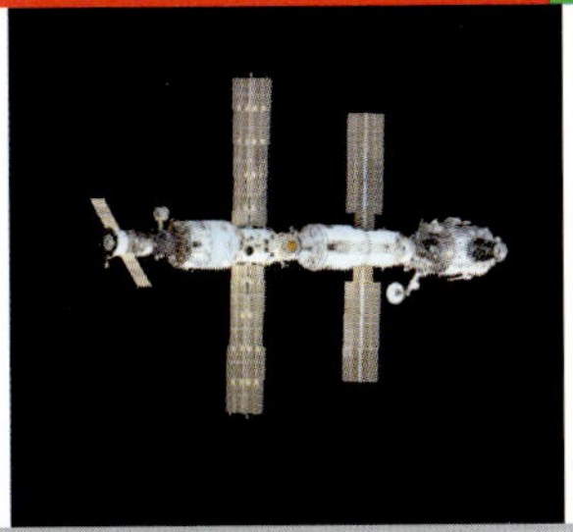

Le pont du Gard est l'aqueduc le plus haut du monde (49 m). Il a pu être édifié grâce à l'invention par les Romains d'un liant résistant à l'humidité. Ce fameux « ciment romain » était fait à partir d'un mélange de chaux et de **cendres volcaniques** : la pouzzolane.

L'élément de base du monde romain est constitué par la cité, qui comprend à la fois une ville et son territoire. Certaines provinces, en particulier dans la partie orientale de l'Empire, comptaient déjà de nombreuses cités avant la conquête romaine. Dans d'autres zones, comme la Gaule, Rome va fonder des cités, qu'elle conçoit comme un profond vecteur de romanisation. Ces nouvelles implantations sont tracées selon un plan rigoureux. Le croisement de deux axes se coupant à angle droit, le *cardo* (N-S) et le *decumanus* (E-O), définit un quadrillage orthogonal, composé d'îlots : les *insulae**.

Plusieurs types de cités existent. La colonie est vue comme une émanation de Rome, dont elle imite les institutions, avec un sénat, des magistrats élus tous les ans et une assemblée du peuple. Les autres cités comprennent aussi des institutions de ce genre, même si elles possèdent plus de latitude par rapport au modèle romain. Ainsi les magistrats suprêmes de la cité, à l'image des consuls romains, sont au nombre de deux dans les colonies*, mais des collèges de huit sont attestés dans certaines cités d'Italie centrale. Les cités les plus anciennes convoitent le statut de cité libre, qui les met hors du pouvoir du gouverneur de province, mais Rome ne l'accorde qu'avec parcimonie, récompensant ainsi ses alliées les plus fidèles.

■ *La rue romaine est longée de trottoirs et bordée de boutiques qui en font un lieu très animé.*

■ *Le capitole d'Ostie domine le forum du haut de son podium. Le marbre qui recouvrait les murs de briques a aujourd'hui disparu.*

Toute cité romaine comporte une place centrale, le *forum*, théoriquement à l'intersection du *cardo* et du *decumanus*. Il est souvent dominé par un temple dédié à la Triade Capitoline (Jupiter, Junon, Minerve), qui se trouve au sommet d'un haut podium destiné à rappeler la colline du Capitole, à Rome même, où se trouve le temple de ces trois divinités. On trouve également une basilique*, édifice civil qui revêt de multiples fonctions : il sert à la fois de tribunal où les magistrats rendent la justice, de halle couverte où les changeurs et banquiers dressent leurs comptoirs, et de salle des pas perdus.

Les constructions de la ville de Rome sont un modèle pour toutes les villes de l'Empire, qui veulent se parer de thermes et d'édifices de spectacle. Leur volonté de rivaliser avec les cités voisines les conduit parfois à se lancer dans des programmes de construction démesurés et à s'endetter lourdement. Pour tenter de remédier à cette situation, les empereurs, à partir du IIe siècle ap. J.-C., chargent des sénateurs de confiance, les curateurs, de remettre en ordre les finances municipales. L'aménagement urbain doit aussi se soucier du ravitaillement en eau, mais la construction d'aqueducs s'avère fort coûteuse. Ceux-ci alimentent de nombreuses fontaines.

■ *Le Forum républicain, centre politique de la ville de Rome, constitue un modèle pour toutes les cités de l'Empire.*

Les ossements des gros animaux ont souvent servi de matériau de construction. Ce fut le cas, il y a 15 000 ans, avec les mammouths en Ukraine, mais aussi et encore récemment avec les **baleines** dont les côtes servaient à clôturer les jardins et les vertèbres étaient transformées en tabourets.

Après les Romains, le ciment cessa d'être utilisé. À la fin du XVIIIe siècle, on redécouvre ses avantages, puis le Français Louis Vicat et l'Anglais J. Aspdin inventent les ciments artificiels. Depuis, ce matériau sous la forme du béton armé ou précontraint a permis la construction des **ouvrages architecturaux** les plus étonnants, tel le viaduc de Millau.

Un habitat contrasté

Les fouilles de Pompéi ont bien fait connaître la *domus* des notables, organisée autour d'un atrium et d'un péristyle. Mais les gens modestes s'entassent dans les petites chambres des immeubles, *insulae*, majoritaires à Rome.

■ *Cette* insula *d'Ostie, port de Rome, est construite en brique, matériau bon marché et facile à fabriquer. Les grandes baies du rez-de-chaussée ouvraient sur des boutiques (*taberna*).*

Le 24 août 79 ap. J.-C., l'éruption du Vésuve, près de Naples, détruit les villes de Pompéi et d'Herculanum : les cendres volcaniques s'abattent sur la première tandis que des torrents de boue recouvrent la seconde. Prises dans leur gangue de lave solidifiée, les deux villes sont ainsi préservées et livrent des renseignements précieux sur la vie quotidienne lorsque les premiers archéologues les redécouvrent au XVIIIe siècle. Elles s'imposent aussitôt comme la première source de renseignements sur la maison romaine.

Les deux cités présentent spécialement beaucoup d'exemples de maisons habitées par les gens aisés : la *domus.** À l'origine organisée autour d'une pièce quadrangulaire, l'atrium*, elle se dote, au IIe siècle av. J.-C., d'un second noyau, le péristyle, cour-jardin entourée

La Cappadoce turque abrite d'étonnantes habitations troglodytiques. Elles furent creusées dans des **cônes de tuf volcanique** façonnés par l'érosion, entre le VIIIe et le XIe siècle, par des communautés chrétiennes grecques qui y aménagèrent des sanctuaires et des habitations parfaitement imperméables et aérées.

Les **récifs coralliens** abritent une faune extrêmement variée dont les poissons-perroquets qui doivent leur nom à leurs dents soudées en forme de bec. Grâce à ce puissant instrument, ils peuvent racler le corail sur lequel poussent les algues dont ils se nourrissent.

d'une colonnade, d'inspiration grecque. Le toit percé d'un trou correspondant à un bassin au sol, l'atrium est entouré de pièces de réception (*triclinium* : salle à manger) et de service (cuisine, chambre des esclaves). Autour du péristyle se déploient les chambres familiales et des salons réservés à l'accueil des intimes. Si l'atrium est plus tourné vers la réception, il ne faut pas en conclure que les parties publique et privée sont séparées de façon fixe et rigide. Selon les moments, les pièces peuvent recevoir des fonctions différentes et le péristyle peut jouer aussi un rôle public. Cette souplesse de l'espace domestique s'accroît au IIe siècle ap. J.-C. lorsque l'atrium disparaît.

▪ *Tablinum : bureau du maître de maison.*

▪ *Résidence de l'élite, la* domus *était conçue pour affirmer la puissance et la richesse de son propriétaire.*

▪ *Péristyle : cour-jardin pour la réception et la détente.*

▪ *Oecus : salon luxueux pour les dîners entre intimes.*

▪ *Triclinium : salle à manger.*

▪ *Parmi les boutiques installées au rez-de-chaussée des maisons, on reconnaît facilement le* thermopolium, *« bar » romain, grâce à son comptoir creusé de trous pour les amphores.*

L'atrium n'en a pas moins été le cœur de la maison pendant des siècles. Il abrite le laraire, autel des cultes domestiques, et les masques de cire des ancêtres, rangés dans des armoires, si la famille est noble. Dans un coin se trouve le *tablinum*, pièce servant de bureau, et tous les matins, les clients du maître de maison se pressent dans l'atrium pour le saluer. Issus le plus souvent de la plèbe, ces clients résident dans des logements bien plus modestes, les appartements des *insulae*. Immeuble de six ou sept étages, construit en brique et en bois, l'*insula* est surtout présente dans les grandes villes comme Rome ou son port, Ostie. Son organisation marie mixité et hiérarchie sociales. Si le premier étage présente un appartement luxueux, les derniers niveaux sont divisés en petites pièces de 20 m², où s'entassent des familles entières. Mais tous les résidents souffrent du bruit : le philosophe Sénèque se plaint ainsi des sons du ballon et des cris des gens qu'on épile provenant d'un établissement de bains voisin (v. 60 ap. J.-C.).

▪ *Sur le seuil des maisons, des mosaïques représentaient des chiens avec l'indication « chien méchant » (cave canem) pour décourager les intrus.*

Dans la tradition indienne, la danse est non seulement un divertissement, mais aussi un moyen de transmettre au plus large public les mythes et la littérature ancienne. Dans cet art où l'improvisation n'existe pas, un **répertoire de gestes des mains** et d'expressions du regard permet d'exprimer une gamme de sentiments que le public reçoit et décode.

Avant l'arrivée des conquistadores, tous les peuples de l'Amérique centrale, comme les **Mayas** ou les **Aztèques**, pratiquaient un étonnant jeu de balle. Il donnait lieu à des paris importants mais était aussi une cérémonie religieuse destinée à assurer la victoire de la lumière solaire sur l'obscurité de la nuit.

Une civilisation de loisirs

▪ *À l'imitation du théâtre grec, certains acteurs portaient des masques, renvoyant à des personnages stéréotypés. Mais la plupart se grimaient plutôt à l'aide d'un maquillage violent.*

> **Vaste ovale de pierre, le Colisée dresse encore sa carcasse à moitié démantelée au centre de Rome, à deux pas du Forum.** L'empereur Vespasien (69-79) décida de le construire à la place de l'ancien palais de Néron, la Maison Dorée, près d'une statue colossale de ce souverain (d'où son surnom). Inauguré par Titus en 80 ap. J.-C., dédié aux combats de gladiateurs, l'amphithéâtre Flavien – tel était son nom officiel – pouvait accueillir 50 000 personnes. Sa présence massive révèle l'importance des spectacles dans la civilisation romaine.

Les Romains distinguent deux types de spectacles mais leur origine est, dans les deux cas, religieuse. Lors des fêtes religieuses, des jeux, *ludus**, sont offerts aux dieux par la cité, sous la forme de pièces de théâtre et de courses de chars. Les magistrats chargés de les organiser, les édiles, y consacrent toute leur attention car leur popularité en dépend. À l'opposé, les combats de gladiateurs, *munus**, sont des cérémonies privées, célébrées lors des funérailles pour apaiser les âmes des morts. Mais les hommes politiques de l'époque républicaine prennent l'habitude d'offrir des combats somptueux pour favoriser leur carrière, et l'empereur Auguste (27 av. J.-C. – 14 ap. J.-C.) en tire les conséquences en instaurant un *munus* public, monopolisé par le souverain. Si les Romains n'ont jamais oublié cette dimension religieuse, il n'en reste pas moins que les spectacles deviennent la pièce maîtresse d'une civilisation de loisirs, qui connaît son apogée au début de l'Empire.

Les spectacles investissent alors une grande partie du temps et de l'espace romains. Les jeux occupent 135 jours par an au IIe siècle ap. J.-C. et la ville de Rome se couvre d'immenses monuments destinés à les accueillir, tel le cirque Maxime, destiné aux courses de chars, fort de 250 000 places. Tout Rome est dans le cirque, quand les cochers, répartis en quatre écuries reconnaissables à la couleur des casaques (bleu, vert, rouge, blanc), effectuent leurs sept tours sur la piste. Leur popularité n'a d'égale que celle des gladiateurs. Composés de prisonniers de guerre mais aussi de volontaires, ces derniers se répartissent en plusieurs groupes définis par leur armement, comme les mirmillons, au casque surmonté d'un poisson, ou les rétiaires, maniant le filet et le trident. Ils combattent à mort et seul

▪ *Sous l'Empire, le munus commençait le matin par des « chasses » : des combats entre des bêtes féroces et des gladiateurs appelés « bestiaires ».*

Quand ils apparaissent durant le XIe siècle, les **tournois** ne sont d'abord que des affrontements en rase campagne entre deux groupes armés de combattants à cheval. C'est seulement à partir du XIIIe siècle qu'ils deviennent des spectacles codifiés organisés par un seigneur : des joutes entre deux adversaires se mesurant dans un champ clos.

En plus des grandes fêtes religieuses, la vie des cités au **Moyen Âge** était rythmée par les carnavals. Ces festivités étaient de véritables soupapes de sûreté, pendant lesquelles le peuple dénonçait les puissants et les injustices passées ; pour un temps, la critique devenait la règle.

Les spectacles se composent des jeux (théâtre et chars) et des combats de gladiateurs. D'origine religieuse, ils acquièrent un rôle central dans la civilisation de loisirs qui s'épanouit à l'époque impériale.

le public peut sauver la vie du vaincu en réclamant sa grâce à l'empereur. Pour les Romains, un tel spectacle n'a rien de cruel car les gladiateurs méritent leur sort : c'est au contraire une école de courage pour les spectateurs.

■ *La forme du Colisée découle de la réunion de deux théâtres mais les architectes romains en ont accentué le caractère ovale pour améliorer la vision des spectateurs.*

■ *Ce quadrige contourne les* metae, *trois bornes qui précédaient le terre-plein central (spina) du cirque. Il doit éviter de les heurter ce qui entraînerait son « naufrage ».*

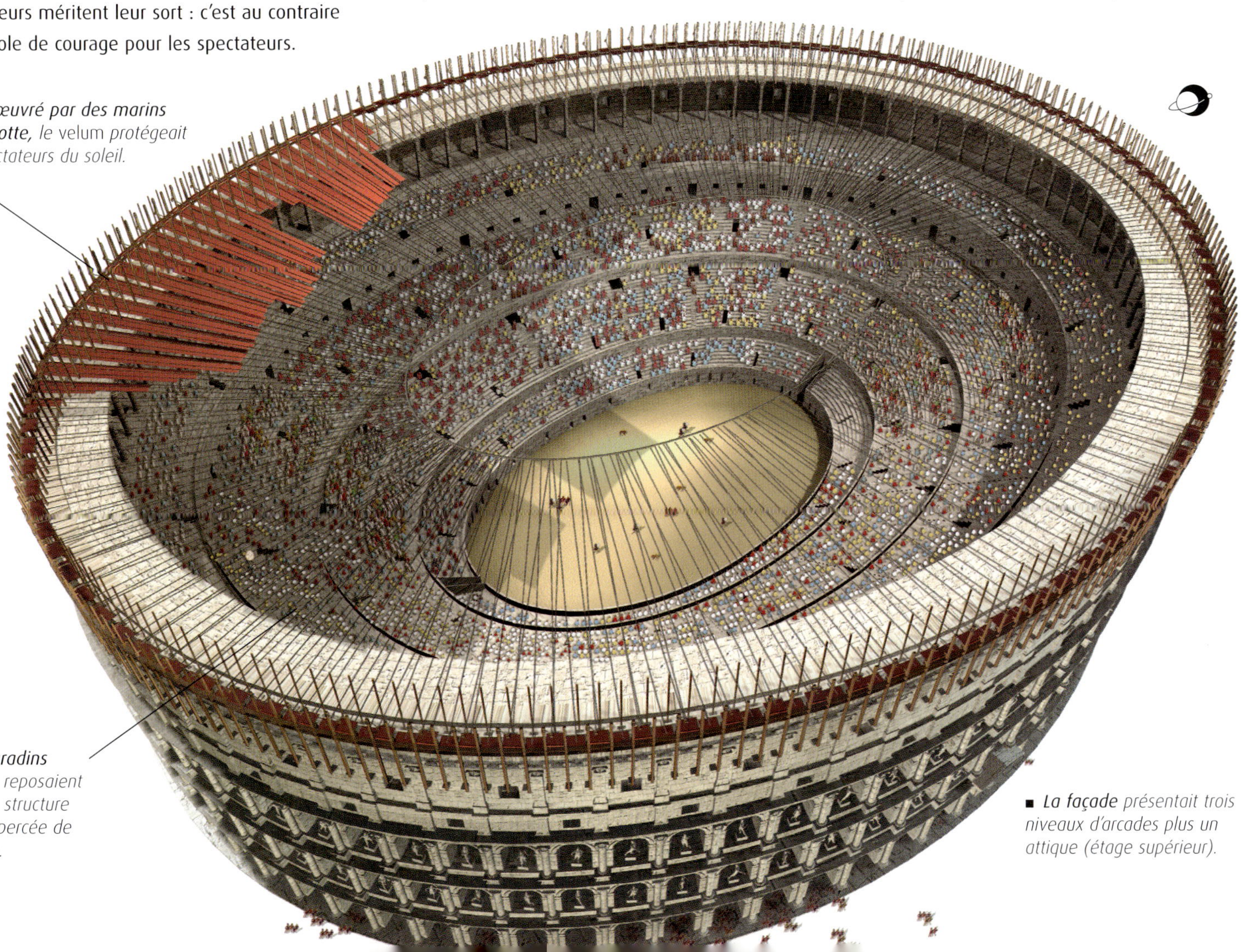

■ *Manœuvré par des marins de la flotte, le velum protégeait les spectateurs du soleil.*

■ *Les gradins (cavea) reposaient sur une structure creuse percée de couloirs.*

■ *La façade présentait trois niveaux d'arcades plus un attique (étage supérieur).*

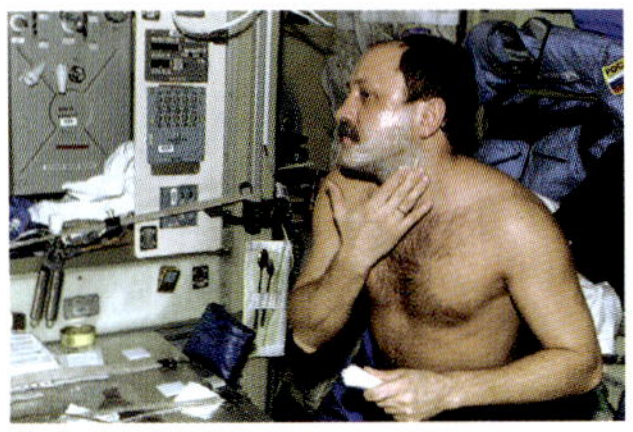

Lorsque les spationautes se lavent à bord de la **Station spatiale internationale,** ils le font en observant quelques règles : ils utilisent des serviettes humides aux propriétés désinfectantes pour le corps, s'essuient avec des serviettes sèches et « recrachent » le dentifrice dans des petites compresses.

Le « grooming », cette habitude qu'ont la plupart des singes de se nettoyer réciproquement le pelage, est pour eux un **moyen essentiel de communiquer.** Les différentes façons dont ils le pratiquent sont toujours des indications sur les interrelations sociales qui existent dans le groupe.

Les thermes :

■ *Même des villes d'importance moyenne comme Pompéi avaient plusieurs édifices thermaux, aux salles décorées de stucs et de vasques de marbre.*

■ *Ces pilettes de brique soutenaient le plancher des thermes. L'air chauffé par une fournaise circulait entre elles.*

> **L'entrée des thermes ne coûte pas grand-chose, elle est même parfois gratuite.** Tous les Romains peuvent donc y avoir accès. Des établissements thermaux sont construits dans toutes les villes de l'Empire et certaines se sont même dotées de plusieurs édifices de ce type. Ainsi, Timgad, en Afrique, avait treize thermes répartis dans ses divers quartiers.

Le plan des thermes suit des principes bien établis et se caractérise par sa symétrie. Il comprend deux moitiés rigoureusement identiques, disposées autour d'un axe central. L'établissement de bains lui-même se situe au centre d'un vaste parc. Les édifices construits rivalisent de somptuosité et de gigantisme. L'empereur Caracalla (211-217) fait édifier à Rome des thermes qui s'étendent sur plus de 110 000 m². Les innovations techniques s'y déploient : un système de chauffage par le sol permet d'atteindre 55 °C dans les pièces chaudes. De tels édifices nécessitent des quantités importantes de bois pour le chauffage, mais également beaucoup d'eau ; aussi des aqueducs sont-ils construits pour les alimenter.

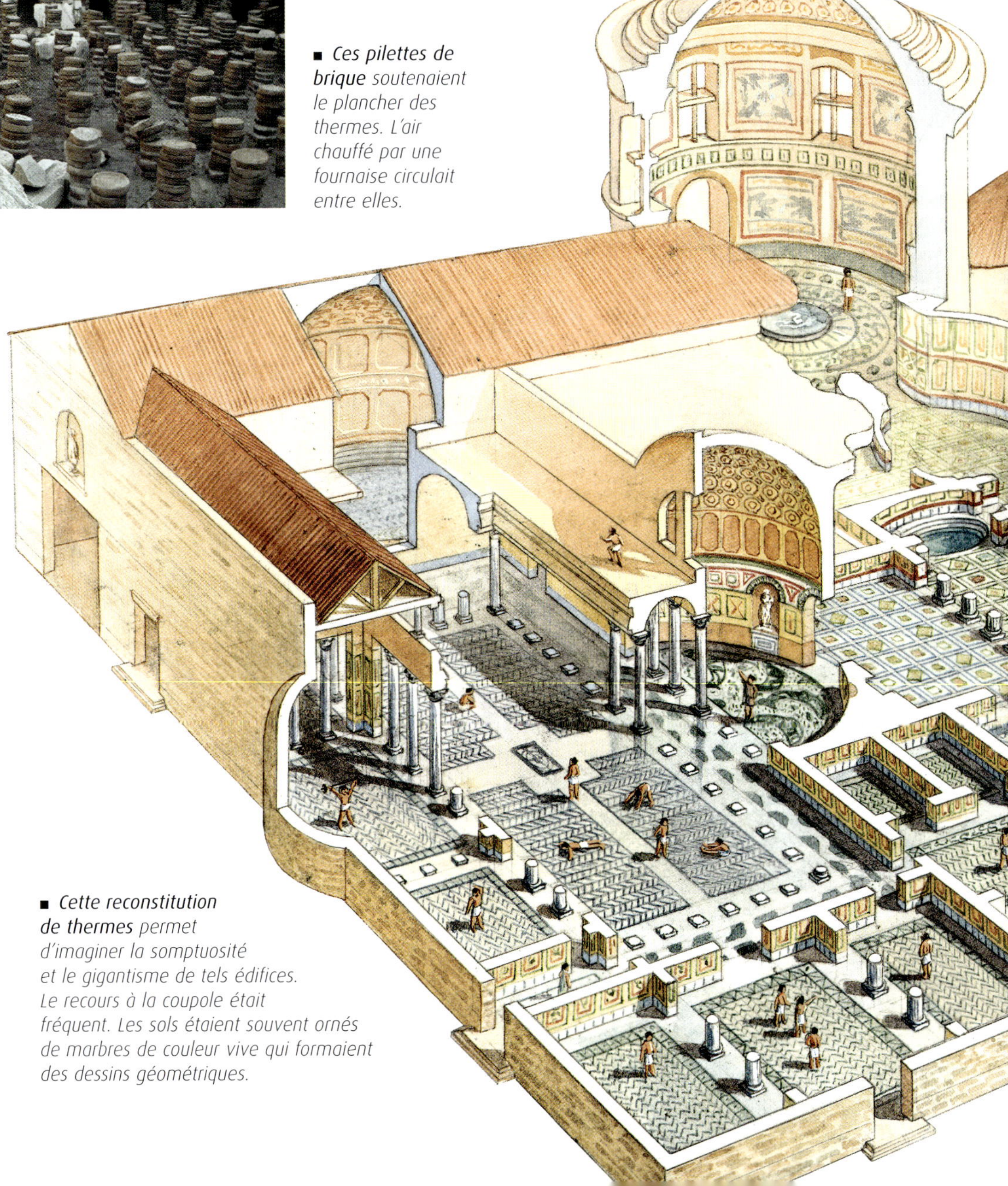

■ *Cette reconstitution de thermes permet d'imaginer la somptuosité et le gigantisme de tels édifices. Le recours à la coupole était fréquent. Les sols étaient souvent ornés de marbres de couleur vive qui formaient des dessins géométriques.*

L'eau douce est un élément indispensable à la survie de tous les êtres vivants, mais c'est aussi une denrée rare et fragile que l'industrie, l'agriculture et l'urbanisation souillent et polluent de plus en plus et finissent par rendre impropre à la consommation.

Les émanations soufrées sont depuis longtemps connues pour leurs vertus curatives et les Romains soignaient leurs affections respiratoires en prenant des bains de vapeur dans des sortes de saunas, construits sur les pentes des **volcans**. Au Japon, on ensevelit les malades sous le sable chaud volcanique pour calmer les douleurs rhumatismales.

un complexe culturel

Les thermes ne sont pas seulement des édifices voués à l'entretien du corps. Ce sont aussi de véritables complexes culturels, où les Romains peuvent passer de longs moments au cours de leur journée, et des lieux de sociabilité.

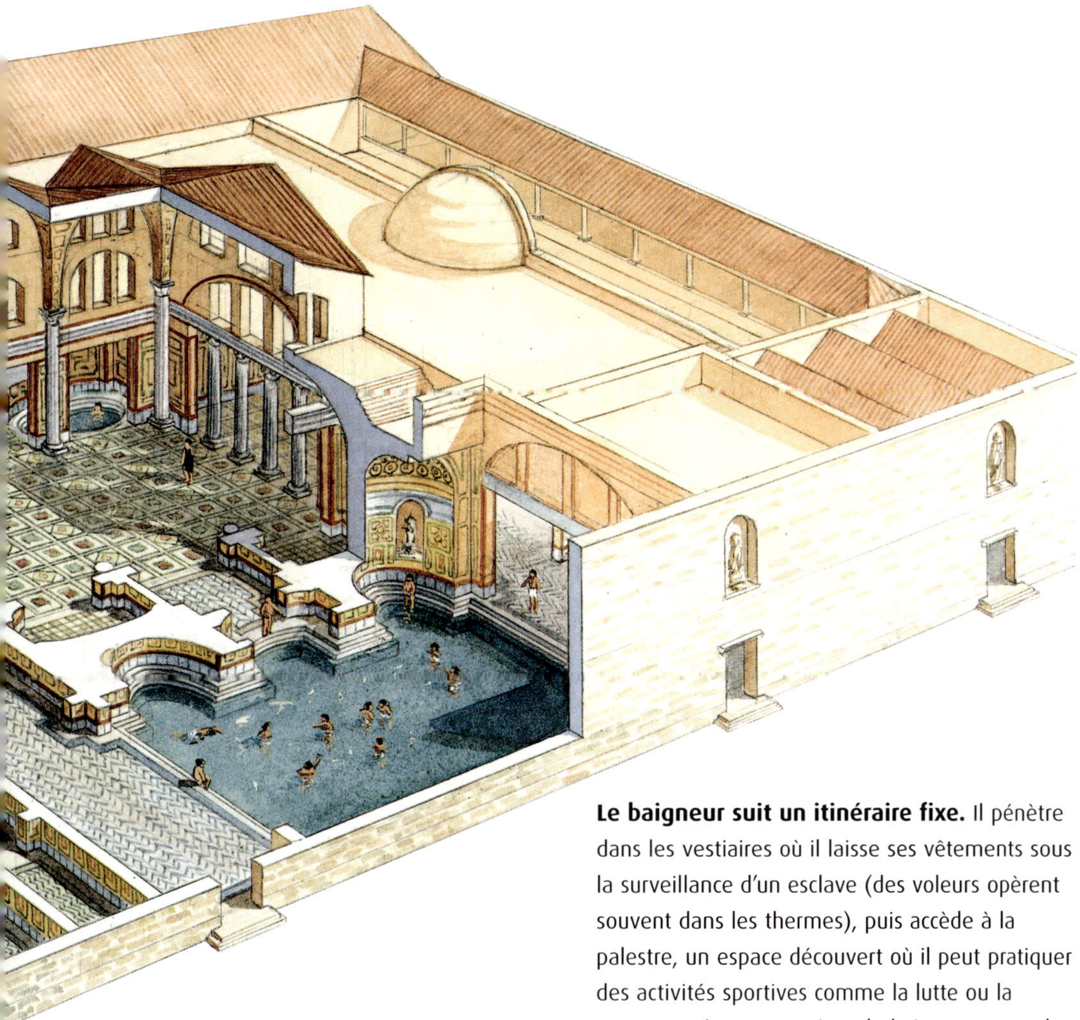

▪ *Cet athlète, après l'exercice physique, nettoie sa peau enduite d'un mélange d'huile et de poussière au moyen d'un racloir : le strigile.*

Le baigneur suit un itinéraire fixe. Il pénètre dans les vestiaires où il laisse ses vêtements sous la surveillance d'un esclave (des voleurs opèrent souvent dans les thermes), puis accède à la palestre, un espace découvert où il peut pratiquer des activités sportives comme la lutte ou la course. Après ces exercices, le baigneur se rend dans le *caldarium*, la salle chaude, puis passe par le *tepidarium*, salle tiède, avant d'arriver dans la salle froide, le *frigidarium*, et de plonger dans la piscine d'eau froide, souvent en plein air. Il peut ensuite flâner et se délasser en se promenant dans les jardins qui entourent les bains. Là sont disposées des œuvres d'art – ce qui fait de ces espaces de véritables musées. Des lectures d'œuvres littéraires et des concerts se déroulent dans des salles annexes, et des bibliothèques sont également à la disposition du public.

Toutes les composantes de la société se retrouvent aux thermes. Pauvres et riches s'y côtoient, et les parasites en quête d'un bon dîner s'attachent aux pas des vaniteux. Les empereurs eux-mêmes aiment à s'y rendre, afin de se montrer proches de leur peuple. La mixité des établissements suscite les critiques des moralistes, et l'empereur Hadrien (117-138) décide que désormais hommes et femmes seront séparés.

Au Japon, le mont Fuji est non seulement le symbole du pays, mais aussi un dieu pour la religion Shinto. Aussi chaque printemps et depuis des siècles, des centaines de milliers de pèlerins gravissent le **volcan** – ce qui fait de lui la montagne la plus visitée au monde.

Mars, qui verra sans doute des humains fouler sa surface au cours du XXIe siècle, est une planète que les hommes observent depuis fort longtemps. Les Romains, pour qui sa teinte rougeâtre due aux composés ferreux de son sol évoquait la couleur du sang, l'avaient associée à une divinité essentielle de leur panthéon : le dieu de la Guerre.

Les dieux sont tombés du ciel

Religion polythéiste, la religion romaine connaît une multitude de dieux, dont la personnalité doit beaucoup à l'influence grecque. Par l'observation scrupuleuse des rites, Rome cherche à s'assurer leur protection, la « paix des dieux ».

■ *Les amours du dieu de la Guerre, Mars (à gauche avec le casque), et de la déesse de l'Amour, Vénus (à gauche, assise), alors que celle-ci était mariée au dieu-forgeron Vulcain, sont l'un des thèmes favoris des peintres romains.*

■ *Déesse asiatique de la Végétation à peine hellénisée, l'Artémis d'Éphèse porte un plastron couvert de testicules de taureau. Sa gaine est décorée d'animaux, symbole de son pouvoir sur la nature.*

Les **Égyptiens** croyaient que la boulette d'excrément que pousse le scarabée sacré figurait la Terre et que l'insecte la roulait du lever au coucher du Soleil. Ils pensaient aussi que ses antennes figuraient les rayons de l'astre et que les 36 segments de l'extrémité de ses pattes représentaient les jours du mois.

Quand les prêtres **embaumeurs égyptiens** entouraient le corps de la momie de bandelettes, ils prenaient soin de placer des amulettes au bon endroit comme un œil oudjat sur le ventre, un scarabée sur le cœur et aussi des nœuds d'Isis ou des piliers Djed.

> **En 249 av. J.-C. lors de la première guerre punique, la flotte romaine se prépare à affronter la flotte carthaginoise** au large de Drépane, en Sicile. Les Romains cherchent à savoir si les dieux leur sont favorables en interprétant l'appétit des poulets sacrés mais les volatiles refusent justement de manger. Excédé, le consul Publius Claudius Pulcher les fait jeter à la mer en s'écriant : « Qu'ils boivent s'ils ne veulent pas manger ! » Quelques heures plus tard, il subit une sévère défaite qui n'étonne personne puisqu'il a défié la volonté des dieux.

Les Romains prétendent en effet devoir leurs victoires au fait d'être les hommes les plus religieux de la Terre. À l'origine, les divinités romaines se présentent comme de simples forces impersonnelles favorisant les activités agricoles ou guerrières mais l'influence grecque leur confère rapidement une personnalité individuelle. Assimilées à leurs équivalents du panthéon grec, elles adoptent leurs traits, leurs compétences et leurs mythes. Ainsi, Vénus, simple déesse des Potagers, est-elle identifiée à la déesse de l'Amour, Aphrodite. Selon le modèle grec, une hiérarchie plus ou moins stricte place au sommet de la foule divine les douze dieux de l'Olympe, eux-mêmes dirigés par Jupiter, dieu du Ciel à la foudre redoutable. Comme tout polythéisme, la religion romaine est accueillante aux nouveaux dieux et l'époque impériale voit le succès des cultes venus d'Orient, comme l'Égyptienne Isis, déesse de la Fécondité et protectrice de la navigation.

Le rapport du Romain aux dieux n'implique ni croyance ni adhésion individuelle. Le but des cultes est d'abord d'assurer de bonnes relations entre la cité et les divinités : la « paix des dieux » (*pax deorum*). Pour y parvenir, il faut d'abord connaître la volonté divine au moyen de techniques diverses, telles que le vol des oiseaux, interprété par les augures*, ou l'examen des entrailles des bêtes sacrifiées, pratiqué par les haruspices*. Il faut ensuite exécuter les rites de façon scrupuleuse, car la religion romaine est une religion du faire et non du croire. Toute modification du rituel entraîne l'annulation, et la réédition, de la cérémonie. Ainsi, deux fois par an, en mars et en octobre, pour marquer l'ouverture et la fermeture de la saison guerrière, les douze saliens, prêtres du dieu de la Guerre Mars, exécutent-ils une danse, équipés de boucliers tombés du ciel. Ils chantent un hymne incompréhensible en latin archaïque, dont chaque parole doit être respectée si l'on veut satisfaire le dieu.

■ *Le dieu iranien Mithra égorge un taureau dont le sang doit sauver le monde, menacé par la sécheresse.*

■ *Installée dans un laraire, cette petite statue de Jupiter représente le roi des dieux sous son aspect canonique, visage barbu et foudre à la main.*

■ *La déesse égyptienne Isis, à moins que ce ne soit l'une de ses prêtresses, porte ses insignes : le sistre (crécelle) à la main droite et le nœud, symbole de vie, sur la poitrine.*

Borobodur, à Java (Indonésie), construit avec 1 600 000 blocs taillés dans une **roche volcanique**, l'andésite, est l'un des plus beaux et des plus grands temples bouddhiques de l'Asie du Sud-Est. Englouti par la jungle, il sombra néanmoins dans l'oubli pendant près de 1 000 ans et ne fut redécouvert qu'en 1814.

En Angleterre, les **hommes du néolithique** ont érigé, entre 3100 et 1100 av. J.-C., le plus célèbre des monuments mégalithiques du monde : Stonehenge. On pense que ces énormes pierres levées étaient une sorte de centre cérémoniel dont l'orientation permettait d'établir la date du solstice d'été et ainsi le calendrier agricole de l'année.

▪ *L'empereur Marc Aurèle brûle des grains d'encens sur un autel portatif, première étape du sacrifice.*

▪ *Le Panthéon était dédié à tous les dieux (sens du mot) mais surtout au culte impérial. Sa coupole symbolise le cosmos, l'univers dominé par l'empereur.*

Au sein du temple : cultes et sacrifices

> **En décembre 69 ap. J.-C., lors d'une guerre civile, le feu éclate sur le Capitole,** colline dominant le Forum, et gagne le temple de Jupiter, sanctuaire le plus prestigieux de Rome. Fondé par les rois étrusques (VIe siècle av. J.-C.), il abrite le culte de Jupiter, roi des dieux, associé à sa femme Junon et sa fille Minerve dans la Triade Capitoline. Le traumatisme de l'incendie est tel que certains y voient le signe de la chute de l'Empire et que le nouvel empereur, Vespasien, aura à cœur de le reconstruire au plus vite.

Au sens premier du terme, un « temple » est un espace consacré mais, dès l'Antiquité, l'habitude s'est imposée de désigner ainsi le monument construit au cœur de cet espace. Au contraire du temple grec, le temple romain s'élève sur un haut podium, mais, pour le reste, le plan du bâtiment a subi l'influence de l'hellénisme. Un vestibule à colonnes, le *pronaos*, précède une pièce, la *cella**, où se trouve la statue de la divinité. La plupart des cérémonies ne se déroulent pas dans la *cella* mais autour d'un autel, placé à l'extérieur devant le temple. Certains monuments plus originaux ont une forme circulaire comme le temple de Vesta, contenant le feu symbole de la vie de Rome, ou le Panthéon, célèbre par son immense coupole construite sous le règne d'Hadrien (117-138). Décorés à l'origine de bas-reliefs en terre cuite, selon la coutume étrusque, les temples romains adoptent le marbre à partir du IIe siècle av. J.-C., mais l'ensemble reste toujours peint de couleurs très vives, bien loin de la blancheur des ruines actuelles.

L'autel externe accueille la célébration du sacrifice, rite central des cultes romains. Le dos saupoudré d'une farine spéciale confectionnée par les prêtresses de Vesta, la bête est assommée puis égorgée par un sacrificateur. Ses entrailles sont brûlées en l'honneur du dieu tandis que les hommes consomment sa viande lors d'un banquet. Le sacrifice opère ainsi un partage entre les dieux et les hommes. Lors des grandes fêtes, un banquet, le *lectisterne*, est offert aux statues des dieux, sorties de leur *cella* et installées sur des lits. Sous la direction du grand pontife*, des collèges de prêtres supervisent le déroulement des cultes, spécialement les pontifes, chargés de la gestion des temples, et les épulons, organisateurs des banquets. Désigné pour la vie, le prêtre n'est pas un personnage sacré comme le prêtre chrétien mais une sorte de magistrat, gérant les rapports de la cité avec les dieux. Cette dimension politique explique que l'empereur ait mis la main sur le grand pontificat dès le règne d'Auguste.

▪ *Après avoir assommé puis égorgé le taureau, le sacrificateur s'apprête à lui ouvrir le ventre pour prélever les entrailles, que les haruspices vont examiner pour y lire la volonté des dieux.*

Si, dans l'imaginaire collectif, les cathédrales incarnent à elles seules **l'art gothique**, elles apparaissent pourtant dès le IVe siècle, bien avant la naissance de ce style architectural. Elles abritent la chaire de l'évêque, symbole du pouvoir épiscopal sur tout un diocèse.

Les **Aztèques** utilisaient deux calendriers. L'un, comptant 260 jours auxquels étaient associés les grands dieux de la mythologie et ceux du panthéon, avait un usage religieux. L'autre, qui comportait 360 jours et 5 autres supplémentaires, rythmait l'année civile et agricole.

Le cœur du temple romain est la *cella*, pièce abritant la statue du dieu, mais le culte se déroule autour de l'autel, situé à l'extérieur. Sous la direction de prêtres représentant la cité, le sacrifice opère un partage entre les dieux et les hommes.

■ ***De plan axial**, garni de colonnes seulement sur sa façade, ce temple est fait pour être vu de face.*

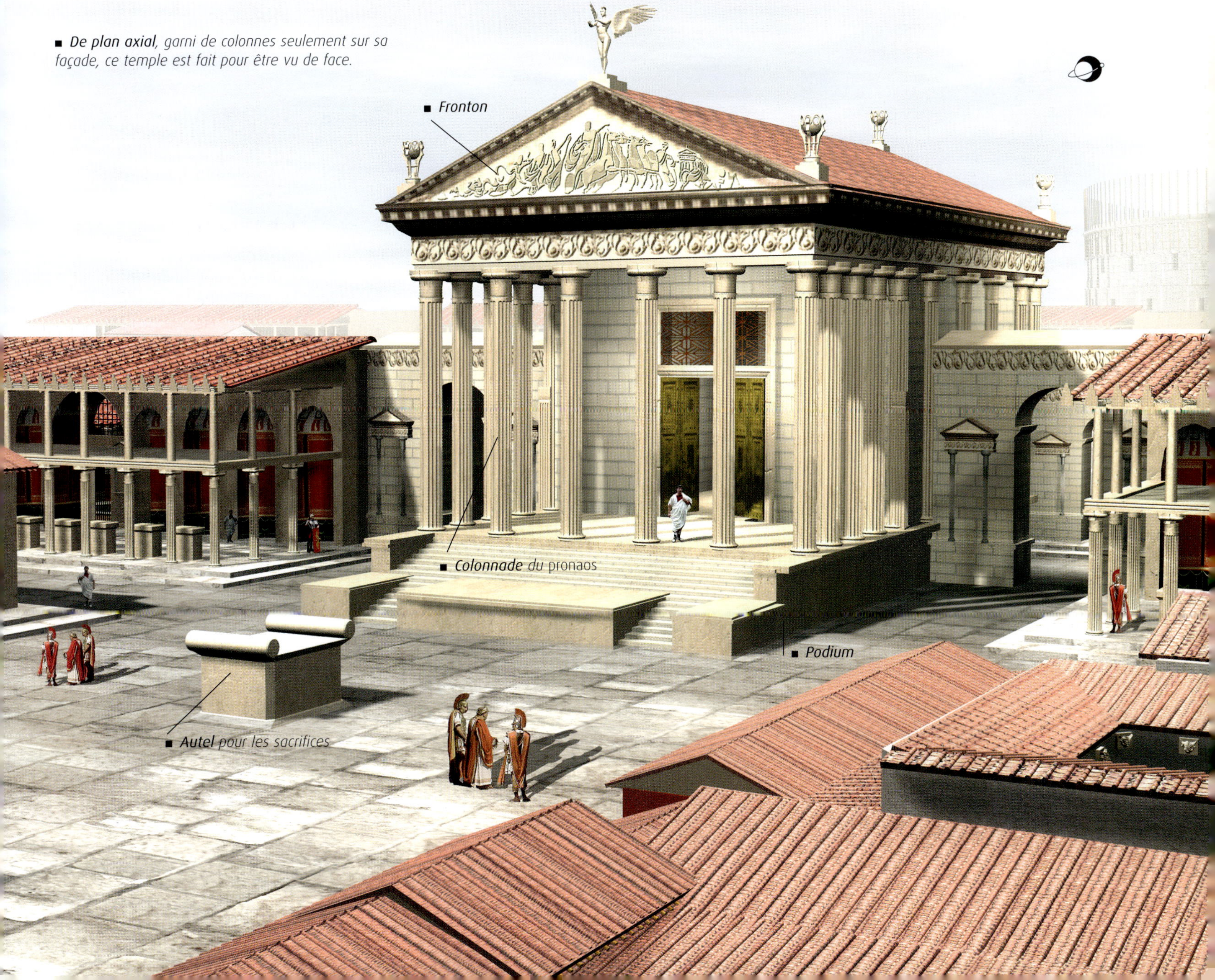

Dans l'un des épisodes les plus fameux de l'Ancien Testament, Moïse et les Hébreux franchissent à pied sec la mer Rouge avant que l'eau ne revienne et n'engloutisse l'armée de Pharaon. Cette ouverture de la mer Rouge est peut-être un **tsunami** qui aurait à l'époque, vers 1200 av. J.-C., ravagé cette région du Sinaï.

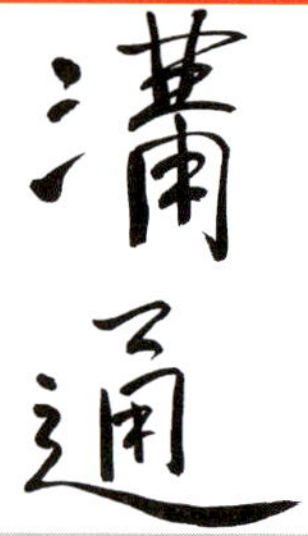

Les premières inscriptions chinoises que l'on date du IIe millénaire avant notre ère, et qui sont les ancêtres des **caractères chinois**, étaient des signes religieux ou magiques. Il s'agissait de marques laissées par le feu sur des os d'animaux et qui passaient pour être des messages des dieux.

Naissance du christianisme

▪ *Cette tête de Constantin mesure à elle seule 2,60 m de haut. Elle appartenait à une statue colossale du premier empereur chrétien.*

À ses débuts, le christianisme ne semble être qu'une secte juive de plus, mais le nombre de ses adeptes va connaître une croissance rapide dans l'Empire romain. La prédication de saint Paul amène la constitution de communautés en Asie Mineure, en Grèce et même à Rome.

Mais ces adeptes d'une religion monothéiste suscitent la méfiance parmi les habitants de l'Empire. On les accuse de pratiques illicites, voire de crimes : ils se réuniraient pour assassiner un nouveau-né et le dévorer ! Cette rumeur n'est qu'une version déformée de l'eucharistie, la communion des chrétiens. Leur refus de rendre un culte à l'empereur les met à l'écart de la société païenne. Des persécutions vont les frapper. Elles sont d'abord ponctuelles et éclatent à l'occasion de

▪ ***Accusés d'être responsables** de l'incendie de Rome en 64 par haine du genre humain, les chrétiens sont condamnés à mort et transformés en torches vivantes.*

Le moine **Martin Luther** (1483-1546) est à l'origine d'un grand mouvement de pensée qui au XVIe siècle remet en cause le rôle du clergé et le comportement des hommes d'Église. Il traduit la Bible en allemand et, soutenu par quelques princes gagnés à sa cause et qui protestent à ses côtés, déclare que seule la foi sauve le chrétien.

En formulant sa théorie de l'évolution, **Charles Darwin** (1809-1882) bouscule les croyances traditionnelles et approuvées par les Églises qui veulent que chaque espèce ait été créée une fois pour toutes afin de s'adapter aux conditions de son milieu.

Le christianisme, d'abord méconnu, puis persécuté au nom de l'unité de l'Empire, s'impose peu à peu dans le monde romain. Après la conversion de Constantin, premier empereur chrétien, il va acquérir au cours du IVe siècle le statut de religion officielle.

▪ *Des scènes tirées de l'Évangile, comme cette multiplication des pains, ornent souvent les sarcophages chrétiens.*

▪ *Les premiers chrétiens enterraient leurs défunts dans des galeries souterraines, appelées « catacombes ».*

▪ *Les tableaux en marbres polychromes, d'origine orientale, étaient très appréciés à Rome. Les chrétiens n'hésitèrent pas à utiliser cette technique pour représenter Jésus.*

crises dans des zones limitées. Ainsi, en 64 ap. J.-C., une rumeur persistante accuse l'empereur Néron d'avoir fait incendier Rome afin de pouvoir se faire édifier sur les ruines un palais somptueux. Néron détourne la fureur populaire sur les chrétiens, qui sont condamnés comme incendiaires.

De ponctuelles, les persécutions se font générales au temps de la crise de l'Empire, au IIIe siècle. Afin de restaurer l'unité de tous les Romains face aux périls qui les assaillent, comme les pestes ou les invasions barbares, l'empereur Trajan Dèce (249-251) ordonne que tous sacrifient en l'honneur des dieux de l'Empire. Ceux qui refusent encourent la peine de mort. Ces mesures s'appliquent dans tout le monde romain. Elles seront suivies d'autres épisodes de persécutions, sous Valérien et surtout sous Dioclétien.

Mais la foi des martyrs et leur résistance impressionnent les païens, et les persécutions n'ont pas réussi à détruire les communautés de fidèles. Bien plus, un nouvel allié de choix va faire basculer la situation en leur faveur. Le jeune Constantin, alors qu'il doit livrer une bataille contre son ennemi Maxence, a un songe. Si ses soldats arborent le signe du Dieu chrétien, la victoire lui sera donnée ! Constantin obéit à cette injonction et vainc Maxence en 312. Désormais, devenu empereur unique, il favorisera les chrétiens et se fera baptiser sur son lit de mort. Cependant il ne fait pas du christianisme la religion officielle de l'Empire. Les empereurs suivants, s'ils s'affirment chrétiens (à l'exception notable de Julien dit « l'Apostat » qui régna de 361 à 363), n'en continuent pas moins à porter le titre de grand pontife*, chef de la religion païenne, et se montrent tolérants envers leurs sujets païens. La situation bascule dans les années 380. L'empereur Gratien abandonne le grand pontificat en 382, et Théodose interdit les sacrifices païens en 391-392. Des temples païens sont détruits. L'Empire est devenu chrétien.

La **peste** dont les populations occidentales avaient eu à souffrir entre le VIe et le VIIIe siècle entre de nouveau en Europe par les ports méditerranéens, entre 1348 et 1351, et tue plus de 25 millions de personnes. Dès lors, le mal ne lâchera plus le continent jusqu'à sa disparition en 1722.

Pendant le **Moyen Âge**, la rançon avait pour but d'humaniser la guerre. Les vaincus n'étaient plus massacrés ou réduits en esclavage mais échangés contre une somme d'argent. C'est d'ailleurs pour payer le solde de sa propre rançon au roi d'Angleterre que le roi de France Jean II le Bon fera, en 1360, frapper une nouvelle monnaie : le franc.

Crise et redressement

▪ *L'empereur Philippe l'Arabe régna de 244 à 249. Il célébra avec éclat le millénaire de Rome.*

Après une période marquée par de nombreux périls aux frontières et une rapide succession d'empereurs éphémères, l'Empire connaît à nouveau une période faste, avec des innovations politiques de grande ampleur et un retour à l'unité territoriale et politique.

▪ *Ce groupe montre les Augustes barbus et les Césars imberbes, distinguant ainsi leur place respective dans la hiérarchie des tétrarques.*

> **Le IIIe siècle de notre ère est présenté traditionnellement comme une période de « crise ».** En fait, la période la plus noire dura une vingtaine d'années, de 250 à 270. Elle fut marquée par l'affaiblissement du pouvoir central. Les empereurs, proclamés par leurs troupes, étaient abandonnés par celles-ci en cas de défaite. Leurs tentatives pour mettre en place une nouvelle dynastie, en associant leur fils au pouvoir, se soldèrent en général par un échec, car le temps leur manqua pour légitimer leur pouvoir.

Les périls aux frontières de l'Empire aggravent la situation. Sur le Danube est regroupée une confédération de peuples, dont les Goths, qui deviennent menaçants, quand l'empereur ne leur verse plus de tribut, et descendent jusqu'en Thrace. L'empereur Trajan Dèce, qui est accouru pour les repousser, est vaincu et tué dans les marais de la Dobroudja au printemps 251. La peste, apparue en Afrique en 250, touche Rome dès 251. Les Perses, en Orient, s'enhardissent et vont jusqu'à envahir la Syrie et prendre Antioche en 256. L'empereur Valérien est vaincu et fait prisonnier en 260 – humiliation suprême. C'est la première fois qu'un empereur romain est capturé par l'ennemi.

Des usurpateurs se proclament empereurs, comme Postumus en Gaule. En 260, il fonde un empire gaulois promis à un certain succès, puisqu'il ne rentre dans l'orbite de Rome qu'en 274, sous le règne d'Aurélien. Une femme, Zénobie, prend le pouvoir dans la grande cité caravanière de Palmyre, dans le désert de Syrie, et rejette la tutelle romaine en 267. Aurélien, à la tête de ses troupes, la capture et la fait défiler chargée de chaînes d'or, lors du triomphe qui proclame que l'unité de l'Empire est enfin restaurée (274).

▪ *Ce camée, réalisé à la demande du roi perse Sapor Ier (à droite), le montre faisant prisonnier l'empereur Valérien (à gauche).*

Après la mort de **Charlemagne** (747-814), l'Empire carolingien, qui regroupait la Gaule, l'Aquitaine, la Germanie et l'Italie, ne resta pas longtemps uni. Ses petits-fils le partagèrent en trois royaumes. Puis leurs descendants furent incapables de maîtriser le pouvoir grandissant des seigneurs féodaux ; le Moyen Âge commençait.

Les débuts du XIVe siècle, en Occident, sont marqués par une crise générale. Famines, épidémies, guerres civiles et révoltes se succèdent. Pourtant les États naissants réagissent et s'affermissent en s'appuyant par exemple, comme en France, sur un sentiment national que cristallise une petite bergère investie d'une mission divine **Jeanne d'Arc.**

Mais la vraie rupture se situe en 284 : un soldat dalmate, Dioclétien, est proclamé empereur. Afin de faire face aux dangers qui menacent toujours l'Empire, il met en place un système original, la tétrarchie* : il s'associe un autre empereur, auquel est conféré le titre d'Auguste, et deux Césars, appelés à succéder aux Augustes quand ces derniers se retireront en 305. Chacun est en charge d'une zone spécifique, mais l'Empire reste indivis. Toutefois, ce système ne pourra subsister longtemps. Constantin et Maxence, fils de tétrarques, espéraient être intégrés au système et sont furieux d'en être écartés. Leur révolte sonne le glas de la tétrarchie. Après bien des péripéties, Constantin est finalement seul Auguste d'un Empire réunifié, en 324. Au cours d'un règne qui dure plus de trente années, il réforme profondément l'Empire, fonde Constantinople, et surtout prend de nombreuses mesures en faveur des chrétiens, longtemps persécutés.

■ *Dioclétien se fit construire un magnifique palais dans sa ville d'origine, Spalato (actuelle Split), sur la côte dalmate, pour s'y retirer après son abdication, en 305.*

Parmi différentes hypothèses pour expliquer la disparition des **dinosaures**, il y a 65 millions d'années, l'une d'elles évoque la chute d'une énorme météorite. Cet impact aurait entraîné sur la Terre toute une série de catastrophes dont une nuit continuelle.

Nul ne sait si la mythique Atlantide mystérieusement disparue a, un jour, existé. Certains pensent qu'elle a pu connaître le sort de la cité d'Akrotiri sur l'île de Santorin, près de la Crète, qu'une **éruption volcanique** a recouverte de plusieurs mètres de cendres.

La chute de l'Empire romain

À cause d'une armée médiocre, Rome ne peut endiguer les invasions barbares qui déferlent sur l'Empire au ve siècle. L'Occident romain éclate entre plusieurs royaumes barbares.

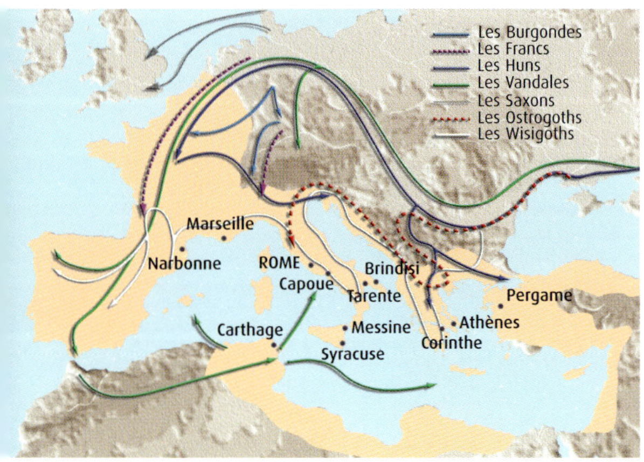

■ *Le dernier empereur d'Occident, Romulus Augustule (475-476), est représenté dans une posture hiératique, signe de son caractère sacré.*

■ *Cette mosaïque de l'église Sant'Apollinare de Ravenne, datant du règne du roi ostrogoth Théodoric (493-526), restitue la façade du palais impérial, cadre d'un cérémonial somptueux.*

■ *Cette carte des invasions barbares montre que l'Occident subit l'essentiel des attaques. L'Empire put subsister en Orient, beaucoup moins touché.*

> **Le 23 août 410, le monde stupéfait apprend que les troupes du roi des Wisigoths Alaric ont occupé Rome :** la ville était inviolée depuis huit siècles ! Le Barbare désire que l'Empire lui cède une province pour y installer son peuple et l'empereur Honorius s'y refuse. Il limite le pillage à trois jours et interdit de toucher aux églises mais ses ordres ne sont pas respectés et de nombreux monuments brûlent. La ville n'est plus la capitale de l'Empire depuis un siècle mais son pillage symbolise la débâcle romaine face aux Barbares.

Sur son lit de mort, l'empereur Théodose a partagé l'Empire entre ses deux fils, confiant l'Occident à l'enfant Honorius en 395 mais le jeune prince doit affronter aussitôt la ruée des Barbares, qui ont franchi le Rhin et le Danube. Poussés par les migrations des Huns, ces peuples germaniques ne veulent en rien détruire l'Empire mais seulement y trouver refuge et bénéficier des bienfaits de la civilisation romaine. Mais leur installation va entraîner à terme son démembrement entre plusieurs royaumes « romano-germaniques ». Après le sac de Rome, les Wisigoths vont s'installer en Aquitaine et en Espagne (418). Les Vandales font de même en Afrique (429) et les Francs dans le Nord de la Gaule. L'armée romaine ne peut s'y opposer car ses effectifs sont trop faibles et ses meilleures troupes sont composées elles-mêmes de Barbares. Dans les provinces, les sénateurs locaux, qui ne vont plus à Rome, préfèrent s'entendre avec les rois germaniques pour partager le pouvoir.

Rome n'est plus la capitale impériale car les empereurs d'Occident préfèrent résider à Ravenne, au nord-est de l'Italie, bien protégée par ses marais. Ils vivent cloîtrés dans leur palais,

Lorsque **Clovis** (465-511) succède à son père Childéric, il n'y a plus d'empereur romain en Occident, et le Sud de la Gaule est aux mains des Burgondes et des Wisigoths. Il se convertit au catholicisme et avec l'appui des Gallo-Romains fait du royaume franc, le plus grand d'Europe de l'Ouest.

L'empereur de Byzance tenait son pouvoir directement de Dieu dont il était le « lieutenant » sur Terre. Aussi le représentait-on non seulement revêtu des symboles de son pouvoir ici-bas, mais également auréolé pour signifier son caractère sacré.

isolés du monde par une étiquette rigide. À la dérive, le pouvoir central manifeste un ultime sursaut en repoussant la menace du roi des Huns, Attila : vaincu par une coalition de Romains, de Wisigoths et de Francs, le Hun doit évacuer la Gaule en 451. Après la mort du dernier descendant de Théodose (455), le pouvoir impérial passe entre les mains de souverains éphémères manipulés par les généraux barbares de l'armée impériale. En 476, l'un d'entre eux, Odoacre, choisit de renverser l'empereur Romulus Augustule, tout juste sorti de l'adolescence, et d'administrer directement l'Italie sous l'autorité lointaine de l'empereur romain d'Orient, résidant à Constantinople. Les contemporains n'en ont pas eu conscience sur le moment mais l'Empire romain vient de disparaître en Occident. En revanche, il va poursuivre son destin en Orient pendant mille années encore sous le nom d'Empire byzantin.

■ *Ce tableau « pompier » du XIXe siècle est censé représenter le déferlement des Huns sur l'Empire, mais les invasions prirent aussi le visage d'infiltrations progressives ou d'installations décidées par les Romains eux-mêmes.*

Pour en savoir plus

DANS LES LIVRES

Œuvres de fiction pour la jeunesse
• *Caïus et le Gladiateur,* H. Winterfeld, Hachette Jeunesse, 2001.
• *Tumulte à Rome,* O. Weulersse, Hachette Jeunesse, 2001.
• *Vercingétorix,* B. Solet, Pocket Junior, 2001.

Documentaires pour la jeunesse
• *Empire romain,* M.J. Corbishley, coll. « Atlas historique », Casterman, 1990.
• *Les Romains,* P. Miquel, Y. Cohat, coll. « La Vie privée des hommes », Hachette Jeunesse, 2002.
• *Rome : une journée dans la Rome antique,* A. Solway, S. Biesty, Gallimard Jeunesse, 2003.
• *Sur les traces des fondateurs de Rome,* P. Castejon, F. Moiraud, coll. « Sur les traces de », Gallimard Jeunesse, 2001.
• *Que sais-tu des Romains ?,* Walt Disney, Hachette Disney, 2002.

Bandes dessinées
• *Alix l'Intrépide,* t. I, (et autres aventures), J. Martin, coll. « Romans Dix et Plus », Casterman, 2004.
• *Astérix le Gaulois,* t. I, (et autres aventures), Uderzo, Goscinny, Astérix Hachette, 1998.
• *Le Mur d'Hadrien*, t. VII, « Prince Valiant », 1949-1951, M. Pagel, H. Foster, Zenda, 1990.
• *Ambre le banquet de Crassus,* t. I, (et autres tomes), *Vae victis,* Mitton, S. Rocca, coll. « Soleil noir », Soleil Productions, 1991.

Ouvrages généraux
• *La Civilisation romaine,* P. Grimal, « Grandes Civilisations Poche », Arthaud, 2002.
• *La ville antique,* t. I, *Histoire de la France urbaine,* G. Duby (sous la direction de), coll. « Points Histoire », Seuil, 1980.
• *L'Antiquité,* t. I, *Histoire des femmes en Occident,* P. Schmitt-Pantel (sous la direction de), Seuil, 2002.
• *De l'Empire romain à l'an mil,* t. I, *Histoire de la vie privée*, Ph. Ariès, G. Duby (sous la direction de), coll. « Points Histoire », Seuil, 1999.
• *L'Homme romain,* A. Giardina (sous la direction de), coll. « Points Histoire », Seuil, 2002.
• *L'Homme romain : des origines au* Ier *siècle de notre ère,* M. Meslin, coll. « Historiques », Complexe Éd., 2000.
• *Ils ont fait l'histoire du monde,* t. I, *De l'Antiquité au Moyen Âge,* Larousse, 2001.

Histoire politique
• *Les Empereurs romains (27 av. J.-C. - 476 ap. J.-C.),* F. Zosso, C. Zingg, Errance, 2003.
• *Histoire romaine,* J-P. Martin, A. Chauvot, Armand Colin, 2003.

Vie quotidienne
• *Les Romains et l'Eau,* A. Malissard, Belles Lettres, 1994.
• *Rome à l'apogée de l'Empire,* J. Carcopino, coll. « La Vie quotidienne à », Hachette Littératures, 1998.
• *La Vie quotidienne du citoyen romain sous la République,* F. Dupont, coll. « Vie quotidienne », Hachette Littératures, 1994.
• *La Vie quotidienne à Pompéi,* R. Étienne, coll. « Vie quotidienne », Hachette Littératures, 1998.
• *La Vie des Romains au temps des Césars,* C. Salles, coll. « Histoire au quotidien », Larousse, 2004.

Religion
• *Le Prêtre à Rome,* D. Porte, Payot, 1995.
• *Aux origines du christianisme,* P. Geoltrain, coll. « Folio Histoire », Gallimard, 2000.
• *Rome et ses Dieux,* R. Turcan, coll. « Vie quotidienne », Hachette Littératures, 1998.

Loisirs et vie intellectuelle
• *Le Monde romain,* t. II, *Histoire de l'éducation dans l'Antiquité,* H-I. Marrou, coll. « Points Histoire », Seuil, 1981.
• *Lire à Rome,* C. Salles, Payot, 1994.
• *Le Théâtre à Rome,* J.-C. Dumont, M. François-Garelli, Livre de Poche, 1998.

Urbanisme
• *L'Afrique antique,* A. Laronde, J.-C. Golvin, coll. « Histoire et Monuments », Tallandier, 2003.
• *L'Antiquité retrouvée,* J.-C. Golvin, coll. « Nouveaux Regards », Errance, 2003.
• *Un voyage dans la Rome des Césars,* G. Chaillet, Glénat, 2004.
• *Guide romain antique,* G. Hacquard, J. Dautry, O. Maisani, Hachette Éducation, 1990.
• *Pompéi, la cité ensevelie,* R. Étienne, coll. « Découvertes », Gallimard, 1998.
• *Rome, ville et capitale de César à la fin des Antonins,* A. Bérenger-Badel, Hachette Éducation, 2001.
• *Voyage en Gaule romaine,* G. Coulon, J.-C. Golvin, Actes Sud, 2002.

Art
• *L'Art de l'ancienne Rome,* B. Andreae, Citadelles et Mazenod, 1998.
• *L'Art romain,* R. Turcan, Paris, Gallimard, 1995.

Œuvres romanesques
• *Les Derniers Jours de Pompéi,* E. Bulwer-Lytton, Hachette Jeunesse, 2002.
• *Mémoires d'Hadrien,* M. Yourcenar, coll. « Blanche », Gallimard, 1990.
• *Moi, Claude, empereur !,* R. Graves, coll. « Folio », Gallimard, 1987.
• *Le Voyage de Marcus : les tribulations d'un jeune garçon en Gaule romaine,* C. Goudineau, Errance, 2000.
• *Quo vadis ?,* H. Sienkiewicz, Livre de Poche, 2001.
• *Du sang sur Rome,* S. Saylor, coll. « Les Mystères de Rome », Ramsay, 2002.

Chronologie

Avant J.-C.	
753	Fondation de Rome
509	Avènement de la République
399-272	Conquête de l'Italie
264-241	Première guerre punique
218-201	Deuxième guerre punique
146	Destruction de Carthage et conquête de la Grèce
133	Tribunat de Tiberius Gracchus
88-82	Guerre civile entre Marius et Sylla
49-44	Dictature de César
31	Victoire d'Octave à Actium, fin des guerres civiles
27	Fondation de l'Empire par Auguste

	Après J.-C.
Règne de Néron	54-68
Règne de Trajan, apogée territorial de l'Empire	98-117
Règne d'Antonin, apogée de la Paix romaine	138-161
Règne de Marc Aurèle, premières invasions barbares	161-180
Crise du IIIe siècle	235-284
Règne de Dioclétien, fondation du Bas-Empire	284-305
Règne de Constantin	306-337
Christianisme religion d'État	391-392
Division de l'Empire entre Orient et Occident	395
Renversement du dernier empereur d'Occident	476

Lexique

Affranchi :
homme libre d'origine servile.

Atrium :
pièce centrale de la maison réservée aux réceptions, dont le sol présentait un bassin pour recueillir les eaux de pluie.

Augure :
prêtre chargé de lire la volonté divine dans le vol des oiseaux.

Auguste :
principal titre de l'empereur, au départ surnom du premier empereur Octave-Auguste.

Basilique :
bâtiment rectangulaire à trois nefs, situé sur le forum, à l'utilisation polyvalente.

***Cella* :**
pièce du temple abritant la statue du dieu.

César :
titre impérial, hérité de Jules César dont Auguste était le fils adoptif. À partir d'Hadrien (136), il fut plus spécialement réservé au prince héritier.

Chevaliers (ordre des) :
ordre romain fournissant certains fonctionnaires sous l'Empire.

Clarissime :
titre officiel des sénateurs sous l'Empire.

Colonie :
cité fondée par les Romains et copiant les institutions romaines.

Comices :
assemblées du peuple.

***Consecratio* :**
cérémonie de divinisation d'un empereur défunt (appelée aussi « apothéose » en grec).

Consul :
magistrat le plus important de la République romaine. Au nombre de deux par an, élus par les comices, les consuls commandaient l'armée et dirigeaient les affaires générales.

***Cursus honorum* :**
hiérarchie des magistratures.

***Domus* :**
résidence urbaine des élites.

Flamine :
prêtre chargé du service d'un dieu particulier (Jupiter) ou d'un empereur divinisé.

Forum :
place principale d'une cité, il joue le rôle de centre de la vie politique, religieuse et économique.

Grand pontife :
chef du collège des pontifes, regroupant quinze prêtres, il contrôle la religion romaine. Sous l'Empire, cette charge prestigieuse est revêtue par l'empereur.

Haruspice :
prêtre chargé de lire la volonté divine dans l'examen des entrailles des bêtes sacrifiées.

Image :
masque de cire des magistrats défunts exhibé aux funérailles de leurs descendants.

***Imperator* (au pluriel : *imperatores*) :**
titre des généraux victorieux puis de l'empereur.

***Imperium* :**
pouvoir des magistrats supérieurs puis de l'empereur, donnant le droit de commander les armées et de condamner à mort.

***Insula* (au pluriel : *insulae*) :**
au sens strict « îlot d'immeubles », mais le terme est communément utilisé pour désigner un seul immeuble.

Laticlave :
large bande de pourpre décorant la tunique des sénateurs.

***Limes* :**
frontière de l'Empire organisée sous la forme d'une zone-tampon, appuyée sur un réseau de routes et de forts.

***Ludus* :**
jeu donné en l'honneur d'un dieu, composé de pièces de théâtre et de courses de chars.

***Munus* :**
combat de gladiateurs donné lors des funérailles d'un aristocrate.

Ordre :
groupe statutaire chargé d'une mission au service de la cité (sénateurs, chevaliers).

Pérégrin :
habitant libre de l'Empire ne possédant pas la citoyenneté romaine.

***Pomerium* :**
limite religieuse de la ville de Rome, correspondant au sillon tracé par Romulus lors de la fondation. La présence de la mort, et donc des tombeaux, y était prohibée.

Prétorien :
soldat de la garde impériale, chargé de protéger l'empereur. Les dix cohortes prétoriennes étaient commandées par le préfet du prétoire.

Procurateur :
fonctionnaire impérial choisi parmi les chevaliers.

Questeur :
magistrat sénatorial chargé des finances.

Sesterce :
unité monétaire romaine. Le sigle HS représente le sesterce.

Tétrarchie :
système politique associant deux empereurs principaux (Augustes) et leurs deux héritiers (Césars). Il fut pratiqué de 293 à 311.

Tribun de la plèbe :
magistrat chargé de défendre les intérêts de la plèbe. Au nombre de dix par an, ils étaient « sacro-saints », c'est-à-dire qu'on n'avait pas le droit de les frapper ou de les agresser.

Triomphe :
cérémonie solennelle au cours de laquelle le général victorieux défile dans Rome à la tête de ses troupes. Sous l'Empire, le triomphe est réservé aux membres de la famille impériale.

Vilicus :
intendant d'une villa.

Villa :
grande exploitation rurale ou résidence de luxe à la campagne et à la mer.

Index

Table des illustrations